CW00695117

Helmsmen and Heroes

William Gosling

Helmsmen and Heroes

Control Theory as a Key to Past and Future

Weidenfeld and Nicolson *London*

Copyright © William Gosling 1994
First published 1994

The right of William Gosling to be identified as the author of this work has been asserted by him in accordance with the Copyright, Designs and Patents Act 1988.

All rights reserved. No part of this publication may be reproduced, stored in a retrieval system, or transmitted, in any form or by any means, electronic, mechanical, photocopying, recording or otherwise, without the prior permission of Orion Publishing Group Ltd.

Filmset by Selwood Systems,
Midsomer Norton

Printed and bound in Great Britain by
Butler & Tanner Ltd, Frome and London
for
Weidenfeld & Nicolson
The Orion Publishing Group
Orion House
5 Upper St Martin's Lane
London WC2H 9EA

British Library Cataloguing-in-Publication Data

A catalogue record for this book is available from the British Library

ISBN: 0 297 81449 4

to

Arnold Tustin (1899–1994)

who reminded all of us that control theory
has a significance which extends far beyond engineering

Contents

Preface

I have long held that technical subjects ought to be capable of explanation in terms everybody can grasp. What cannot is most likely not yet fully understood, even by authorities in the field. This view is unpopular with many who claim expertise, undermining their sense of belonging to an elite whose deep mysteries are incommunicable. Recently, though, eminent scientists have published books which seem to support my thesis, making lucid topics in mathematics, cosmology and physics previously thought impossibly difficult.

Sadly, the information sciences have received little coverage in accessible form, despite their significance for every aspect of contemporary life. This is a book about one of them: control theory. Its rudiments are easily grasped, and give insights into many things. Falling in love or having a fight, launching an invention or building an empire, 'arms races' between nations and the industrial revolution – control theory speaks of them all and deserves to be heard. It makes more comprehensible our survival in a hostile universe, shows how we achieve our objectives in the challenges of life – and why we sometimes fail. There seems to be a place for a book of this kind.

In the interests of readability, I have obliged myself to get by without any mathematics, although at times it has been a sore trial to be parted from this valued old companion. Even so, I managed it, and hope this will smooth the reader's path. As for my sources, where there has been a choice between history or gossip I have chosen the latter, since it is always more interesting and often more accurate.

To end, a few words of grateful acknowledgement: Michael Clark, Wyn Crompton, Melanie Edwards, Helen Haste and Geoffrey Holister read my text at various stages, and made helpful and perceptive comments. Above all, but for my beloved wife Patricia's urging I would never have begun, nor would I have persevered through dark times when I wondered if I really had anything to say.

Introduction

Three ways of knowing dominate our world. The first is formal knowledge, enshrined in the written word, or perhaps in pictures of many different types and kinds, in mathematical formulae or computer software. The second is common knowledge, comprising the routine necessary things we carry in our heads about the world we live in, ranging from taking it for granted that winter is cold and summer hot or that we shall be more acceptable to mothers if we smile at their babies, all the way to an awareness that somebody who tries to sell us a gold brick at a knockdown price is probably not entirely honest. Finally the third way of knowing is about all that we know but cannot tell, things we could never hope to articulate, such as the skills of eye, hand, foot and brain which enable us to place a two tonne car within a dozen centimetres in a parking space, having manoeuvred it around several others just like it in order to do so.

However, human beings are not isolates, even the most misanthropic, and our knowing is always dominated by its social dimension. Although formal knowledge invariably wishes to be thought universal, nevertheless that part of it to which any one of us is able to gain access depends critically on the identity of the social groups in which we claim membership. In the case of common knowledge much the same is true; the groupings may be different but they are no less significant. Common knowledge in Lagos is different from that in London, even although in important ways the two overlap. Common knowledge is time-dependent too: at the beginning of a certain century any fool knows that the sun goes round the earth but towards the end of the next century only a fool would think so.

Scholars and academics naturally tend to believe that formal knowledge is the most important way of knowing, and perhaps in the long term, on the time-scale of the rise of civilizations, they are right, yet even so it is not formal but common knowledge which informs nearly all the day-to-day decisions and actions people take, even the most learned among them. Indeed, this leads Harry Collins to argue the view that it is because computers, being social isolates, cannot access common knowledge that they are forever barred from fully emulating human thought processes.[1]

Collins' book is part of the vigorous debate taking place at present about the 'can a machine think' question, and usefully draws attention to the indispensable social dimension of human thinking. Sadly, all too many other books and papers on this topic are hardly worth opening. Two faults are common. First, authors fail to say what they mean by 'think' though it emerges that what they have in mind is something like 'emulate a human being in all mental processes'. Put like that the question becomes trivial; it is obvious that machines cannot do so since this would imply that they share human socialization, which they do not, as Collins points out. The second trap, which most others fall into but Collins partly avoids, is to assume that machines must operate in a deterministic manner, by inevitably linked cause and effect. Not so, not so at all; it is perfectly possible to build stochastic machines which incorporate some randomness in their operation, as the human brain most certainly does. Failure to take this into account limits many erudite arguments, including those of Roger Penrose (in his fascinating book), who proves convincingly that a wholly deterministic machine cannot think like a person.[2] To establish that is useful, but not enough, for why should we expect a deterministic machine to be able to emulate something stochastic? So—can a machine think? There is only one sensible response: it depends entirely on what you intend

1 H. M. Collins, *Artificial Experts* (1990).

2 Roger Penrose, *The Emperor's New Clothes* (1989).

> by the words 'machine' and 'think'. Once a specific meaning is given to both words the answer to the question generally becomes self-evident, but trying to do that raises far trickier problems of satisfactory definition than might at first be thought. Alan Turing understood this very well, tried to define them and failed. His famous 'Turing test' for machine intelligence was a cop-out, the best he could propose as a solution in the absence of water-tight definitions.[1] It is ingenious and quite seductive at first sight, but really only shifts the ground of debate to whether the test is adequate and what it means. By itself it solves nothing.

Held jointly by most people in a given society and at a particular historical epoch, it is the body of common knowledge which largely regulates our lives. Nothing could be more important to us, collectively and individually, therefore, than its progressive evolution. The indications are good in this respect: over time common knowledge has shown itself able routinely to absorb and integrate insights from the formal domain, particularly from technology and science, so that what is known only to an elite in one century may be the common possession of everybody in the next. Thus today all the world knows that an object once set in motion will continue to move until something stops it, that it moves 'under its own momentum' as we say. But this view is culled directly from the Newtonian theory of motion, which was finally accepted by the scientific community only at the end of the seventeenth century. It replaced the previous Aristotelian orthodoxy, which held that objects move for just as long as a force is acting on them and without it they stop, like a spoon in treacle. Present day common knowledge has no difficulty at all in accepting that Aristotle's earlier view—the treacle spoon—was a special case, lacking generality, 'the exception that proves the rule'. Indeed, if we did not all of us have a reasonable unconscious grasp of Newtonian mechanics, particularly as it relates to stopping distances, we could not safely drive our cars or cross busy streets. An Aristotelian car would stop dead as soon as the foot was lifted from the accelerator, but it does not exist in nature.

Similarly common knowledge tells us today that electricity, which can give people bad and even fatal shocks, passes freely along metal

1 Alan Turing, 'Computing machinery and intelligence', *Mind* **59** (1950).

wires but is stopped by their insulating plastic sheaths. It is easy to forget that these ideas about conductors and insulators were hot from the research laboratories at the end of the eighteenth century. Finally it is now accepted into common knowledge that under some circumstances matter can be converted into energy by 'splitting the atom', and that when this happens the amount of energy released is prodigious but the process is accompanied by the production of radioactive material which can be dangerous to life. All of this was discovered as recently as the turn of the last century.

This appropriation of formal into common knowledge is no matter of merely abstract knowing, but is of intensely practical significance. Awareness of the laws of motion preserves us from sudden death in city streets, we know that to touch bare electrical wires would put us in peril, and we understand that we must conduct ourselves with appropriate circumspection near nuclear power plants. Children who do not fully share access to our common knowledge are perceived as being at risk, and we hasten to explain it all as best we can, meanwhile protecting them from the possible consequences of their ignorance.

Indeed, it is not too extreme to argue that the various societies in which we live do not collectively 'know' aspects of science or technology until their discoveries have entered the domain of common knowledge, and certainly before that we cannot handle their political and human consequences adequately. Democratic states, in particular, depend on the good sense of the voters to discriminate between the courses of action offered to them by politicians, and their conclusions are profoundly influenced by the store of common knowledge on the basis of which they are made. It is reasonable to hope that, as more science is transformed into common knowledge, politicians will be helped to develop advantageous new policies and the electors will grow more competent to choose the better from the worse.

Whilst it is likely that science and technology in their fullest detail may always remain the preserve of a few, nevertheless technical ideas which are not assimilated to some degree into the realm of common knowledge remain a potential hazard, because we cannot even begin to judge their significance for our lives. It may be true that only an astronomer will really grasp the totality of knowledge about the natural history of stars and the structure of the universe, and that only an engineer will be able to design the complexities of a computer or the software that vivifies it. The ordinary citizen, though, will become more secure by learning enough to have reliable instincts about these things when they impinge on his life. Thus an activity of great social and political importance is the reordering of the important ideas drawn from science and technology, their shaping and recasting, so that they are fitted for absorption into the body of common knowledge. This is why education in science and technology must now be a required part of the national curriculum for all children, not just the ones with a scientific penchant, and also why those who popularize and explain high technology and science to the general public have a vital social function. It is work which needs to be done no less well than the advancement of high and formal knowledge through scholarship and research, and both are never-ending tasks.

> Sometimes politicians and government officials, aware of their own lack of understanding, will turn to experts in science (very rarely technology) for advice in formulating policy. This may be unavoidable, but it is a poor substitute for their own understanding nevertheless, since the advice given is by no means value-free, but is influenced by the predilections, often unconscious, of the experts who happen to be selected. To suppose that scientists, by virtue of their calling, are independent, impartial and unmoved by the passions that sway lesser people is to be ignorant of the turbulent history, psychology and sociology of science, which give no comfort at all to any such view.
>
> Like government advisers, the popularizers of science have their prejudices too, necessarily shaping what they say, but there is a free market in their opinions and people can select between many competing gurus, which mitigates the dangers.

Translating formal knowledge into what everybody understands is not without its dangers, needless to say. Trying to express scientific ideas in such a way that they can be comprehended easily by the nonscientific, and even the non-numerate, can lead to oversimplification or downright error, so that the common knowledge view of difficult technical ideas is very likely to be astray at critical points. However, with the passage of time the errors are slowly flushed out, and even before they vanish altogether it is likely that an imperfect understanding may prove better than total ignorance.

Some sciences have been better served by popular dissemination than others. Medicine has succeeded best in spreading its message, although physics, chemistry and aspects of biology have also had their successes. Quite often it is mere chance, the lottery of circumstances, which seems to dictate what will be widely heard. The Chernobyl disaster did more to teach people about the perils of radioactivity than any other single event, and the 'salmonella in eggs' scare of a few years back, although hard on chicken farmers, had its positive side as a public educator in microbiology. These rather hit-or-miss processes, though, mean that some topics of the greatest importance remain relatively unexplored for a long time. Until quite recently, for example, most people's ideas about diet were informed more by traditional beliefs than science, and although happily this situation is now changing fast it is only thanks to some determined efforts by a concerned few. Sadly, however, other important areas of new understanding remain to this day the preserve of a small minority, despite everything.

Of particular concern is information technology. Some of the greatest technical advances of the nineteenth and twentieth centuries have been in the dissemination, handling, storage and processing of information. Scholars might assign a very early date to the beginning of information technology—the invention of printing, perhaps, or even the early mass production of books in the scriptoria of monasteries—but the technology in its modern form came to prominence from the introduction of the electromagnetic telegraph by William F. Cooke and Charles Wheatstone in 1837, an innovation which (along with its successor, the telephone) transformed the nineteenth-century world.[1] In our own century, radio and optical communication have continued to make unbelievable strides, but arguably even more important has been the introduction of computing machinery, the miraculous information processors which have transformed our world and upon which the infrastructure of civilized life now utterly depends.[2]

As a result of the advance in these technologies much important new science has also developed, and among them specifically the theory of

1 William Gosling, 'A short history of electrical communications', in Derek Walker (ed.), *Great Engineers* (1987).

2 N. Metropolis, J. Howlett and Gian Carlo Rota (eds), *A History of Computing in the Twentieth Century* (1980).

control and of automata, as well as communications theory and software science. These new information sciences stand on their own; they are not a branch of physics or any other earlier field of study, not least because they speak of wholly new and unfamiliar things, such as the so-called 'software objects' within computers which have no immediately obvious physical form yet can determine issues of human life and death. Sadly, most of what these new sciences say has so far had to be expressed in a recondite and mathematical style, and little has yet entered the domain of common knowledge, the science behind information technology remaining the preserve of the expert. This is a great pity, because its impact on ordinary people's lives has already been vast and will be far greater yet. What is more, like all worthwhile science, these new ideas and theories not only illuminate the things that they were initially created to explain but also cast a broad and helpful light on other puzzles and curiosities, social, psychological, political and economic, enabling us to comprehend them better and live more easily in our world. It seems wrong and even dangerous that such valuable insights should continue much longer to be restricted to the elite which created them.

This book will therefore attempt to expound the beginnings, the first intimations and no more, of one such area, the theory of control. The subject is very far from being only of technical interest since attempts at control, successful or otherwise, are associated with every aspect of life, and at all levels from physiology to world politics, as we shall see. The ideas involved are not impossibly difficult to understand, and even if their detailed application can get distinctly sticky they remain of the greatest possible practical utility, so it is worth the effort of coming to terms with them. Control is the art of being and doing; it is inseparable from life itself.

1

The improbable now and the challenge of time

It is a wonder that we are here at all. Even the universe itself is an incredibly improbable thing. Had the laws of physics been minutely different from what they actually are then either none of the stars and planets we know would have come into existence at all, or else they would not have lasted long enough for life to evolve, certainly not intelligent life.[1] There would have been no Earth, and no human history, had almost any of the major constants of physics been just a very little unlike what we now measure. It is a disconcerting thought, but then much in postmodern physics and cosmology is more than a little disturbing.[2]

> Postmodern physics, dating from the 1980s, is the study which followed on after the great early twentieth-century milestones of relativity theory and quantum mechanics, seeking to unify them and to answer at a deep level many questions that they left unresolved. In one of its thrusts of enquiry it treats of entities smaller than the atom in the same ratio as the size of the atom itself is smaller than the objects about us.

Scientists debate with vigour just why things fell out the way they have. Hypotheses include the weak anthropic—which merely says that since we manifestly are here, it happens that the laws of physics must have been propitious—and the strong anthropic which sees our being

1 John L. Casti, *Paradigms Lost* (1989), particularly Chapter 6.

2 David Peat, *Superstrings and the Search for the Theory of Everything* (1988).

here as what the game is all about, so the laws of physics had to be like that for our benefit. The first is unhelpful and the second raises more questions than it settles, but at least opens up some interesting lines of enquiry.[1,2] Anyway, that does not seem to be the most pressing topic just now, for there are other issues, nearer to home.

We evidently do have a viable universe in which intelligent life has proved able to emerge, yet our continued existence (as individuals, but no less as groups, organizations and societies) is always under attack. It would not do to think too often or too deeply about the degree to which we live our lives on a knife edge of survival. 'Whether we pass the night or no, I'm sure is always touch and go,' said the Rev. Eli Jenkins.[3] Our coming into the world is hazardous enough. A myriad of things determine absolutely whether or not we are successfully conceived and born—anatomy, physiology, biochemistry, neurology and psychology (just to name a few)—and considered dispassionately most of them look to have long odds against us. Quite as many different factors again settle how long we live, and how effectively we function as human beings while we are here. All these vital parameters have to be continually regulated to within a quite narrow range of the ideal if a long and full human life is to be enjoyed.

Yet it is a fundamental and seemingly inescapable principle of science that, over time, all order tends to disorder, and everything well-conditioned becomes progressively more and more impaired. This is the famous second law of thermodynamics, but it is valid in this simple form only for a totally closed system, such as the universe taken as a whole. Human life, though, is lived in systems which are not closed, since energy and information can flow in and out of them, and therefore we just as often experience reducing disorder. Indeed, evidence has been emerging which suggests that on a localized basis certain categories of complex systems may quite commonly proceed from disorder to order. Perhaps this is how all life began; nobody can be sure. The study of self-organizing systems—complexity theory—is fashionable just now.[4]

1 Paul Davies, *The Mind of God* (1992).

2 John D. Barrow and Frank J. Tipler, *The Anthropic Cosmological Principle* (1986). Some mathematics is required to read this difficult but intriguing book.

3 Dylan Thomas, *Under Milk Wood* (1954).

4 Roger Lewin, *Complexity—Life at the Edge of Chaos* (1993).

Be that as it may, it is evident that the setting of the biological, physiological and psychological conditions for our survival, though, cannot be a static thing, got right at the beginning of our lives and thereafter forever let be, but instead requires unceasing monitoring, correction and control. Life is like a juggler balancing a stick on his nose, his body in permanent movement so that it does not fall.

Nor is it the end of our problems merely to get all those things right, for even if bodily and psychological wellbeing are surely an essential precondition for the good life, they are not enough on their own, necessary but not sufficient. No more than the world within, the world about us can never be taken for granted, neither the mundane experience of home and work nor yet the wider perspective of the national and global economy, of international relations and the condition of our planet, in short the totality of the environment in its fullest sense. We are not disposed, and have never been, to accept the world passively, just as it happens. Although other animals show controlling behaviour also, even at its most developed it is profoundly less sophisticated than ours. Since our remotest ancestors diverged from the other apes, no longer subsisting on the fruits of the trees in which they lived, a distinguishing mark of humankind is a grand obsession with taking the environment and moulding it to our needs. Sometimes we do it wisely, more often we botch the job in part at least, but the effort to assume control of the world makes us recognizably what we are.

Long before our technology established its firm links to science in the eighteenth century, humankind had already long been changing the environment, slowly but determinedly. The appearance of tools and of weapons, both for war and hunting, the invention of agriculture, building and other technologies: these are the traces of our presence in the record of the planet. In the long process of bringing the world under our control, some argue for the historical primacy of weapons, but it now seems no less plausible that the earliest technology may have been the manipulation of plants and animals. Thus sheep, we know, were domesticated from 9000 BC. Agriculture and animal husbandry, along with the building skills that made them practicable, created a population explosion in Bronze Age cultures, from about 3800 BC, notably in Iran and Mesopotamia. As the titles assigned to archaeological periods suggest, the progress of the use and manufacture of materials was crucial, even at a very early date. Other technologies of critical importance were shipbuilding and seamanship, culminating in the production and use of ships capable of transoceanic voyages. The earliest ship for which there is firm archaeological evidence was built for the funeral of the Pharaoh Cheops (3960–3908 BC).

> The accepted archaeological divisions of prehistory are: Old Stone Age (Palaeolithic) to 10,000 BC , New Stone Age (Neolithic) to about 3000 BC , then Bronze Age, and Iron Age from 1500 BC. The classification was first suggested (1836) by C. J. Thomsen (1788–1865).

All the advances in early technology were achieved by an evolution of practice, without the least deep or scientific knowledge. Our forefathers knew how, but not why. But can this really be technology without science that we are seeing? The idea is such an unfamiliar one to many that its implications deserve to be explored. Today we link science and technology so routinely (some even thinking the words practically synonymous, running them together) that many no longer understand that they are quite different things, once totally divorced from each other. *The Concise Oxford Dictionary* (Seventh Edition) defines science as 'systematic and formulated knowledge' and natural science as 'dealing with material phenomena and based mainly on observation, experiment, and induction...' In short the essence of science is seeking to know how the material universe about us works, in effect to simulate its structure and functioning in the human mind. By contrast, technology (in its first definition) is 'practical or industrial arts', although there is then mention of 'application of science'. The essence of technology is therefore doing and making, with the business of knowing seen as a means, but not an end. Whilst technology may depend on scientific knowledge it can also be perfectly well based on a less analytical understanding, and it often is. The success of technology is measured by its ability to make things well, which can be achieved without needing to have knowledge in its deepest sense. It is enough to proceed by knowing thoroughly how to do things, and while it may be interesting it is not strictly necessary, so far as technology is concerned, to know why they must be done so.

> All of this is getting to be *Zeitgeist* talk. Thus, Lewis Wolpert makes the distinction between science and technology well,

> even if from the scientist's standpoint.[1] Technologists should agree with him; many of us still find most rewarding the parts of technology which the sciences cannot reach. Incidentally, Wolpert, like many scientists, apparently thinks that ultimate explanations of everything will always be in terms of the interaction of matter and energy. Not so, for the universe has three equal pillars: matter, energy and information. Undervalue the last and many subtle errors follow. Of course mass, energy and information appear together, but in a particular situation the significance of one or other is to the fore, so all three are indispensable concepts. In particular, Wolpert is to be taken with a pinch of salt in what he writes about disciplines such as psychology, psychoanalysis and computer science which are primarily concerned with information.
>
> Copp and Zanella describe a series of case studies, a long list of innovations, and distinguish clearly between the science and the technology that lies behind them. Most often, they say, technology came first and science followed.[2]

Traditional craftsmen, above all, are a category of technologists who have no scientific theory of their task at all. They proceed in ways they were taught during an apprenticeship, where they learned rules and recipes for achieving the desired results without the least knowledge of why they succeed. Why is a sailing ship built thus and thus? Because it has always been so. Indeed, the traditional view holds that to ask why is not profitable. In technologies of this kind progress is by trial and error, and comes very slowly. Medieval masons, whenever they were obliged to innovate, learned entirely by trial and error how to build new kinds of structures that could be depended upon not to fall down, sometimes constructing a few which actually did fall before they got the trick of it. Salisbury Cathedral spire had to be built three times before it stayed up. As the perfection of many traditional artefacts—tools, weapons, buildings—demonstrates, technology developing this way, learning from its mistakes, can ultimately reach a very high standard, despite the fact that all were made without understanding of the

1 Lewis Wolpert, *The Unnatural Nature of Science* (1992).

2 Newton H. Copp and Andrew K. Zanella, *Discovery, Innovation and Risk* (1993).

science underlying them. Inventors there must necessarily be in this traditional technology, but their names are neither honoured nor even recorded, indeed the very fact of innovation may subsequently be concealed, or attributed backward to supernatural beings at the dawn of time.

Modern technologists proceed differently: they use science essentially as a means to a cheaper and quicker way of innovating than trial and error, since deep knowledge can help to avoid all but a few of the initial failures. Yet even today, and in the most thoroughly scientific technologies, it is invariably the case that the available science is insufficient to give quite all of the answers that may be required to make the looked-for innovation possible, and some degree of trial and error is still commonplace. Modern innovators in technology use science to begin their climb to the peaks of problem solving, and it carries them a very long way, but they return to the techniques of their traditional predecessors as they approach the summit. That is an intriguing thought to turn over in one's mind when sitting in an aircraft halfway across the Atlantic, which is one of the reasons why engineers do not talk about this sort of thing much in the presence of laypersons. Indeed, to do so is seen as somewhat indelicate; better by far to collude in the myth that our profession is all based on a solid scientific foundation.

The truth is that science and technology are frequent and firm allies, but they are not at all the same thing. Technology is far older and grew unceasingly, if with less vigour, long before science emerged in its modern form. Indeed, even in the recent historical record new technology has more often led to new science than the other way round. In the nineteenth century it was practical experience with the transatlantic telegraph cable that led Lord Kelvin to formulate his theory of extended networks. In the early 1920s it was the success of long-distance radio transmission (contrary to the ideas then accepted) which led to theories of ionospheric radio propagation. Still more recently the practice of computer software engineering developed empirically for a decade before being codified into theory. These are just examples drawn from information technology; many more are found in every other field of engineering and technical endeavour. The early eighteenth-century invention of the steam engine was the origin of the science of thermodynamics; studies in applied metallurgy led to the modern physics of solids. Perhaps the most glaring example of this evolution from applied knowledge into a new science is in pharmacology, where drug design has only in the last few years really begun to emerge from its empirical beginnings and take a systematic form. Nuclear power is one of the few contrary examples.

The long collective love affair of humankind with technology is no accident, but a true measure of what we really are. Our characteristic preoccupation is the attempt to govern the external world, both living and inanimate, hoping to make it conform to our wishes. In all of this, human action mimics the internal world of physiology, neurology and psychology in its concentration on the need to control. Spiritual leaders warn of the dangers of trying too hard to command the world in which we live—'Consider the lilies of the field, how they grow; they toil not, neither do they spin: and yet I say unto you, that even Solomon in all his glory was not arrayed like one of these.'[1]—and we know very well that, at the last, time will claim all. Both within us and without, one day the effort at control must ultimately fail, of that there can be no rational doubt, yet not even the saints and gurus live in total passivity.

Control is the stuff of which our lives are made, the means of our preservation and the ever-implicit object of our actions. It begins before the infant's first leap in the womb, and for good or ill it lasts as long as life itself. This driving compulsion marks what we do as individuals, our interactions with people as well as things, and also, no less, our collective actions, from the life of a primitive tribe to the politics and economics of developed societies. Indeed, when we cannot achieve operational control through the action of cause and effect, in times past we have often resorted to petitionary prayer to God as the only available alternative, unwilling even to contemplate the prospect that there might be literally nothing to be done to mitigate our impotence. At the same time, the need to control is both our glory and our peril, for by a fruition of control great works of art or science are created and great acts of altruism carried through, yet it was also 'the triumph of the will' that made possible the Gothic horrors for which the terrible twentieth century now passing will doubtless be best remembered, the brutal totalitarianism, the persecution, the wars, genocide and holocausts.

So we fight for mastery over circumstances, but the outcome of our

1 *Matthew* 6. 28–9 (Authorized Version, 1611).

struggle often remains a puzzle to us still, for what we intend does not always happen, our best-laid plans come to nothing, and all too frequently we are left confounded and dismayed. Sometimes, indeed, the world can seem full of the defeat of high hopes: a car smashes into a truck and a life is senselessly lost; the marriage begun in love collapses in painful divorce; the intended Utopia for which dedicated idealists struggle and suffer ends as an authoritarian nightmare; the revolution made for liberty, equality and fraternity descends into blood and terror. At times it almost seems that however hard we try, however noble our intentions may be, the outcome is at best a disappointment and all too often a disaster.

The problem has long challenged the understanding of philosophers. St Augustine's doctrine of original sin is one response; it teaches that nothing of purely human origin is capable of perfection, not merely because of our carelessness, ignorance or inattention, but more fundamentally because there is something lacking in us which forever prevents the achievement of a totally faultless outcome. Some find this a gloomy doctrine, others quite the reverse, because it releases them from the intolerable need to be perfect, and also helps to mitigate the disappointment of inevitable failures in day-to-day life.

St Augustine (354–430), from 396 to 430 Bishop of Hippo Regius (now Annaba) in Algeria, was born in Souk Ahras, at the time a small Roman town. Educated at Carthage in rhetoric (in effect, in legal advocacy) he became a lecturer there, then in Rome, and finally Milan, where imperial government was located at the time. After a brief flirtation with Manichaeism, in 386 he was reconverted to Christianity, was baptized by Ambrose, Bishop of Milan, and returned to North Africa. Ordained somewhat against his inclinations in 391, he became bishop five years later. His subsequent career was full of controversy because he was obliged to battle with various Christian heresies, notably Pelagianism and the Donatists. What he taught remains to this day the basis of Christianity in the West, Catholic and Protestant. Augustine argued that because of original sin none of us can entirely govern our own motivations. Thus, in his view, it is the help of God's grace which enables people to do what is right, and if they depend solely upon their own powers they will certainly fall short. Of his many writings the two best known are his *Confessions* and *City of God*. Augustine's clear theological vision was one of the things that helped Western Christianity to survive barbarian invasions in the fifth century and establish itself as the religion of medieval Europe. Without him, Islam might well have conquered the West.

The contrary assertion, of the intrinsic virtue of human beings and their consequent perfectibility solely by the exercise of their free will, was taught in Rome by Pelagius (around the year 410) but later condemned as a heresy (417) and its author excommunicated.[1] Known as 'the English heresy', Pelagianism was stripped of theological subtlety and forged into a component of revolutionary political thinking by his disciple Celestius within a few years, and it has continued thus, in one disguise or another, to the present day. Notably it did so in Jean Jacques Rousseau's writings; through his mediation, interpretations of Pelagianism, involving varied notions of human perfectibility, have had great impact on the twentieth century, inspiring both socialism and fascism.

Jean Jacques Rousseau (1712–78) gave ideological inspiration to the French Revolution. His mother died when he was born, and he was brought up by an aunt under a harsh regime. Showing the classic symptoms of paranoia, he routinely attacked those who befriended him. In *Emile*, offered as an ideal pattern for child rearing, he argues for natural human goodness which asserts itself if not prevented. (The book was purely theoretical because his own children, by his mistress Thérèse le Vasseur, were all sent to an orphanage soon after birth.) His social thinking (in *The Social Contract*) was based on the notion of a 'General Will' of society (not at all the same as the majority opinion, which may be quite wrong). This is (or should be) embodied in the State, he argued, which thus necessarily acts to secure freedom, equality and justice. Since he did not specify how the General Will was to be revealed, his ideas soon became a tyrant's charter, in effect a licence for those who claim to act on behalf of the General Will to persecute and kill opponents. Rousseau would surely

1 John Ferguson, *Pelagius: A Historical and Theological Study* (1956).

have been horrified by these bastard intellectual heirs, but he fathered them nevertheless.

Are we obliged, then, at the end of a century full of ideological failures and unparalleled atrocities, to abandon the Pelagian dream and accept that St Augustine's answer says it all? Is fate and our fallen nature truly against us, and are we doomed forever to play games with the Devil, the Prince of Cheats, who has already marked our cards? Maybe so, maybe not, but the truth may be more complex, and at the same time less discouraging.

Even if there were indeed an inherent human tendency to failure, its domain is not necessarily so wide as sometimes appears to be the case. While it is doubtless true that not everything going wrong can be attributed to a lack of intellectual comprehension, even now much still can. Many of the bizarre consequences of our well-intended actions, which presently seem so puzzling, might perhaps make perfect sense if we were able to view them in a different light, freed from old habits of analysis which have not served us well. Faced with the practicalities of living our lives, it could indeed be the case that we shall properly understand neither ourselves nor the world we have created until we gain insight into the inner nature of the processes of control we try to deploy, untangle their complexities, and comprehend why it is that our struggles to build a new heaven and a new earth so often produce an outcome we had not intended.

This applies at the most mundane level as well as the most elevated, and often it is easier to gain insights by starting with the simplest things. Thus, for a long time I used to get unsatisfactory baths in the morning, the water mostly ending up either too hot or too cold. In those days my habit was to turn the hot tap half open while adjusting the cold to a precise setting, arrived at by experiment. In theory I could then attend to something else—shaving maybe—and when I returned to the bath I ought to have found it filled with water at just the right temperature, all without the need of further intervention on my part. Sometimes it worked, but more often I was disappointed.

The causes of my failures were various and unpredictable. There were days when my wife took a shower before me, with the result that the temperature of the water in the hot tank was reduced and I had a tepid bath. On one memorable occasion a defect in the water supply led to exceptionally low pressure in the cold tap, while the hot, fed from an overhead tank, was unaffected. A tub full of scaldingly hot water was the consequence. Now, happily, everything is different. I do the sensible thing: run the water as before, but check its temperature with my hand once or twice part-way through filling, and readjust the taps if necessary. Working out the way to get a fill of water into my bath tub at the desired temperature presents a problem, though a very simple one, in control theory.

> For decades regulation of the temperature of bath water has been an obsession in elementary textbooks of control theory. Control engineers are neither more cleanly nor more fussy about the water temperature than others, so the reasons for this preoccupation are shrouded in obscurity. A passage on the topic has been included out of deference to tradition, although in real life it is tempting to opt out completely and use a shower with a thermostat. The Americans invariably do, and find this fixation on what they call 'the tub' oddly European and dated.

Control technology began long ago, with the construction of automata and other self-regulating mechanisms.[1] James Watt's fly-ball governor for his steam engine (1788) is one of the best-known early examples, but by no means the first. However, no early theory of control was ever perfected, although nineteenth-century astronomers began to use mathematics to study how to regulate the pointing of telescopes at stars in the seemingly moving heavens, George Airy apparently among the first of them in 1840. From 1860 to the end of the nineteenth century there were many studies of automata, but mathematically they were developed in terms of classical solutions of differential equations, which was the mind-set of the time but did not prove to be the path of the future in this subject. The formal theory of control in its modern form is a twentieth-century development[2,3] and has now progressed to the point where it includes a complex and extensive body of theory which can be fully comprehended only through a lifetime of study. Despite that, its implications are intensely

1 Otto Meyr, *The Origins of Feedback Control* (1969, English translation 1970).

2 R. C. Oldenbourg and H. Sartorius, *The Dynamics of Automatic Controls* (1948)—the first textbook on the subject. Some mathematics is required to read this book.

3 John C. Doyle, Bruce A. Francis and Allen R. Tannenbaum, *Feedback Control Theory* (1992). Some mathematics required.

practical because throughout our lives we spend much of our time trying to control things, big and small. It is therefore, as has been argued, eminently suitable and timely for incorporation, in part at least, into the stock of common knowledge.

The domestic routine is full of control problems, of which the water in the bath is only one. My house, for example, is heated by hot water flowing through radiators. Each has a special tap, which opens or closes according to the temperature of the air around it, regulating the flow of the water. In theory it should regulate the room temperature to a constant value, and in practice it does work quite well. At an earlier date a single thermostat in one room would have turned the circulation pump on and off instead. This was found unsatisfactory because it sets the temperature correctly only in the room in which the sensing device is situated. The snag is that any heat source there, even people (six to a dozen of whom approximate to a one-bar electric fire, depending on what they are up to), must cause the thermostat to reduce the total heat input to the whole house, so that all the other rooms grow cold.

The temperature of the water in the hot supply tank is also controlled to a preset value, although the mechanism is a little different from the room thermostats. Indeed, regulating temperatures is one of the most common, if rather unexciting, of mechanical automatic control problems. Other control tasks in the house are somewhat more enterprising. Increasingly sophisticated devices determine the succession of operations carried out by the washing machine and the dishwasher, a much more complicated problem to address, which involves not only having to get water temperatures right but also completing a whole sequence of programmed operations. These days, it is economic for a small computer to be used for this purpose.

Out of the house, driving the car is largely a matter of regulating its speed and direction. Apart from my own control actions, the automatic gear-change and power steering are autonomous control systems which assist me in doing just that. Many cars have air conditioning—temperature control again—and some have automatic cruise control to regulate the car speed, despite fluctuations in road gradients. Indeed, almost all contemporary means of travel rely increasingly on automatic control systems. Even pleasure boats may have artificial helmsmen, to keep them on course, and airline pilots simply could not fly their planes without the highly effective and elaborate control mechanisms built into them. The automatic pilot in an airliner flies the aircraft so much more precisely than a human pilot that it saves a considerable proportion of the fuel that would otherwise be consumed. Partly for this reason, passenger aircraft carry three auto-pilots so as to overcome problems that might follow a failure. Because of the precision with which they are flown, vapour trails left in the sky by airliners (on auto-pilot) are perfectly straight and level, in contrast to those from military combat planes, which are all loops and curls.

Information systems present a control design challenge, no less than transportation. When I punch a number into my telephone I direct the setting-up of circuits in my local exchange and the worldwide network to give me a connection to the person I wish to call, a refined problem of control. If I hanker for music and decide to play a compact disc, a sophisticated control mechanism is needed to keep the laser beam which reads the disc accurately aligned on the long string of minute pits in the aluminium surface (each a hundredth of the diameter of a human hair in size) which carry the encoded record of the music.

The list of control problems that have to be solved if contemporary life is to be enjoyed to the full seems almost endless. Power stations, fuel supply, industrial production—all are totally dependent on the successful application of control technology. Without sophisticated automatic regulating systems many manufacturing processes in the oil, steel and chemical industries would be neither effective nor even safe. At another extreme, modern horticulture demands control mechanisms to regulate the greenhouse light, temperature and humidity, often in complex cycles, to promote the healthy growth of plants. Nor is control important only at the mechanical level. Running a business, for instance, has much more to it than just getting satisfactory engineering into place in the factory, as company directors well know. The whole organization, the firm—itself a system composed of the people and the machines that support them—also has to be regulated and steered optimally if it is to perform its operations in a cost-effective way, sensitive to the demands of the market. But in the scale of tasks where control is crucial, business, even the very biggest, is by no means at the upper limit. Control problems come far bigger than that.

There is the matter of the economy, for example. Politicians, government officials and central bankers spend a good deal of their time trying hard to control the national and worldwide economy. By tinkering in various ways with the more sensitive parts, they strive to engineer stable prices, high levels of activity and an acceptable distribution of wealth between different social groups and geographical areas, all at the same time. Regrettably, they seem unable to achieve these objectives for long. It would be nonsense, of course, to suppose that intractable economic questions are entirely explained away by control theory; however, it does succeed in resolving some of the puzzles. Economics is illuminated by control science, just as by mathematics, yet is not subsumed by either; in this it is like many other disciplines—physiology, industrial management or engineering, for example.

Yet although it may be the largest, the world economy is still by no means the most sophisticated problem of control. Living creatures are positive wonders of immensely complex and highly successful automatic control, and humans foremost amongst them. Thus from the moment of my conception, all my growth and development were meticulously regulated so that I should mature into a human being rather than a dolphin or a giraffe. While I live, every aspect of my body function is dominated by automatic control mechanisms of which I am quite unaware, unless they go wrong. If the iris and lens in my eye were not always closely controlled to the correct settings I would be as good as blind, and if my body temperature or the salinity of my blood passed outside a strictly limited range I would soon be dead. My heart, which has already beat about two billion times in the course of my life, is itself a miracle of control, each beat precisely triggered and the average rate adjusted to give just the right blood supply that I need for my activity level at the time. Even my mental function is perpetually guided by instinctual drives and regulated by complex internal mental objects and constructs, like the fear of death which prevents me from choosing my own destruction. In any living being there are so many control mechanisms, both physiological and psychological, ranging from simple regulators to complex sequential controllers, each capable of precise operation as it is needed, that even listing them is an impossible task. All life, human and animal, individual, social or economic, floats on a sea of control activities, without any of which it might very well be 'solitary, poor, nasty, brutish and short'.[1]

Internal psychological entities, including things like Freud's

1 Thomas Hobbes, *The Leviathan* (1651).

> id, ego and superego, are not material but 'software objects', pure packages of information which happen to have their embodiment at that time in the neurophysiology of the brain. Our whole personal identity—what defines 'me'—is a complex ensemble of these software objects. For this reason the very old will sometimes assert that the 'real' inner them is still young—they are right; software does not age like hardware (the body, in this case) so the inner personality does not age with the passage of time. It does evolve and develop, though, so they may be wiser than once they were, and it is subject to random corruption on rare occasions. Furthermore, if those software objects which are me for some reason were no longer stored in my brain, or were permanently unable to interact, I would no longer be there, dead and gone even though the body might be kept functioning by some artificial means. This is sometimes called 'brain death' although it can happen when the brain retains quite a lot of function, and 'software death' would be more accurate. Note, though, that because the brain contains software objects, just like a computer, it does not necessarily follow that the brain functions much like our digital computers, or indeed that the mind is usefully to be compared with one of our present computer programs. The matter is hotly disputed; among others, John Pollock[1] would argue for these propositions, while John Searle[2] gives compelling reasons to think differently.

While it is true that the human body is nothing like a factory, and neither of them much resembles the workings of the economy of a nation, nevertheless a remarkable discovery of our century was that there exists a unifying thread of control theory running through all of them. Each is concerned with regulating the variable factors in a situation to achieve (and go on achieving) certain objectives seen as of critical importance. Of course, it is also undeniably true that to understand the factory fully it is absolutely necessary to have some knowledge of engineering, for comprehending the workings of the body physiology is the prerequisite, and economics is needed for the

1 John Pollock, *How to Build a Person* (1989).

2 John R. Searle, *The Rediscovery of the Mind* (1992).

fullest understanding of the wealth of nations, yet for all of them a grasp of the mechanics of control is also critical if they are to make sense. Control theory became an evolved scientific discipline in its own right soon after 1930, when it was realized that all of these systems—mechanical, organizational or biological—have a certain conceptual unity, despite their vast diversity of detail.

Little wonder, then, seeing its generality and the broad sweep of its claims, that modern control theory is complicated and highly mathematical. Open even an undergraduate textbook of the subject and the prospect is forbidding. Yet labyrinthine as it has become, the science is still far from complete and many control activities vital to our lives have yet to be comprehended by a fully effective theoretical treatment. Even so, just as those of us who are neither physicists nor chemists can pick up enough of both sciences to make a little more sense of the world we live in, so equally there are comprehensible basic principles running through all control situations, and grasping just a few of these simple ideas makes it possible to understand much that would otherwise be obscure.

In the past people often picked the subject up unawares, a component—often ad hoc and rule of thumb—in the generality of their professional knowledge, the pill hidden in the meat of their subject so that it was taken unwittingly along with all the rest. It is more constructive, though, to look directly at the issue, and what is learned as a result proves to have a generality which is a reward in itself. Certainly control science cannot provide simple explanations for all the complex issues that plague us, and never will, but it helps to give insight into many strange things that sometimes happen.

2

More than one way

I put my hand in my bath water to judge its temperature, so that I can readjust the taps if necessary. When I do so I am using an indication of the variation of the actual situation from what I seek to achieve—the error, that is—in order to modify the control actions I adopt trying to achieve it. The accepted term for this is feedback, and a great divide exists between those control systems using feedback and those which do not. Feedback involves routeing some aspect of the result, the outcome of the controlling activity, back to influence the controlling action itself, around a loop as it were. Controllers using feedback are therefore called closed-loop systems, whereas those without feedback, by contrast, are called open-loop. These are the two basic kinds of control, and both are equally important for without either we could not live.

One of the first to study feedback from a modern standpoint, working in the United States in the years after 1920, was Harold S. Black (1898–1983),[1] who saw that properly understood it might solve problems then being encountered in long distance telephony. In 1927 he developed a mathematical theory of feedback, later used in the actual design of a feedback system. In Europe, Klaas Posthumus attacked the same problem, taking out a patent in 1928.

My own interest in this topic is far from merely intellectual, for most of the biological life-support control systems in my body are of the

1 Elizabeth Antebi, *The Electronic Epoch* (1982), p. 130.

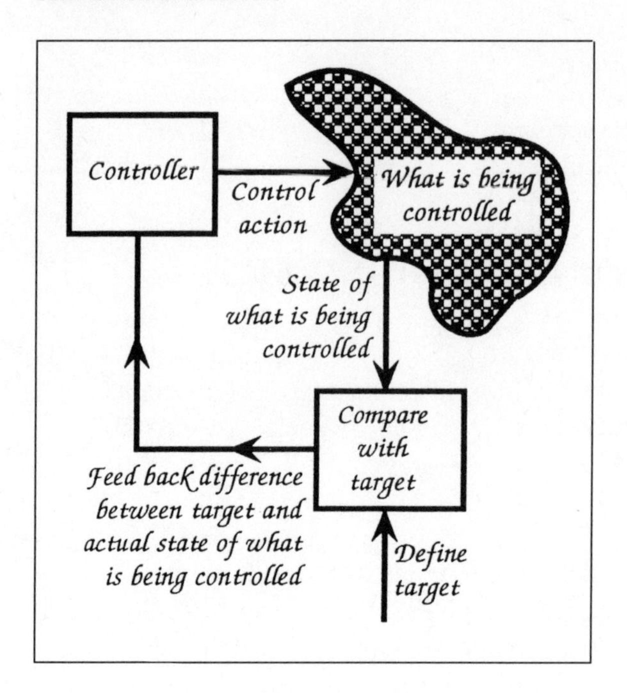

Fig. 1 A closed-loop controller

closed-loop type, employing feedback. Thus, when certain sensors inside me detect that my temperature is getting too high the sweat-glands function more vigorously, bringing it down again. The sweating is regulated by feedback from my temperature—a closed loop. To take another example, the amount of light falling on the sensitive retina at the back of my eye regulates the opening or closing of the iris of the eye, so determining the amount of light admitted in the first place, in a similar closed-loop control action. The iris of my eye closes a little if the light around me gets brighter, the consequence of feedback from the light sensors in the eye, with the effect of bringing the intensity of the light falling on the retina nearer to its optimum value.

Physiological closed-loop feedback is not always quite so benign, however, as those of us who try to lose weight by dieting are likely to find out. A sharp reduction of calorie intake in consequence of a downright penal diet sometimes produces only a temporary weight loss, and after a few weeks the bathroom scales are telling their old doleful story once again, despite continued misery in the dining room. What has happened is that a closed-loop control system (of which we are quite unaware) has reduced the level of physical activity in line with the reduced calorie intake, so the body weight returns close to its previous value. To lose weight it is necessary to break the loop, by reducing food intake while at the same time maintaining or increasing bodily activity, which many find hard. Alternatively it would be nice to instruct the internal control mechanism to aim for a lower target body weight, but it is doubtful that anybody knows how to do this.

Because, in all these cases, the feedback is in such a direction as to oppose and correct any deviation from the desired norm which may be taking place—any error, in short—it is called negative feedback. Ideas about negative feedback were first formulated explicitly in economics, where they were used to explain the supposed self-regulating character of a free market economy, and perhaps first of all by David Hume.[1] Long before that, though, technologists had been successfully building a variety of mechanical devices involving feedback, and without the benefit of any developed theory. Negative feedback spreads its web much wider than either economics or mechanical devices, too, for it is the great stabilizing force of both the natural and the human-built world, which, once set in motion, tirelessly corrects all deviations from the target value. Thus, consider the thermostat on a central heating radiator, increasing the flow of hot water if it senses that the surrounding air is cooler than it should be, or think of a falcon in flight, adjusting its speed and trajectory in accordance with its visual perception of the distance from its prey in order to achieve its aim, which is to close and make a kill. These are but two examples of ubiquitous negative feedback.

'Negative feedback'—the name sounds a little depressing, and maybe it was not well chosen. The feedback is negative, but not in any destructive interpretation of the word, only in that what is fed back is of such a sense that it counters the original stimulus—the perceived error, or distance from the target. Certainly the application of negative feedback is commonly altogether positive in its consequences, and often seems able to perform veritable miracles.

Sometimes, indeed, it achieves with ease what might rationally seem quite impossible. It is perfectly feasible, indeed routine, for me to leave my garage and drive my car five hundred kilometres only to park within

1 David Hume, *Political Discourses* (1752).

ten centimetres at my destination. Comparing the precision of the final location with the total distance I have travelled, a tenth of a metre in five hundred kilometres is equivalent to one part in five million. This remarkable precision of accomplishment looks impressive, and so it would be if I tried to complete my journey by open-loop control, starting out with a long sequence of instructions which took account of dimensions and curvature of every branch and bend in the road and the precise distance travelled between them. In reality, though, such a journey is quite easily completed because I control my car in an entirely different way. Throughout I continually compare where I ought to be (both position on the road and on the map) with where I actually am, check my speed against what it should be in the circumstances of road and traffic about me, and drive my car to minimize the error in any of these things. This is closed-loop, negative feedback control; properly followed it gets me safely there and home again.

Some years ago former United States President Ronald Reagan approved the so-called Star Wars or Strategic Defense Initiative (SDI) programme. It was proposed to defend the United States against nuclear weapon attack by destroying the incoming ballistic missiles with anti-missiles and laser guns, fired against them from space platforms. Many sought to decry the idea, and one argument used at the time made much of the impossible accuracy required to hit a target which might itself be less than a metre across at a distance of many hundreds of kilometres. This was probably a fair criticism of the open-loop controlled weapons, lasers and particle beam 'guns', but it seems that these were always little more than a bluff anyway, most unlikely to have worked in the foreseeable future. The real threat from the SDI platforms in space would surely have been from anti-missiles, which would certainly be subject to closed-loop control, steered like the hunting falcon to minimize the perceived miss distance from the incoming enemy warheads, their targets. With a closed-loop controller the required accuracy is easy to obtain, provided only that the target can be exactly located, something entirely possible in this case using precision radar.

The consequences of this approach were demonstrated clearly enough during the Gulf War, when Iraqi Scud missiles were successfully disabled by Patriot anti-missiles fired toward them, using closed-loop navigation in just this way. The anti-missiles were sophisticated—each Patriot round cost about a million dollars—but they were very successful. It is widely believed that fifty-one out of fifty-three Scuds fired towards United Nations forces were hit. Patriot was originally designed for use against ordinary aircraft, not as an anti-missile weapon, so the result achieved is particularly impressive.

> The then Soviet Union had its own 'Star Wars' research programme, from which it learned that a defence of this kind might indeed just about be feasible, but also that the cost would be way beyond its own capacity to match. It therefore mounted a campaign of propaganda and exhortation in the West—directly and through proxies—aimed at preventing any such development, fearing that if the programme went ahead the military balance could shift irretrievably against it.
>
> History may well characterize the Cold War as one of mutual economic attrition; it seriously weakened the economy of the United States but devastated the Eastern bloc. Reagan's 'Star Wars' was the final turn of the screw. Part bluff, part reality, aimed at driving the Soviet Union into yet more ruinous defence expenditure, it served its authors well, for that war is history now, lost and won.

One reason why the military have been more enthusiastic about missiles than guns in recent years is because by employing negative feedback control of their flight path missiles can be depended upon to come close enough to their targets to destroy them every time. In 1991 grimly memorable pictures appeared on our television screens in the West of an Iraqi military column which had been fleeing from Kuwait towards Baghdad at the end of the Gulf War; it had been systematically destroyed by helicopters using air-to-ground missiles. Hovering safely a few kilometres away, barely visible above the horizon, the helicopter crews lined up their missiles on target after target. Virtually all of them were hit first-shot and destroyed. The scale of the devastation was limited only by the logistics of loading helicopters with missiles and getting them into the air. The carnage was appalling, although at the time the use of stand-off weapons made the scale of human suffering invisible to its authors. Perhaps it was just as well for the morale of the UN forces; historical experience suggests that in situations where there is no risk to the attackers it is difficult to persuade the military to kill fellow creatures on this scale. By contrast soldiers who feel threatened and see close comrades killed by the enemy are able to be quite merciless.[1]

By contrast, guns are essentially open-loop controlled. They are carefully aimed in the right direction but once fired the flight of the shell cannot be deflected. In the past artillerymen have cleverly approximated to closed-loop control by firing a number of rounds and correcting the aim on the later ones according to the miss distance of the earlier. A traditional tactic, it works well, but only provided nothing changes from shot to shot, for example the wind does not alter direction and the target does not move. Effective as it has often proved, the modern military appears to think that this is just not good enough. However, guns do retain the advantage of being relatively cheap, and for this reason hybrid 'terminally guided munitions' have recently been invented, fired from a gun like a shell but navigating themselves like a missile once near their target. This hybrid of open-loop initial aiming followed by closed-loop terminal guidance has significance far beyond the military domain; indeed, in some areas of control it is virtually the unchallenged master strategy, as we shall see. Its adoption largely overcomes the weaknesses of open-loop control.

As for the closed-loop controller, whether in a terminal guidance role or much more generally, versatility and conceptual simplicity are important parts of its attraction. Another, no less far-reaching in its consequences, is that it can achieve success in situations which are not wholly predictable when the control is set up. It is not necessary to foresee everything that might happen: closed loops guide the anti-missile to its target regardless of any evasive action, something that could not be known in advance, and similarly in our bodies closed-loop systems regulate the processes of life despite widely fluctuating and unpredictable levels of activity, environment and nutrition. How significant this physiological feedback is can easily be seen in circumstances where it fails and an attempt is made to replace it by open-loop control. Consider the illness diabetes, for example.

Diabetes mellitus was known in former times as 'the pissing

1 Charles Carlton, *Going to the Wars* (1992). This comment relates to ordinary soldiers under normal military command; specialized murder squads, like the Nazi SS or the Soviet NKVD, are of course quite another matter.

sickness' because if untreated it leads to the passing of very large volumes of water. It is due to the pancreas secreting too little insulin to maintain a normal blood glucose concentration. The insulin-dependent form often starts in childhood. Its incidence increases with age, and it is more common in females and the poor. Unless insulin is supplied externally the sufferer will develop high ketone levels in the blood, with risk of heart failure, while coma from high levels of blood glucose is also likely. After the isolation of insulin by Banting and Best in 1921, death from diabetes declined dramatically in developed countries. The disease may affect some 150 million people worldwide and despite modern treatments could still be the cause of up to five million deaths each year, a larger number than road traffic accidents.

Whereas a normal person can produce internally his own requirement of the hormone insulin, the amount strictly regulated by closed-loop control, in the case of insulin-dependent diabetes the patient does not do so. Since the hormone is essential to the correct metabolism of sugar, fats and proteins, wellbeing is threatened and ultimately perhaps even life itself. The only satisfactory treatment is for the patient to receive injections of insulin daily. However, the dose is fixed in advance for the day to come, so these shots can only allow for an average level of physical activity. If this is significantly exceeded in a particular day the result may be very low blood sugar levels, with unpleasant symptoms and even unconsciousness. The open-loop control proves unable to adapt to changing circumstances in the way that the closed loop would for a healthy person.

In practice, however, experienced insulin-dependent diabetics can sense the onset of low blood sugar, and deal with the problem by carrying confectionery with them, which they can eat to counter the danger. They re-establish a closed-loop control by using feedback from their perceived physical state to regulate the sugar available to them instead of the insulin. Adjustment of the insulin dose and control of physical activity are other ways of recovering closed-loop control. On its own the open-loop approach proves simply not flexible enough.

All this may make it seem that closed-loop controls can solve all problems as if by magic, but that is certainly not the case and they do not always appear by any means so successful. In part it depends on what constitutes success; for example, if incoming missiles carry nuclear warheads even just one failure to destroy would be intolerable, which was the fundamental dilemma of the SDI programme. But perhaps the most obvious case of an at least partially ineffective closed-loop control is the management of the economy.

One task of those who try to regulate the national economy is to keep a check on the money supply. If it appears to be growing too fast they raise interest rates to reduce it, conversely lowering them if the amount of money available seems inadequate to sustain economic activity—yet another example of negative feedback closed-loop control. In theory it should work, but to the bystander it does not seem by any means like an outright model of effectiveness. Recessions and inflation follow each other in seemingly endless business cycles, and the extent of control various governments seem able to impose ranges from bad to unimpressive. Despite the excellence of the closed loop in theory, this is one example of inadequate control which is all too apparent.

> It is a gross oversimplification, of course, to write as if interest rates were the only means for regulating the economy that governments have at their disposal, even if some choose to play it that way. Needless to say, there are all kinds of other possible means of regulation, from fiscal policy to public works.

Yet although constraints of various descriptions may enter, in other applications the closed-loop controller mostly succeeds very well, with no obvious limit to its accuracy, whether in hitting a target in space or setting my bath water temperature. If it can hardly be denied that the economic regulatory process does not always work well, this must evidently be due to a number of as yet unidentified factors which make it malfunction. It is essential, therefore, to seek to understand just how good we can expect that the degree of control will be in any particular case, supposing that we have a closed loop governed by negative feedback.

Sadly, the question is not simply answered, because several conditions must be fulfilled simultaneously for the control system to succeed. One of the more obvious is that the residual error—the difference between what is desired and what has been achieved—needs to be reliably measured, and that is a large part of the difficulty in the management of the economy. For finance ministers and central bankers the available means of measuring what they are trying to control (the money supply) are neither well defined, quick nor accurate. Other intractable problems also dog the economic regulators, principally arising from lag in the functioning of the feedback loop, the consequences of which will emerge shortly.

However, one further condition for the success of a closed-loop control is not too difficult to guess at. For a given stimulus, the outcome of the controlling action must surely depend on how much feedback is generated, how vigorously the loop responds. We need, here, to begin to be quantitative. How do we actually measure whether the feedback effect is strong enough to give the wanted result, achieving the object set for it? Seeing its distance from the prey, how hard will the falcon have to struggle to accelerate itself toward the capture? If my bath water is too hot or too cold, by how much do I adjust the taps for each degree of error? If the money supply overshoots by twenty per cent, should interest rates be increased by one per cent, or three, or five?

Because this relationship of the magnitude of the feedback effect to the stimulus producing it is one of the most important characteristics of any closed-loop system, it is given a name: the loop gain. This is simply the ratio of feedback to stimulus (which could be less than unity, that is less feedback than stimulus, but for negative feedback is generally much greater). In the examples quoted, it is not difficult to guess that the larger the loop gain the more emphatic the effects of feedback will be, and therefore the closer the control system will approach to achieving its aim, at least in principle.

> Strictly, to measure loop gain we should temporarily break the loop at the point where the feedback returns to the part of the system at which the original stimulus is applied. If not, feedback and stimulus will interact and the situation becomes confused. With the loop broken a stimulus can be injected and the feedback observed without complicating effects. However, in some important cases, of which the economy is one, any such procedure is impossible and it becomes necessary to infer the loop gain by more indirect means.

This, though, is not the end of the list of snags and difficulties. Time, the old enemy, is the most important of all the complicating factors. Closed-loop negative feedback control systems have been depicted so far as having many advantages, including the ability to respond to unforeseen circumstances and an accuracy of control which could, in principle, be made as close to ideal as we please, simply by raising the loop gain. This is all true, though, only if everything in the loop happens so quickly that it is possible to ignore the effects of the passage of time, for time, as we shall see, is the great tyrant of all negative feedback systems.

Harry Nyquist (1889–1976) first understood and quantified the effects of things taking a time to work that could no longer be neglected; his insights were an intellectual watershed, at last making comprehensible much that had previously been mysterious. The publication of his paper on feedback is considered to mark a major step in the emergence of control theory as a distinct science in its modern form.[1] Nyquist was a Swedish-born migrant to the United States who worked for AT&T (1917–34) and at the Bell Laboratories (1934–54). The Bell Labs at their height constituted a classic example of massive research spending funded out of a near-monopoly (United States telephones) and their achievements were legendary. The monopoly was ultimately broken up by legal action and after that the funding of the Bell Labs no longer seemed quite so bottomless as before. Whether this will prove to have been in the long-term interests of the United States remains to be seen.

While working for AT&T, Nyquist discovered (1932) the conditions for stability in a feedback system (the Nyquist criterion). In this he was influenced by Harold S. Black, who had earlier succeeded with a less general analysis of the effects of feedback. Later, after joining the Bell Labs, Nyquist is also credited with discovering how close in time must be the points at which a signal has to be sampled for satisfactory digital representation (the Nyquist rate), another crucial insight. Digital coding of signals (representation by a string of numbers rather than a continuous quantity) is the basis of modern telephony, broadcasting and recording.

To get a real feeling for the problems Nyquist addressed there is nothing quite like experiencing them in practice. I recall a day in the early 1980s, under the hot California sun, when I visited the laboratories of a major United States defence contractor, one of whose interests was the building of submarines. As part of their design facility

1 H. Nyquist, 'Regeneration theory', *Bell System Technical Journal* 11 (1932).

they had established a submarine simulator. Simulators are a means by which the characteristics of a vehicle (be it plane, car or ship) or even of an industrial plant may be experienced and investigated, yet without the thing itself actually being constructed. They consist of a mock-up of the controls—the cabin of an aircraft, control centre of an industrial site, the bridge of a ship—which can be manipulated just as if they were the real thing by those using the simulator. Linked to them is an unseen computer, continually working out what the real-life consequences would be of the actions that the simulator users are taking. In the case of an aircraft simulator the cabin even rolls and tilts under the command of the computer to heighten the sense of the realism with which a flight is replicated. To an almost uncanny degree, the simulation may even produce the right noises in the cabin and coordinated pictures at the windows, still further to heighten the illusion that this is the real thing.

Having already tried an aircraft simulator—widely used for training air crew—I thought I could guess how things would work out, but this was the first time I had experienced a simulated submarine. We climbed down into what seemed very like the bowels of a vessel and I soon found myself sitting in front of a control column, responsible for the navigation of the ship in the vertical plane, up and down, with another person seated at my left who would steer to port and starboard, like the helmsman of a surface ship. Our simulated voyage began, and receiving the order to dive I eased the control column forward and watched the depth gauge. Precisely nothing happened, so I pushed the stick in my hands forward a little more. Still nothing! Another forward push, and all of a sudden we were diving, much too fast. I pulled the stick back hard, but it was too late. In supposed shallow water our simulated submarine drove hard into the sea bottom. I had wrecked the ship, and that within moments of starting my try-out as depth helmsman. What deceived me was the long time it took for the vessel to answer to the controls. Thus I pushed the stick forward so far that when the ship finally did respond she crash-dived. I had no hope of correcting matters because the opposite action of the controls took just as long, and could not correct the dive before the collision with the simulated sea-bed. The better strategy, as I soon learned, was to make a small movement of the column and then wait for what seemed a very long while to give the submarine time to answer. Only then was it safe to make a further small movement, or to draw back, as the depth achieved might dictate.

I left the simulator that day with immense regard for the people who crew such ships, navigating them around the world with skill and precision. Of course, with my hands on the submarine controls and my eye on the depth gauge I had been trying to make myself part of a negative feedback closed-loop controller, keeping the ship at a constant depth, but in this attempt I was frustrated at first by the loop delay. The solution to the problem, taught me by hard experience, was to try to anticipate the actions of the ship. I was able to do this because quite quickly I formed in my mind a model, as it were, of how she would respond, and did to the controls whatever I anticipated would make the ship in my mind's eye behave as I wanted. The contractors, at that time, were researching the possibility of modelling the behaviour of the ship in a computer rather than in the mind of the helmsman, so that the crew could control her in an altogether simpler and more intuitive way. This turned out to be feasible and was a valuable advance for submariners. A computer model of almost any system proves to be an important aid to dealing with difficult control situations, permitting a degree of offset of the effects of time-lag by intelligent anticipation.

The simulated submarine is a typical example of a closed-loop control system with a long time delay. No less, my troublesome early morning bath water is yet another. I test the temperature of the water with my hand only once or twice, with a long lapse of time between. If it should be too cold the first time and I consequently increase the flow of hot water to put matters right, I am quite likely to find at the next trial that the temperature is too high—I have overshot the mark with my bath water just as I did with the submarine simulation. Notice that in this case a large loop gain—in the submarine a large movement of the control in response to a small perceived depth error, or in my bath a large increase in the flow of hot water in response to feeling water that is only a little cool—will make matters worse, not better. This is not a problem to be solved by trying harder.

When a time-lag is present in a negative feedback closed-loop controller it is very commonplace for the system to 'hunt' in this way. Instead of settling to a steady state where what is being controlled—the temperature of my bath for example—is acceptably close to the desired value, it cycles continuously around the optimum condition, overshooting first in one direction and then in the other. The bath water is first a little too hot, then a little too cool, then a little too hot

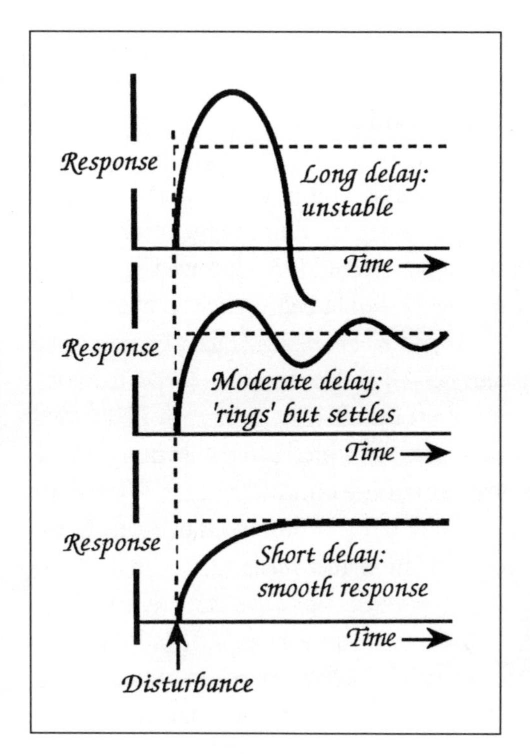

Fig. 2 The response of a negative feedback system to a disturbance, such as a change in what it aims at, depends critically on the delay in the loop.

again, hunting on either side of the right temperature for as long as the attempt at control goes on. In the worst cases the hunting gets larger and larger and the system goes completely out of control.

Nyquist's discoveries of 1932 included the proposition that all those negative feedback control systems where some time delay occurs in the loop will hunt unstably, provided only that the loop gain is large enough. Just how large it has to be in any particular case may be deduced from Nyquist's criterion, the statement of which was one of the most important milestones in the development of control theory.

For Nyquist's purpose the loop gain is assumed to be measured with the loop opened, using a sinusoidal perturbation. Nyquist's criterion, for a linear system with only a simple time delay, may then be put in an elementary form as follows:

> *If the loop gain is unity or greater at that frequency of the input sinusoid where the time delay in the system is equal to half of a cycle period, the system will be unstable.*

> Another way to look at it is that under these conditions the feedback is delayed by just the critical time which leads to it arriving when the correction should actually have been in the opposite sense, so that what should be negative feedback has been turned by the delay into positive feedback (for which see below) and the system will no longer be stable (provided the loop gain is sufficient in magnitude).

Control systems all around us are unstable, others hunt but ultimately settle. The hunting is, for instance, a common cause of cyclicity in the market price of a product, of which the archetype is the celebrated pig cycle. In simple market theory if the price of pigs rises (because of buoyant demand for pork, ham, bacon and sausages) farmers will see that good profits are to be made by rearing pigs, the supply will therefore increase and the price will fall back once more. Just so: if it worked this would be a perfect negative feedback control system. However, merely deciding to increase the supply of pigs does not create them overnight; certain formalities must be gone through first. For a start, breeding sows in a receptive frame of mind have to be located and introduced to an interested boar. After nuptials are completed there follows an extended pregnancy, then delivery, the nursing of piglets, the weaning of piglets and finally their fattening to a marketable weight, all taking much time. This extended delay is incorporated into the feedback loop, which has a large gain, partly because there are many potential pig breeders who all read the same market reports in farming magazines and partly because modern sows produce large litters. The predictable consequence is that the price of pigs never settles to a steady value but hunts continually, going through peaks and troughs at regular intervals of a few years.

This is vexing for the pig-breeding industry because the farmer always seems to find himself with a good supply of pigs when the prices are low and hardly any to offer when the prices are high. What could be done to put matters to rights? To stop a system containing a time delay from hunting it is necessary, according to Nyquist, to reduce the loop gain below the critical value given by his criterion, but in practice this may sometimes mean that the gain is so low that the control is not very effective. The critical value of loop gain before hunting sets in is, however, almost always higher the shorter the time-lag in the system. If action can be speeded up, therefore, it should be possible to raise the gain and improve the performance of the system without running into hunting.

Evidently to end the hunting of the pig cycle it is necessary either to reduce the loop gain or (better) the time delay. This is not easy, for obvious reasons, but it is not impossible. Governments, ever mindful of the votes of pig breeders, may decide to buy (and cold store) pig carcasses when the supply is plentiful, in order to release them to the market when their availability is poorer. This has the effect of reducing the system loop gain (since it is as if the increase in supply at times of glut had not been so great) but also, more importantly, in times of dearth the stored carcasses can be released to the market immediately and in times of glut withdrawn just as fast, thus greatly decreasing the time delay in response. Practised on a large enough scale, buy and store could thus suppress hunting altogether, by speeding response and reducing the loop gain below the Nyquist's criterion value. Even if not carried this far it will reduce the extent of the problem.

The pig-rearing industry is one of the best documented in which price hunting occurs, but by no means the only one. Manufacturing silicon microelectronic circuits, or chips, is a high-technology industry bedevilled by similar problems, and for much the same reasons. A decision to increase the supply of silicon chips can rarely be implemented instantly because it will normally involve building and equipping a new silicon fabrication plant, and this can easily take a couple of years. The silicon chip manufacturer too often has the galling experience of bringing a new factory on stream just at the time when the price of chips is heading towards an all-time low. To add to the problem, the pig-cycle solution of market intervention, by taking product into store for release at a later date, will not work in this case. Silicon chips are subject to rapid technological development, with the consequence that stored chips lose much of their value in a few months, due to technical obsolescence. One answer is to start to construct new fabrication plants when prices are bad (rather than very good, as one would be instinctively inclined to do) but it is difficult to persuade a board of directors to accept any such proposition. It takes strong nerves, sympathetic bankers and a contrary spirit to extend the plant of a silicon chip business when it is actually losing money because the available market price is so weak, yet this could be the most rational course to pursue.

Another example of a negative feedback system which continually hunts because of excessive gain and long time delays is the regulation of money supply in the economy, already mentioned. The attempt is made to control money supply by changing interest rates and the effect is to produce economic cycles of boom followed by recession. When money supply rises too fast, causing inflation, a rise in the interest rates should reduce it, and conversely when the supply is too low a drop in rates should remedy the situation. However, the control system is characterized by long delays and excessive loop gain, so it hunts between inflation and recession with a rather irregular cycle (in the UK) of a dozen or so years from trough to trough. Why so?

Control loop dynamics is not the only factor involved, but the argument goes somewhat as follows. The decision to put up interest rates is politically unpopular, so governments stall any such move as long as possible, turning a blind eye to indicators of increasing inflation while they plausibly can, and then a little longer. Finally, in crisis, they see at last that something must be done. Interest rates are then raised steeply, in the hope that drastic action will squeeze the economy quickly and get the whole unpleasantness over fast, well before the next election. This is represented as the government taking a firm and unflinching line in the national interest. Characteristically, there has been long delay followed by excessive response, implying a high loop gain.

When the time comes to drop the rates again, this too is postponed. Central bankers counsel prudence, and advise making sure that the serpent of inflation is really dead before vigilance is relaxed. The politicians, who have been through a period of unpopularity and certainly do not wish to repeat it, are vulnerable to this cautious-seeming advice, which has the effect of introducing yet more lag. When the belated cut is at last made a big one is attractive, because it signals clearly that the good times are coming back, which is electorally useful. By then there is also a general acceptance that room for a large cut exists, in direct consequence of the long wait. Once again the loop gain is set very high, therefore. With long delays and high loop gain the system cannot but hunt, and so it does and for a long time has, between boom and recession. Part of the trouble is psychological: fear is a great procrastinator, so prudence is equated with caution which is thought to be synonymous with postponement. Doing nothing seems safer than doing something, but in a closed-loop control system this is not the case. Delay promotes hunting, or even hitting the bottom hard, like my simulated submarine.

The problem is made still worse because interest rate changes are employed for two distinct and unrelated purposes simultaneously: at the same time as they are expected to perform a regulatory function they are also used to transmit messages to the world—'the government's determination to stamp out inflation' at one extreme and 'the clear success of the government's anti-inflation policies' at the other. To send these political messages in a noticeable way a large change in interest rate is more effective than a small; such a pity that big changes mean large loop gain, and hence destabilize the system.

A more rational economic control strategy would be to make frequent very small changes in interest rates, and do it slightly before they seem altogether unavoidable. The result would be to reduce both loop gain and delay, so that hunting should be much diminished. It would be interesting to see the results of a regime where central banks were obliged by law to change their base rates not more than once per week, but could only increase or decrease by the fixed increment of, say, one eighth per cent. Whatever defects such a system might have, its loop gain should be low enough to preclude inflation–recession cycles (at least those due to this cause). Having to make very small up or down decisions not more than once per week might also encourage an attempt to foresee the coming need for change, since the option of a big jump sometime in the future would have gone. This would have the effect of reducing loop delay. In fact, around the world, governments which are more successful economic managers already appear to favour small increases and decreases in interest rates. For a time the UK government seemed like a recruit to this exclusive club at last, keeping changes of interest rates small from the start of 1990 until the middle of 1992, and this despite the Opposition and some friends alike urging them to the contrary.

Finally, a problem with understanding feedback systems is that their operation can often be counter-intuitive, so that common sense is a deceptive guide to their mode of function. Indeed, the action of the closed loop can make them seem very contrary. Thus, if I eat an egg for my breakfast, evidently one chicken less will hatch (assuming the egg was fertile). Do we therefore reduce the world chicken population by eating eggs? Not so; it is quite obvious that if nobody ate eggs there would be precious few hens. The number of birds is set by a closed loop (operating through the market) which attempts to regulate the number of eggs produced to equal the number consumed, although it works imperfectly, as with pigs. Thus, contrary to first appearances, eating eggs should actually increase the chicken population. All closed-loop systems have this kind of tricky character, and many difficulties that people experience in understanding economics come from not being able to tell chicken from egg in the real world of trade, industry and wealth creation.

3

Open loops, closed loops and hybrids

We have seen that successful application of negative feedback, working in a straightforward manner merely to minimize the distance between the objective (or target) and the actual current achievement, does three things: it attains defined objectives, offsets the consequences of unpredicted change and gives repeatability of results between nominally like systems despite minor variations. These are great virtues, and our world would fall apart without negative feedback closed-loop controls. However, such controls, despite their strong points, cannot be universal. In some cases, indeed, closed-loop control is out of the question and open-loop the sole option.

The most obvious example is when the controlled actions take place later in time, perhaps long after, the controlling strategy is determined. A classic example of an open-loop controller is thus a computer program. Once it has been fed into the machine the subsequent behaviour of the computer is according to a fixed pattern set by the program; while it is running there is normally no feedback or adjustment made to the sequence of statements which make up the program. Although the program may contain instructions which command feedback actions within it, or may be used as part of a feedback controller, for example managing a chemical plant, the actual program itself is invariant once written, its commands unchanging, and is at the end what it was at the beginning, the archetypal open-loop controller.

As a consequence, everybody who has ever written software knows how difficult it is to get the list of instructions just precisely right.

Even the smallest deviation from the ideal program results in things happening which frustrate the writer's intentions, and to make such a mistake proves all too easy. This illustrates the principal shortcoming of open-loop control: since there is no adaptation to changing circumstances, absolutely everything that is required must be foreseen and correctly provided for. Yet despite all that, open-loop controls are also widespread in the real world, and often highly successful.

> Although what has been written is true of most computer programs now in use, just a very few experimental ones do have the capacity to rewrite themselves as a consequence of observing how well they are doing. This adaptive software is rare as yet, but it has the important capacity to learn by its mistakes.
>
> Human software—the content of the mind—is massively adaptive, which is an enormous point of difference between the brain and present-day computers. Psychotherapists exploit the adaptive capacity of human software; by using various of its technical characteristics, such as transference and counter-transference, they provoke adaptations and hence modify the patient's software. Sadly, it is a very slow process, but there is no more direct way to access and change the defective software. Perhaps it may be just as well; to be able to do so would be a frightening power in the wrong hands.

Genetic inheritance is quintessential open-loop control, for no animal can reach back and retrospectively change its own genetic codes in a feedback process. Animals and plants are programmed to develop in a given way, the whole pattern contained within the genetic code passed on to them by their parents, and this process of transmission is already complete when their life begins. Lizard, horse or human being, they will be what they were predestined to become, and if that should prove a poor match to the environment in which they are obliged to live, too bad for them. It is because of the intrinsic limitation of the open loop, its inability to respond to changing circumstances not allowed for when the control was set, that from time to time species of living creatures become extinct, as the dinosaurs did when it became too cold for them, following a sudden environmental cataclysm.

> This is according to one theory of dinosaur extinction, but nobody really knows what finished them off, and there are

other hypotheses. Charig, in a paper presented to the geology section of the British Association, lists a hundred proposed mechanisms of dinosaur extinction, not all entirely serious.[1]

However, extinction happens only rarely, when circumstances change particularly fast, because, although the major characteristics of individuals are set by open-loop control through genetic determination, by contrast so far as the species of animal is concerned a slow closed-loop control mechanism does exist. It works because there is always considerable inherited variation between the individuals of a particular species, amounting to a statistical distribution of the characteristics of their particular genetic packages. Those best adapted to their environment will have the best chance to reproduce. Thus in the next generation (neglecting for simplicity distinctions between genotypes and phenotypes) the least well-adapted genetic packages are less likely to be present, whilst the better adapted will be in greater proportion. On average, as the generations pass, the distribution of genetic packages will drift in a direction such as to increase the representation of those which are more successfully adapted. This process of natural selection is indeed, therefore, a form of closed-loop control, but it takes many generations to have a major impact. Species of animals are consequently extinguished from time to time when natural selection produces adaptation too slowly, compared with changes taking place in the environment, so that the genetic stock of the species cannot evolve fast enough to offset the problems being encountered.

Selective extinction, a kind of 'natural selection', is also commonplace far outside the natural world.[2,3] Thus, the numerous programs produced commercially for desk-top computers, many with closely similar functions, can be regarded as a 'population' competing for survival. Examples generally have a limited life, to be extinguished and replaced as soon as users are no longer prepared to buy them. In this way the population of available desk-top computer software adapts itself both to the evolving requirements of users and the developing capabilities of their machines. Such programs are often written in

1 A. Charig, *The Great Dinosaur Mystery*, British Association, Plymouth (1991).

2 R. J. Richards, 'Natural selection and other models in the historiography of science', in M. Brewer and B. Collins, *Scientific Enquiry and the Social Sciences* (1981).

3 George Basalla, *The Evolution of Technology* (1988).

software houses which get little meaningful feedback on how their products are doing. They design to what they think will be needed, but this evidently constitutes an open-loop control situation. Selective extinction is the only way a software population of this kind can adapt to the users' actual needs. More generally, selective extinction is the most important way in which a market economy adjusts goods and services to match the preferences of consumers. One of the disadvantages of allowing political factors to interfere with this process is the growing consequent mismatch between what consumers seek and what is available to them.

All in all, it is sometimes difficult to be sure whether the control loop is truly open or closed, and indeed there is a tendency for loops to find their own avenue of closure if only through selective extinction; nevertheless the importance of understanding the character and shortcomings of open-loop control cannot be overstated, and for an unlikely reason: human beings find the open loop psychologically seductive, greatly exaggerating its virtues and often treating its desirability as almost axiomatic. The surprising observation is that most people find the actual practice of open-loop control highly rewarding when they manage it successfully, and what is more the attempt to do so is a challenge which many find hard to decline. It is for this reason that all the most popular games we play or watch exploit the challenges of open-loop control.

Thus once the golf ball has left the club there can be no use for feedback, because nothing can control it in flight. What counts is getting that first impact of the club just right, the carefully executed stroke which achieves the seemingly impossible in terminal accuracy. The same is just as true between the football and the boot, or the tennis ball and the racquet. But it is not only in the performance of well-judged open-loop control actions that we revel. There is much pleasure for us to be had in merely watching others do such things well, as the attendance at Wimbledon or the audience for televised snooker matches clearly demonstrates. We are in love with the dream of perfect open-loop control and make heroes of those who appear to have the knack of it.

The obsession with open-loop control is seemingly dominant in all games, even if a closed-loop element is present also. In tennis the service is a quintessential open-loop activity, but the skill of responding to the ball that comes over the net is an open-loop stroke executed by the player thanks to closed-loop control skills in hand and brain. In more detail, the skill of moving and placing the tennis racquet, so that it will hit the fast-approaching ball at the desired angle and with the intended impact, is a matter of precise closed-loop regulation, but after the impact on the ball the player has no further control. So then, to speak precisely, the shot is played open-loop as a result of an impulse applied to the ball under brief closed-loop control.

In some games, it is true, the closed-loop aspect apparently has a larger place. Poker players can succeed by adapting their play to the cards opponents hold, so they do all in their power to infer what these may be. Players cultivate a 'poker face', trying hard to reveal nothing about cards in their hand in the hope of breaking the feedback loop for opponents. It might seem, therefore, that this is a wholly closed-loop game, but those who play well tell me that this is not true, that the masters have secret strategies conceived in advance, which are essentially open-loop. Be that as it may, what is sure of all games is that closed-loop play is perceived at best as skilful but open-loop play as heroic, and we particularly admire, even in those games which have a closed-loop component, the players who can so dominate the strategy that they reduce the significance of their opponents' responses to a negligible level.

Open-loop control retains its seductive quality far outside the boundaries of sport, too. In politics there has been a predilection, widespread throughout history, to follow the open-loop practitioner. Great kings, heaven-sent emperors and charismatic leaders, men of destiny called to power in a moment of historic need, it is all these who are admired and followed. Whether they succeed or not they are long remembered, celebrated indeed in poem and legend, their failures invariably attributed to misfortune or to the malice of their opponents, rather than to their own shortcomings. Heroic images of Napoleon Bonaparte as Emperor, painted with genius by David, all too often correspond to how we would secretly like our leaders to be, and we even count it a virtue in them that they make their own plans and go their own way, led by the gods or by their genius. In short they control events open-loop, guided—and sometimes driven—by a unique inner vision, without too much regard to the immediately apparent consequences of what they do.

Jacques Louis David (1748–1825) was the great French painter of the Revolution and Napoleonic era. His first masterpiece was 'The Oath of the Horatii' (1784), neoclassical in style like all his work. David backed the Revolution ardently, was elected to the National Convention in 1792, and voted to execute Louis XVI. After Robespierre was guillotined David, like so many others, narrowly saved himself only by lies and deceit. Napoleon soon took him up though, and he produced many portraits of the great man in a heroic, flattering style. When the Emperor fell David fled France for Belgium and painted no more of any worth.

Not everybody had such a flattering view of the Emperor. Mlle Georges, of the Comédie Française, is said to have remarked, 'Dormir avec Napoléon, dormir avec le vainqueur du monde! Mais M. le Duc était de beaucoup le plus fort!'[1] She meant Arthur Wellesley, Duke of Wellington, of course, and that of which she spoke, she knew.

Preference for, and admiration of, open-loop actions seems a universal human trait. It may be that it has its origins in the struggles of the infant to individuate itself, asserting its own (open-loop) control over its environment rather than simply responding (in closed-loop) to its mother. At the beginning, as Donald Winnicott pointed out,[2] psychologically 'there is no such thing as a baby', only an entity which is mother and baby together. Later the infant individuates itself, in part by exercising control over objects. In doing so it is conscious only of its own open-loop control action, the myriad of closed loops in the musculature and nervous system which make the action possible remaining quite unsuspected. Thus individuation is linked with processes of open-loop control.

It is also at this stage that the infant becomes fully aware of the father, perceived as one 'out there' who causes things to happen in the external world and the archetype of the heroic open-loop controller (because the infant is unaware of any constraints on the father's actions). Perhaps this explains the later tendency foolishly to suppose that the

1 Quoted in Arthur Bryant, *The Great Duke* (1971). 'To sleep with Napoleon is to sleep with the conqueror of the world! But the Duke was by far the more vigorous.'

2 D. W. Winnicott, 'Anxiety associated with insecurity', in *Collected Papers* (1958).

heroic open-loop domain is an exclusively male preserve, women's 'natural' control mode being closed-loop (as in good mothering). It is all nonsense, of course, but—in Western societies at least—a very evident mind-set. In this context, God is, needless to say, the ultimate open-loop controller. As the Koran (written 610–32) expresses it 'Everything is possible if Allah wills'. He can do whatever He pleases by His will alone and 'nothing shall hinder Him'. God is also, we are told by theologians, omnipotent, omniscient, omnipresent and omnicompetent, which is probably just as well in the circumstances.

> Some feminists find the use of 'He' for God objectionable, and are rarely mollified by being told that it is not meant to be gender-specific. Actually it is theologically impossible for God to have gender because that would be in conflict with His attributes of omniscience and omnicompetence. Jesus, the second person of the trinity, presumably had gender only while he was incarnate.
>
> Early Christian writers, however, often referred to the Holy Ghost as 'she'. I like this because the Holy Ghost is said to have brought the gift of tongues, and of course we all receive the inestimable gift of language from a woman—our mothers, needless to say. Although the Holy Ghost, as third person of the triune deity, does not have gender either, perhaps we could get into the habit of using 'she' in this context.

There is also an obvious connection with the belief in the primacy of free will, as against determinism, in regulating human behaviour. The former asserts the possibility of open-loop control of behaviour by the individual concerned, whereas the latter reserves the open-loop initiative to God alone. Judaism, Islam and most of Christianity make a strong stand for free will.[1]

In politics an inclination towards open-loop control, with all its problems, arises not merely because we have a psychological predilection towards charismatic leaders, important though that is. All too often in the past, it has also been widely believed that open-loop control of society was both more efficient and, strangely enough, more moral. The notion of a command economy, in which the scale and direction of virtually all economic activity is rationally determined in advance by

1 Melanie Edwards explained this to me.

a master plan, articulated either by the genius of the Great Leader himself or by some all-wise State planning body, was a central issue of political aspiration for a major part of the twentieth century.

By many the superior efficiency of the command economy was regarded as so obvious that it had axiomatic status in their political debate. When experience of actual planned economies showed that this was untrue, indeed an inversion of reality, for a long time the facts were not accepted. Either flat denial or rationalizations based on the assertion of false reporting, or even sabotage, achieved wide acceptance, until the reality could no longer be disputed. During World War II it was widely assumed in Britain and the United States that the German Nazi regime must naturally be more efficient than the market economies on the opposing side because it was believed to feature a ruthlessly planned economy. There was genuine surprise in some quarters when investigations after the conclusion of hostilities showed, beyond doubt, that for war purposes the German economy had been less efficiently mobilized than those of the democracies.

> Those who favour open-loop control of economic activity call what they aim at a 'planned economy', while those who oppose prefer 'command economy'. With the failure of so-called 'real socialism' (i.e. communism, as we would say in the West) the latter is now the more fashionable term.
>
> In Marxist eschatology 'communism' denotes an ideal state of human society only to be reached in the distant future, beyond the stage of socialism. Thus within the Soviet empire (and in China to this day) people believed (or affected to believe) that the government they lived under was building socialism, and they called it 'real socialism' to distinguish it from the Western bourgeois democratic version, which they denounced as bogus or ineffective.

Its proponents argued that the planned economy must be more efficient, since it could avoid the devotion of resources to wasteful and undesirable activities while coordinating the magnitude, timing and direction of those it favoured, so as to optimize what could be achieved. In the 1930s the only political question of significance for many in Europe was whether it should be the inspired Leader or the Vanguard Party which gave approval to the plan, believing as they often did that the last great political battle would necessarily be between fascism and communism in some future ideological Armageddon. Today, when the differences between these two appear slight, and of degree rather than kind, this seems a quaintly dated notion. Even so it was once widespread, and still survives here and there.

Others of those who favoured central planning emphasized a different dimension: the moral superiority of the planned economy. Because it was driven by commands which were the expression of the General Will (as embodied, naturally, in the Vanguard Party or the Leader), such a system would be able to ensure that what ought to happen, what was morally right, did in fact take place. At one and the same time needless waste could be eliminated while the right and the good would be made to prevail, all at a stroke, simply by decree. It followed that in a planned economy no longer would the poor starve while the rich searched for new extravagances on which to waste their money. No longer, either, would popular entertainers (in different epochs movie idols or pop stars) earn vastly more than productive workers or academics (a group who have long believed themselves seriously under-rewarded and who write books explaining how these things happen). In the eyes of many the planned economy, amounting to the abandonment of closed-loop market control in favour of open-loop control through government direction, was the solution to achieving a society both efficient and moral.

Now it is of course manifestly true that the moral failings in many societies are clear enough, and should be entirely unacceptable. The sufferings of the poor in nineteenth-century England were well chronicled even at the time,[1] and ought not to have been tolerated by a civilized nation. In fact the widespread hardship arose because the market consistently delivered too low a price for labour, which was all the poorest had to sell. Rather than providing a reason for abolishing the market altogether, in the event this failure of the imperfect labour market as it then operated proved capable of correction by government action. Reducing the length of the working lifetime and cutting back the working day and year played a useful role in draining away the oversupply of labour, although the slowing down of workers' migration out of agriculture and from Ireland were doubtless more important factors. Contrary to the bizarre expectations of economists of the day,

1 Henry Mayhew, *London Life and the London Poor* (1851).

better rewards for labour proved of great benefit to the poor.

However this was a largely twentieth-century phenomenon; the nineteenth-century idea was of a radically new order of society which would eliminate poverty at a stroke and was encapsulated in a slogan, said by some to define socialism: 'from each according to his ability, to each according to his worth'.[1] Unfortunately, moral philosophy has not yet progressed to the point where the worth of a human being is capable of objective computation. Nor is it clear how each person is to be induced to give according to his ability. In practice the fascist, Nazi and communist States were remarkably unanimous in the solution they chose to these problems, using repression and terror in the attempt to elicit the contribution of the individual citizen according to his ability and selecting loyalty to the leaders of the State as the measure of his worth. This experiment led to perhaps sixty million needless deaths in all, and some of the most immoral, unjust and terrible societies ever seen.

Since the collapse of communism in Eastern Europe, and also the decline in influence of democratic socialism in the West, many attempts have been made to redefine socialism. The debate is often interesting, but frequently the proposed political scenarios coming out of it seem to have little connection with the socialism of history. Michael Rustin,[2] for example, bases his own proposed reconstruction of socialist ideas on that strand of psychoanalytical psychology which derives from Melanie Klein. This has good sense behind it because her theories are particularly concerned with paranoid phenomena—the very stuff of politics. The outcome, though interesting and constructive, is a book which makes references in its index neither to capitalism (though cannibalism is there) nor to the means of production, distribution or exchange of wealth, nor yet to class war or indeed class itself. Despite a reference to Engels (but not Marx, though he does appear in the text) the word 'socialism' sits oddly in such company, and one wonders why the author feels he must use it—from

1 Karl Marx's version, 'according to his needs', *Criticism of the Gotha Programme* (1875), applied to an idealized communism, not socialism.

2 Michael Rustin, *The Good Society and the Inner World* (1991).

> nostalgia perhaps? Or is it a club of which he has been so long a member that it would be churlish to resign just because the roof has fallen in? It seems that for some people 'socialist' has become no more than a term of approbation, devoid of other meaning, as did 'Christian' in great-grandfather's day.

Seeming so self-evidently right, nevertheless the social experiment proved a disaster, morally as well as in respect of economic efficiency, as control theory might have predicted. The power to direct from the centre fell into the hands of a clique, which invariably used it for their own advantage. Open-loop control could not adequately respond to the needs of a changing economy and society, becoming mired in bureaucratic complexity by its attempt to do so. Popular dissatisfaction was met by repression, yet those in charge felt entirely justified in such measures, since it was axiomatic that their open-loop control was morally superior to the 'squalor' of the market economy. Those who opposed them must be either mad or motivated by the basest reasons and therefore entirely merited whatever unpleasantness, punitive or psychiatric, fell to their lot.

It would be wrong to condemn those intellectuals who championed the planned economy too readily, however, for the idea of open-loop control is always seductive. Its claims to greater efficiency and morality, however ill-founded, once seemed persuasive, and besides that its very simplicities have an appeal to political system builders: it makes for the evolution of a very tidy hierarchical organization. This invariably takes a tree form (like a family tree), with information and instructions flowing only one way, and this lack of complexity has a strong appeal to the ideologist anxious to articulate the governmental structure of a new society. The progression of command is from the centre, where the regulatory framework is constructed, out through intermediaries where it is articulated and detailed, to the periphery where it is applied in interaction with the world outside. Once such a pattern is in place a pervasive internal orderliness seems possible, making easier the attack on incipient disciplinary problems and facilitating the dissemination of the latest elaboration of the regulatory code, devised by the Party which is the acknowledged vanguard of the working class, or perhaps by the Emperor who has the mandate of Heaven, by the supernaturally inspired Leader of the People, or in all cases largely by the bureaucrats acting in their name in actual fact.

> Societies which have developed organically, rather than being established by decree or existing in imagination alone, rarely show much tree-like structure,[1] but have a bewildering pattern of interrelationships and cross-links between individuals and groups. In mathematical terms they might perhaps be described as hyperdimensional semi-ordered lattices.

Open-loop control strategies, because they are determined at the outset, have to make full allowance in advance for all possible variable factors bearing on the task they are trying to regulate and on the goals they are trying to achieve, which is so difficult that in real-life and practical situations it proves scarcely feasible at all, except as a poor approximation. Attempts at control tend in consequence rapidly to become very complex, in the pursuit of an unattainable perfection. Thus bureaucrats, whether in economic planning departments or elsewhere, invariably proceeding by open-loop control, evolve ever more complex statutes, regulations, ordinances, codes of practice and guidelines to say in advance of the event just how things should be done. When mishaps of control occur within such organizations they are always seen either as resulting from failure of individuals to carry out the correct procedure—a question of discipline—or as pointing to a need for yet further complication of the regulatory code, to take into account possibilities and factors not previously considered. It is hardly surprising therefore that the communist states rapidly became a jungle of bureaucracy. Yet despite the failure of 'real socialism' in our time, hierarchical bureaucratic organizations applying open-loop control techniques and supported by repression have proved remarkably durable forms of social organization, the only major threat to them coming from their inefficiency and lack of capacity to adapt fast enough to rapid change in the world outside. Provided that they can be a little universe all to themselves, impervious and not challenged from beyond their borders, they prove very long-lived.

Doubtless the classic example is the Chinese Empire.[2–4] In the fifth

1 Christopher Alexander, 'A city is not a tree', *Design* **206** (1966).

2 Joseph Needham, *Science and Civilisation in China* (1954).

3 John K. Fairbank and Dennis Twitchett, *Cambridge History of China* (1978–87).

4 Michael Loewe, *The Pride that was China* (1990).

century BC, after a period of slowly decaying central government under the Zhou dynasty, civil war became endemic in China (403–221 BC). The country broke into warring regions, virtually free of central control and bent on conflict with their neighbours. Whole societies and governments became subject to selective extinction on a short time-scale, constituting closed-loop control of the most rigorous kind, which propelled new social groups to positions of authority in the state. Under the pressure of the necessity to survive, talent, not birth, increasingly became the criterion for employment. The feudal system died, giving way to tightly run centralized mini-states which could compete effectively in the winnowing environment of the time. Much new technology evolved: a plough with an iron ploughshare was developed, drawn by oxen, and also new techniques of irrigation. These were only two of many factors improving agricultural productivity. A money economy began to develop out of the growth of trade. Government officials, chosen for their competence, were given regular salaries, while peasants began to pay taxes on their land. Although a period of social chaos, with the avalanche of change and consequent hardship such times inevitably bring, the late Zhou dynasty was also an era of technical, administrative and intellectual innovation, and the start of China's golden age of philosophy.

All this finds parallels much later in twelfth-century Europe, when there was a striking growth in application of new technology. The widespread introduction of the solid horse collar increased the drawing power of a horse by up to five times (compared with the old 'choker' harness, hardly changed since the Roman era)[1] making possible the use of a new plough with wheels and a deep ploughshare, and hence the ploughing of heavier soils. The invention of the post windmill (which could be turned to face the wind and would therefore work most days) and its use for irrigation and drainage, together with the new plough, greatly increased the land area cultivated in Europe. These two technical innovations produced an explosion of wealth; indeed, it was medieval advances in technology which funded the Renaissance. However, Europe never came under the control of a unified bureaucracy, and this made all the difference to its subsequent history.

In China, by contrast, what happened next was a major setback,

1 Lefebvre de Noëttes, *L'Attelage—le cheval à travers des ages* (1931).

although it looked like deliverance at the time: government in China was unified and peace returned. Shi Huangdi, the First Sovereign Emperor, created a centralized administrative system replacing the semi-independent states of the late Zhou, and although his own Qin dynasty proved short-lived (221–206 BC) the system he established was reinforced and became permanent under the succeeding Han (202 BC–AD 220). With the pressure of competition between states removed, the way was clear for the organization of China as a classic monopolistic bureaucratic structure. In the interaction between society and government the closed loop fell back before the open. The articulation of a code of conduct to be obeyed throughout all China inevitably followed, together with measures to tighten internal discipline. The system of writing was unified throughout the country, as were weights and measures. Almost as a first action of the new order, an attempt was made to eliminate all doctrines not officially sanctioned by the State, through a decree for Burning of the Books—a practice followed by authoritarian governments down to our own century, in which the German Nazi Party was its enthusiastic proponent. Much of China's earlier literature vanished from history as a result.

True, there were reverses to the growth of imperial power and some necessary adjustments. So great was the opposition generated by the early Qin centralization, and so heavy the taxes exacted, that it was overthrown by the Han in only fifteen years. Yet it was the same policy of centralization that the Han pursued once the power of the State was theirs. They strengthened government further, but in a way more sensitive to the welfare of the peasants, aware now that there were limits to what would be tolerated. For all that, the Chinese Empire had come into being with the Qin and was to endure almost until the present day. In effect what had happened was that the bureaucracy had organized a monopoly of governmental power, a monopoly which lasted for thousands of years with brief interruptions only. As in this case, the endurance of such systems is impressive, but the price they exact for it is high. In China the ultimate cost was failure to participate in the industrial-scientific revolution, as we shall see. The dictators of the twentieth century paid the reckoning sooner, and in blood.

In all authoritarian societies the problem of bureaucratization stemming from open-loop control is serious, and becomes progressively more acute the longer they endure. Few indeed are the brave souls prepared to offer feedback on defects in the functioning of organs of the State when the secret police may soon be at the door to dispute the matter in their characteristically persuasive fashion. In such circumstances closed-loop control of any government function via the populace is virtually impossible and sooner or later the whole of society is inevitably driven open-loop, and hence rapidly bureaucratized. The price of 'protecting the revolution' by the repression of dissent is therefore very high. In the fascist regimes of the 1930s it was bad enough. As already noted, studies by Allied experts after World War II demonstrated conclusively that the German economy was much less well mobilized for war than that of the United States or Britain, in part due to corruption amongst Nazi officials. Yet even so, to the extent that they left industry and commerce in the hands of private business, the economic consequences of the regime were only moderately damaging, utterly repugnant though such societies were in other respects.

However, the Soviet Union from 1926 (when Stalin reversed Lenin's New Economic Policy[1]), and also Eastern Europe after 1945, were another matter. Following the theories of Karl Marx (in a corrupted form) they drew the whole organization of the economy totally within the orbit of government planning and control. What was worse, they tried it in the context of an authoritarian organization of society, something Marx never envisaged and which the German socialist Karl Kautsky (see below) vehemently denounced. The communist experiment amounted to an attempt to run the whole of society from the centre using open-loop controls reinforced by terror.

> Karl Heinrich Marx (1818–83)[2] was the son of a Jewish lawyer who converted to Christianity to save his government job in Prussia. After a time as a student at the University of Berlin, and a period of drifting, in 1842 he became editor of the *Rheinische Zeitung*, a liberal newspaper which he pushed so far to the left that it was banned by the Prussian government in 1843. With Jenny von Westphalen, his bride, Marx left for Paris, then in 1847 moved to London, picking up an earlier

1 Alan Bullock, *Hitler and Stalin* (1991), particularly Chapter 4.

2 David McLellan, *Karl Marx, His Life and Thought* (1973).

association with Friedrich Engels. In 1848 their *Communist Manifesto* appeared.

Marx was constitutionally unable to hold down a job. His family lived in poverty on hand-outs from Engels, what his wife could beg from friends and relatives and her small inheritance (which did not, however, inhibit his philandering). In 1867, Marx published the first volume of *Das Kapital*, which characterized all history as class struggle. At his funeral Engels spoke of him as 'the best-hated and most-calumniated man of his time', which he would have liked, but towards the end of his own life Engels expressed the view that Marx had made errors.

Idealistic, if inadequate, Marx would surely have been horrified by what subsequently happened to his ideas, particularly in Lenin's hands. Vladimir Ilyich Lenin (1870–1924), his father a provincial director of elementary education, was much influenced by the hanging in 1887 of his older brother Aleksandr for plotting against the Tsar. Expelled from the University of Kazan, Lenin later qualified in law and practised briefly. In 1895 he was exiled to Siberia but was allowed to go abroad in 1900.

Like Engels, Lenin recognized the obvious failure of Marx's prediction that the workers would be radicalized, but asserted that political consciousness had to be created by a vanguard revolutionary party—his first major departure from Marxism. Rejecting alliance with liberals, in 1903 he organized the Bolshevik faction of the Russian Social Democratic Labour party. Hoping to create difficulties for the Tsar, when World War I was in its last stages the German authorities helped Lenin return to St Petersburg (1917) and by the year end he had exploited the political chaos to consolidate the Bolsheviks in power. Almost his first move was to establish a secret police (the Cheka, forerunner of Stalin's infamous NKVD), a second long step away from the future Marx had foreseen.

Lenin reorganized the ruinous economy along Marxist lines and it quickly deteriorated still further, so he instituted his New Economic Policy—a return to capitalism and yet another departure from Marxism. His agricultural policies were directly responsible for the 1921–3 famine which killed 5.9 million people. Lenin's politics really had more in common with Robespierre than Marx, and the Soviet Union was never more than notionally Marxist. A heavy cigarette smoker, in 1922 Lenin suffered a stroke; he died in 1924 and soon an official hero cult became widespread.

Joseph Vassarionovitch Stalin (1879–1953) was his terrible successor. The abuses of his era were a logical consequence of Lenin's antidemocratic theories, bravely denounced by Kautsky. A peasant by background, educated as a priest, Stalin soon came to prominence among the Bolsheviks, although there is evidence that he was a Tsarist agent. He rose to control of the Party apparatus (1922), working his way to the supreme power (1929) after Lenin died. There is nothing agreeable or amusing to say about Stalin; combining opportunism and indifference to human suffering, he progressively eliminated his competitors for power, which he then enjoyed unchallenged for a quarter of a century. The catalogue of horrors under his tyranny is too extensive and too awful to repeat. Some thirty million people perished; for comparison it is doubtful that the French Revolution—Robespierre, Terror and all—killed more than thirty thousand.

It appears certain that Stalin died, like Lenin, from a stroke, although there were rumours that he was poisoned by his close colleague Vyacheslav Molotov (1890–1986, nephew of the composer Scriabin). Stalin was planning a new Terror at the time and Molotov's Jewish wife was already in a prison camp for alleged Zionist activities. After Stalin's illness began he lay twenty-four hours without medical help because nobody dared to call a doctor. Svetlana, his daughter, who was present to the end, describes graphically the terrible, lingering death that he suffered.

Stalin's henchman Lavrenty Beria (1899–1953), who controlled the secret police, first the NKVD then the equally terrible MGB which followed, tried to seize power. Because the police could not be trusted, Beria was arrested by a posse of eleven high-ranking military officers. Led by Marshal Zhukov brandishing a pistol, they were all armed and ready to fight if need be. Shortly afterwards, incarcerated in Air Force headquarters and taunting his interrogators with what would happen to them when the MGB took action, Beria was shot dead informally, across a committee table.[1] Later a double played the part of the deceased at his trial for treason; Beria and two colleagues were found guilty and he was posthumously condemned to death.

Not all twentieth-century Marxist revolutionaries were so despicable. Karl Kautsky (1854–1938) was a German socialist who, while approving revolutionary Marxism, courageously condemned the Bolshevik Revolution in Russia as antidemocratic. He quickly lost all influence because he would not underwrite the fashionable fantasy of the Soviet Union as the workers' paradise, 'the last, best hope of mankind'. In this at least he was justified by history, and deserves more respect than he presently receives.

In power communism can best be understood as a veneer of socialism over actual fascism, which enabled its proponents to disarm criticism (from their own consciences as well as the world at large) that they must otherwise have suffered as overt fascists. 'Progressives', such as the Webbs and H. G. Wells[2] in England, Georges Sorel in France and Benedetto Croce in Italy, were at first sympathetic to many of the ideas brought together by Giovanni Gentile (1875–1944) to become the philosophy of fascism.[3] However, after Mussolini established his power in Italy a general disenchantment followed, and fascism was reclassified as a right-wing aberration.

Benito Mussolini (1883–1945) (named after Benito Juarez, champion of the liberal cause in Mexican politics) was the son of a Marxist-socialist blacksmith who shared his father's politics. In World War I he initially opposed Italy's entry (in line with Socialist Party policy) but later had a change of heart, called for alliance with France and Britain and himself served in the army, which cost him his membership of the party. In

1 Viktor B—, private communication.

2 David C. Smith, *H. G. Wells* (1986).

3 Giovanni Gentile, *The Theory of Mind as Pure Act* (1917).

1919, with other war veterans, Mussolini founded the Fasci di Combattimento. The movement gained wide support and after his 'march on Rome' in 1922 (unopposed), Mussolini formed a government. In 1925 he imposed a fascist dictatorship, his 'Corporate State', supposedly based on a 'deal' between industry, workers and government, and hence on open-loop control of the whole of society. Mussolini kept Italy out of World War II until 1940 when he sided with the Germans, whom he thought bound to win. In 1945 the war ended in defeat; Mussolini and Clara Petacci (his mistress) were captured by Italian communists and shot, their bodies subsequently strung up for public exhibition.

The communists were lucky that the philosophy of fascism had not been articulated at the time Lenin was putting his own ideology together, so that he never overtly broke with Marx. Through the historical accident of having obscured its true nature in a pseudo-socialist wrapper, communism retained the allegiance and practical help of 'progressives' in Russia and worldwide (not least as spies and traitors) far longer than it otherwise might have done. In the out-turn, the conduct of communist governments did not prove morally superior to that of the fascists, but rather worse.

As we have seen, to many in our century the idea of a planned economy was a seductive one. Instead of being a prey to 'blind' (that is, closed-loop) forces the economy could be directed in such a way as to carry out the will of the people, or at least of the vanguard party acting, naturally, in their name. Now at last morality and efficiency could jointly govern the workings of commerce and industry and a wholly new and better kind of human society would emerge. In the event, though, things turned out very differently. Particularly because rapid technological change during that period made the penalty for inflexible and inefficient control all the greater, the result was a progressively developing economic and social disaster. The collapse of 'real socialism' (or communism, in everyday Western parlance) after 1989 doubtless had many causes, but the congenital inability to adopt effective control strategies in industry and commerce was one of the more important.

Why did their governmental organizations develop in this way? It is hard for State and public bodies to operate closed-loop controls, since they see themselves as existing primarily to carry out actions arising from the policies and instructions of governments, who are their masters. To argue, as some might, that the bureaucracy serves the needs of the people precisely by carrying out government policies is a Rousseauesque fantasy which puts too large a burden on the prescience and infallibility of governments, something for which we have little evidence. But in any event, from whom, even in genuine democracies, would bureaucratic structures derive feedback if they did try to close the loop? Does the government department responsible for welfare payments to the poor, for example, exist to satisfy the poor, or the government? Ignoring public pronouncements, which are only words after all, and studying how such organizations actually behave, it seems as though the latter were true, even though we may think it should be quite the other way.

The question is generally conceded to be too difficult to resolve, and open-loop control appears by far the less hazardous option. The alternative, indeed, is thought hardly realistic, and still less are its virtues understood, which is a pity. Because in complex and changing situations open-loop controls must always fail to greater or lesser degree (due to unexpected changes in the operating environment and also to unforeseen or wrongly estimated factors which appear after the controls are set up), bureaucrats are characteristically engaged in unending exercises to tighten internal discipline or to modify the regulatory framework, and the more well-meaning and conscientious the individuals concerned the more rapidly and completely this inward-looking orientation develops.

So it is that, despite their durability and stability, bureaucracies are by common consent unfriendly things to those who are not a part of them, even in democratic societies. Driven by an orderly internal logic, by open-loop control, they do not respond in other than wholly stereotyped ways to those with whom they come into contact. Nobody loves a government official, and many foreigners think the British term for him—civil servant—is just sly English humour.

Recently, trying to ease bureaucratic problems, the UK government has initiated the experiment of dividing civil service departments into those promulgating policy and those which provide a service (to other government bodies or to the world

> outside). The latter are organized as Agencies, run on quasi-commercial lines. Provided that Agencies have the wit not to frustrate the forces driving them towards operating under closed-loop controls, this looks like a worthwhile exercise in damage limitation.

The market economy, by contrast, puts into the hands of customers the ability to send effective feedback signals to suppliers of goods and services by buying or refusing to buy what they offer, and thus facilitates closed-loop control. Friedrich von Hayek seems to have seen the market principally as a magnificently effective means of communication, disseminating the economic facts of life to all those who participate in the game.[1]

> Although expressed here in control theory terms, the arguments concerning free market versus command regulation of the economy echo Hayek, who was a great prophetic voice of the twentieth century, whether one likes what he said or not. Friedrich August von Hayek (1899–1991) opposed all government interference in the market, arguing that a command economy is incompatible with political liberties. His ideas are now widely regarded as seminal; to think about social issues in the late twentieth century without having read him is to be gravely handicapped. Hayek shared the 1974 Nobel Prize for economics with Gunnar Myrdal (1898–1987), who held quite different opinions.

For the management of a business in a market economy, the profit and loss account overshadows all things. Scrutinized and agonized over at monthly board meetings in thousands of enterprises, it is the inescapable means by which customers generate powerful feedback into the business control systems. The maximization of profit demands increasing volume of sales at favourable prices, and thus, within the important and necessary limiting constraints of the law, drives industry towards supplying goods and services which prove widely acceptable to the consumer at the price asked, and also to progressively reducing the cost of providing what is offered so as to improve the profit margins.

Changes in consumer preferences (expressed through the market), the developing technology or changing legal requirements are all

1 Friedrich von Hayek, *The Road to Serfdom* (1944).

examples of the changes in external circumstances which have an immediate impact. Any business enterprise ignores them at its peril, and in consequence the essence of business life is a process of never-ending adaptation driven by risk and uncertainty. It cannot be denied that to work within an economic system which is closed-loop controlled by the market like this, although it certainly makes for efficiency, is to be obliged to tolerate a future unpredictable in the highest degree, and is therefore never comfortable for the individual concerned. Driven by the fickle lash of changing market preference, no manager can ever relax. Something of a dog's life, people accept it when they can see no alternative, and certainly not from any kind of natural virtue.

Just as Adam Smith once pointed out, '...people of the same trade seldom meet together, even for merriment and diversion, but the conversation ends in a conspiracy against the public or in some contrivance to raise prices'.[1] Unless effectively restrained by law, businessmen will always try to combine together, and it is monopoly and vested interests acting as quasi-monopolies which foul things up. The reasons why the monopolistic path seems attractive to the participants are obvious, though. If the parties manage to pull off this trick the cartel they create by it will be able increasingly to dominate and ignore the market. Less and less subject to feedback, its managers will be quick to change over to open-loop controls in the expectation of a more profitable, predictable and above all more comfortable life. The improved profitability, however, will be transient, since once relieved of the pressure on costs previously created by market feedback the monopoly will increasingly find new and more ambitious ways to waste money. Not the least common of these is the failure to adopt new technology and working methods, so making life easier for management by lessening the innovative burdens they have to carry and the skill requirements they are obliged to demonstrate.

There is no shortage of examples, either, to support the view that this opting for the familiar and against change proves perfectly capable of flourishing side by side with excessive and ill-directed research spending, often undertaken for its perceived value as bestowing prestige on the company rather than with a view to the utility of its outcome. In consequence a golden glow of intellectual merit falls on the monopoly's

1 Adam Smith, *An Inquiry into the Nature and Cause of the Wealth of Nations* (1776).

senior management, needless to say, who thus have the pleasure of being able to pose as patrons of learning and to be fawned upon by academics. Spending on research activities with little relationship to the real needs of the organization, particularly 'pure' or basic research (seen as more prestigious), is a sure symptom of escape from market control. Governments, the greatest monopoly of all, frequently spend in this way, as a glance at United States research funding from the end of World War II will clearly demonstrate.

Under the banner of enlightened working conditions, a monopoly will also find it easier to tolerate inefficiency in both its work force and management than to take the disagreeable actions needed to correct them. Its relationship with its suppliers, too, will be more and more that of an ill-informed benefactor facing a determined freeloader, and will be characterized by 'trophy hunting' on the supplier's side and acquiescence, or in the later stages downright corruption, on its own.

In the past, one way for a business to achieve the desirable monopoly trick was to get itself nationalized, which had the added advantage of implicating the politicians of the day in the process of swindling the consumer, and hence winning useful allies against any possible later retribution. However, since the collapse of 'real socialism' this is no longer fashionable. Also an important disadvantage of nationalization in bourgeois democratic societies has proved to be the political sensitivity of top salaries in nationalized industries. Chief executives can award themselves salaries ten times higher if their business is in the private domain, which is therefore much to be preferred.

A successful alternative approach to achieving effective monopoly status, still hugely popular, is to establish a special relationship with a single large customer, persuading him, by whatever special pleading, to collude in the elimination of competition. This is particularly easy if the customer is a government official, to whom competition may seem wasteful and disorderly, compared with the open-loop dominated structure of his own organization. In various developed countries the relationship of defence contractors to the procurement agencies of governments, or that of suppliers of equipment to State-controlled telecommunications organizations, has therefore often been of this type. In less developed countries, particularly those with notionally 'socialist' governments (which have considerable scope for political interference in the operation of the economy), corruption of senior politicians performs a similar role of rigging the market in favour of one or two suppliers.

The residual dangers to a well-established monopoly are only three: technical change undermining its unique position, legal process based on antitrust laws, and the possibility of political intervention driven by outraged public opinion. To fend off the last, when consumers begin to revolt against what they are being offered, professional soothers—public relations consultants and design houses—may typically be used to improve the corporate image. Better still, from the manager's point of view, a communist or fascist social form in which the control of industry and the political function are intertwined, makes it possible to use the power of the State to delay technical innovation, avoid legal process and suppress public resentment at poor service. This is why societies of this kind have a built-in tendency to inefficient, monopolistic and dated forms of industrial organization.

The most attractive monopoly of all, needless to say, is a monopoly of government. Government is one of only two kinds of businesses which have the potential physically to coerce those who do not wish to buy the services they offer, organized crime being the other. The dangers of a monopoly of government have long been understood, and go back well before Hayek. Indeed they form a central theme of Montesquieu's *De l'espirit des lois* (1748) and, through the wide acceptance of his ideas at a critical time, profoundly influenced the writing of the United States Constitution, which enshrines the principle of separation of powers.

> Charles Louis de Secondat, Baron de la Brede et de Montesquieu (1689–1755) is remembered today primarily for this one brilliant book, *De l'espirit des lois.* Wealthy from an early inheritance, Montesquieu was educated as a lawyer and held high judicial office in Bordeaux. Moving to Paris in 1726 he soon became a member of the Académie (1728). He then toured Europe before retiring (1732) to his chateau at La Brede.

As so often in every field of intellectual and practical endeavour, as already indicated the Chinese were among the first to explore the exciting possibilities of monopolistic State power and over the centuries have done so wholeheartedly. At a time in Europe when political authority was at best patchy and localized, in China a vast State monopoly of power was achieved long ago, with the coming of the Qin and Han dynasties. The Qin foundation of the historic Chinese Empire (221 BC) has already been described as a classic monopolistic bureaucratic structure. In fact it began the building by government officials of a centralized State so resilient that it could withstand numerous subsequent changes of dynasty unharmed. Indeed, even three hundred years of chaos which followed the collapse of the Han dynasty—the so-called Period of Disunion (AD 220–589)—did not blot out the memory of an effective centralized power. Thus it was that the short-lived Sui dynasty (581–618) followed by the Tang (618–906) were able fully to re-establish the monopoly of government and to extend its effective area. At its height, Tang bureaucracy controlled an empire stretching from Korea to Iran.

This kind of heaven-sanctioned empire (such as China, for most of its history), the one-party State (much of Africa from the end of colonialism to the 1990s), military dictatorship (Oliver Cromwell's 'Protectorate' of England, from 1653 to his death in 1658), 'Peoples' Democracy' led by a 'vanguard party' (Eastern Europe 1945–89 and the Soviet Union 1917–89), a command economy (mid twentieth-century India and South Africa), a State-sanctioned belief system to which adherence is obligatory (England and Spain during the sixteenth century), the conquest and subjugation of other societies as colonies (European colonies in the nineteenth and twentieth centuries, although the British were often tolerant of alternative centres of power in subject territories, a practice enshrined in the concept of 'indirect rule')—all of these are ways in which the governmental monopoly may be established or extended. In fact anything will do which denies the people alternative or multiple sources of power in society, to which they could give their allegiance and which might be set against each other to compete for influence.

By contrast, multiparty systems, separation of powers, regional autonomy which the centre cannot subdue, very limited control of the information media, vigorous cultural and religious groups which do not depend on State power or patronage, strong and genuinely independent private business enterprises—these are the commonest indications that a State monopoly has not been achieved, and that there exists a plurality of independent forces within society. The result is a 'free market of power' in which power seekers and wielders can compete and refine themselves, even by selective extinction processes if no other, although hopefully by the extinction of institutions (as in business take-overs) rather than that of individuals. However imperfect it may be in some respects, beyond doubt the closest approximation that we have seen so far to this political pattern is the United States of America.

The first of these two categories of society—the monopolistic—is driven open-loop from the centre, although invariably using localized negative feedback to stabilize some particular aspect of social behaviour, but always with the goals of regulation set from the centre as part of the overall open-loop control (like the tennis player who controls his racquet closed-loop in order to make his open-loop shot). In the second, pluralistic, category it is primarily closed-loop control via the populace which is taking place. Mostly this will be negative feedback, necessary to avoid social chaos, but sometimes it will involve positive feedback with a loop gain greater than unity, making possible dramatic changes and profound transformations in the way things are done. No two strategies could be more different in their outcome than these two ways of running the State.

Having asserted so much, however, it is time for a caveat. There is nothing magical about a market economy, despite the enthusiasm of its proponents. It is just the one way so far convincingly demonstrated of ensuring that industry or government operates under closed-loop controls set by the consumer. Perhaps other viable ways of achieving this end are possible. If they exist they might be just as effective; we simply do not know. Those who dislike the capitalist form of society, for whatever reason, could do worse than to give this point their thoughtful attention.

Failures of the market are not, after all, far to seek. In international trade, the free market has for years depressed the price for commodities relative to manufactured goods, to the ruin of the less developed countries. Many also consider that throughout history the market has consistently delivered too high a price for money but too low for labour, relative to what is socially equitable. John Maynard Keynes certainly thought so.[1] Yet what option have we? Because they depend on open-loop control, socialism and fascism (all questions of morality aside)

1 John Maynard Keynes, *The General Theory of Employment, Interest and Money* (1936), Chapter 22.

deliver miserable economic performance, drown in corruption and bureaucracy, and offer unjustifiably high material rewards to those who seize political power. They are thus hopelessly flawed. We stand in urgent need of a good new idea, though it will have to offer closed-loop control of the economy, whatever else.

A starting point in developing a new approach might be William Keegan's view of the state of capitalism in the post-Marxist world, seen from an economist's standpoint.[1] Andrew Samuels, by contrast, comes at the problem from psychology, but develops his ideas from a basis of unexamined egalitarian assumptions about the objectives of political action.[2] Although only yesterday they would have been regarded as a kind of axiomatic orthodoxy—indeed in some quarters perhaps still are—these traditional assumptions are now under heavy attack from a 'new liberal' position.[3] The widely held egalitarian belief that through political action it is possible to deny, even suppress, distinctions between young and old, parents and children, male and female, successful and unsuccessful, rulers and ruled, is seen by Janine Chasseguet-Smirgel as at base a manifestation of perversion (as understood by contemporary psychoanalytical theory),[4] and when acted out must therefore necessarily result in the nightmare world which communism and nazism alike created—in short that, in this case as so many others, good intentions pave the road to hell. But if the psychological siren-song of the left is perversion, that of the right may well be narcissism—by its nature alienating and uncaring—which at heart is convinced that there is no such thing as human society, only a mere aggregation of individuals.[5,6]

1 William Keegan, *The Spectre of Capitalism* (1992).

2 Andrew Samuels, *The Political Psyche* (1993).

3 David Graham and Peter Clarke, *The New Enlightenment* (1986).

4 Janine Chasseguet-Smirgel, *Creativity and Perversion* (1984).

5 Heinz Kohut, *The Search for the Self*, 1–4 (1979–91).

6 Béla Grunberger, *New Essays on Narcissism* (1989).

4

So which should we choose?

A wildfowler who shoots at a bird knows that a sudden change in its flight path or in the wind can mean the shot misses and is wasted. The ultimate destination of the round is set by open-loop control, so everything must be perfectly precalculated, and in practice even fine shots do not expect to hit their target every time. By contrast, a traditional desert Arab, his falcon on his wrist, knows that a kill is highly likely provided only that instinctive hunter is properly aroused before being let loose at her prey. The falcon sees the bird she is attacking and closes with it by subtle adjustment of her own flight in near-perfect closed-loop control, using visual negative feedback. Matched against a sufficiently good pursuer, neither change in the wind nor evasive manoeuvre offers much hope of escape for the quarry. Yet in Europe, although falconry was once commonplace for wildfowling, it has now mostly given way to guns.

First developed for war, by the early seventeenth century firearms were in wide use as sporting weapons. Commonplace in Europe between the tenth and seventeenth centuries, falconry began to decline in popularity with the progressive improvement of guns. Why so? The answer is complex. First, the advantage of the closed-loop control is somewhat exaggerated in the argument I have presented in its favour.[1] In fact the edge in the chase which the falcon enjoys over its quarry is quite small. She must start with a height advantage from which to gain

1 Michael Clark, private communication. I am indebted for expert advice on these points.

speed, and if this is inadequate she will not kill. The wind may favour the quarry more than the hunter, as may the terrain, and the fitness and experience of the falcon are also critical, no less than the strength of the grouse (there being all the difference in the world between an old cock grouse and a so-called 'squeaker'). By no means least important, it takes the falcon time to 'lock on' to her prey, to be 'in yark' as they say, and if she does so too slowly the quarry may be over the hills and far away.

Secondly, our circumstances in the West dictated the change. Falconry originated in central Asia around 2000 BC, and was introduced to Europe by invading 'barbarians' during the decline of the Roman Empire. Knowledge of the rearing and training of hunting falcons quickly became widespread. It demands enormous time and application, as well as considerable skill.[1] Once satisfactory guns had been evolved they proved cheaper and far easier to learn to use. They are not perfect, even now, but are still good enough to send the average competent wildfowler home with a full bag at the end of the day. Open-loop control, although certainly less consistently accurate than a closed-loop technique might be, is nevertheless good enough for the purpose, and cheaper to implement. This is by no means to say that the desert Arab was unwise to keep to falconry in his very different circumstances, though. The bird was a more economical choice than a gun for him because until relatively recently he did not live in an industrial society capable of mass-producing ammunition at low cost, whereas he did have the labour available to rear and train the birds.

The actual laying of the wildfowler's gun on its target line, before the trigger is pulled, is of course a closed-loop control activity, so the open-loop phase is only the very short time of the flight of the shot, and therefore does not greatly worsen the outcome. Particularly is this true if steps are taken to ensure that a small degree of error will not frustrate the kill. For this reason, the hunter mostly does not choose to use a rifle but prefers a shotgun, firing a cloud of pellets which spread over an area, and therefore capable of bringing down a bird even when not quite on the target, as a rifle shot would need to be. The military also used spread-shot at one time: canister and grape shot fired from cannon against men and horses. Now they find its destructive

1 T. H. White, *The Once and Future King* (1958).

power inadequate, but achieve a similar effect by using repeating weapons.

> A practical machine gun was invented in 1862 by Richard J. Gatling. His version, using a hand-cranked ring of barrels, became the most successful repeating gun of its time, and sophisticated versions of it are still being made today. Recent mechanically driven Gatling guns fire sixty heavy calibre (30 mm) rounds per second, throwing precisely aimed metal at a rate equivalent to three tonnes per minute.

So then, open-loop or closed-loop: which is the better method of control? Sometimes we may not have a straight choice, but in those cases where we do the answer is often easy. The basic and inescapable trouble with open-loop controls is that everything that could bear on the outcome—literally everything—must be accurately foreseen in order for them to work with total success. That is a very tall order. By contrast, within limits set by the loop delay, a closed-loop controller can be made as accurate as may be desired and can also adapt to changing external circumstances. There are certainly horses for courses, but it is not by chance that animals and plants have evolved and optimized themselves through millions of years using closed loops very extensively, to keep themselves stable and functional. It could be argued that the development of closed-loop temperature control in animals, permitting the warm-blooded creatures to flourish, was a decisive step towards the evolution of advanced life forms, bird and mammal. For simple control tasks, where a single parameter is held at the desired value and everything works very nearly in 'real time', a closed-loop negative feedback controller will always win.

However, there may be complicated situations in which the optimal solution proves to be a mixture of open- and closed-loop, each handling a different aspect of the control task. Long ago, when the world was young, two organizations began to set up training programmes to give suitable qualifications to younger people entering their profession—let us call these two the Institute and the Association. I would not have it thought that they are actual organizations, however heavily disguised, for in reality they are entirely fictional, mere figments of my imagination. Even so many will recognize the distinctive styles, and academics in particular should do so. The story is, in short, a kind of parable.

From the beginning the Institute was obsessed with open-loop control, perhaps because those most involved, inwardly fearful people, were nervous of uncertainty. Anxious that things might get out of hand, they tried to specify completely and exhaustively what the content, style and teaching method should be for their training course, as well as articulating in the finest detail what qualifications and prior experience were required for those teaching every distinct part of it. As might be expected, the labour involved in working all this out was enormous and the Institute's Training Committee felt snowed under by the task. As they began to fall behind anxieties ran so high that soon factions developed, backing one approach or another, and before long the disputes grew acrimonious. There were resignations from the committee and tenure of office by chairpersons grew short. Political manoeuvring became rife as each faction sought control, and the Institute's Executive Committee had to intervene more than once. Even when the first students were due to be received the course design was still not complete, despite the mounds of numbingly detailed paperwork that had been produced and endlessly debated. So many of those who had expected to teach the courses were either alienated by the committee battles or had been assessed not suitably qualified in some respect that it seemed impossible to go on.

In total contrast, the Association, its members more relaxed and self-confident, was dedicated almost as a matter of ideology to a non-directive approach. They proposed to start the course with nothing at all decided, only the sketchiest curriculum and no detailed description of the constituent parts, letting everything emerge out of dialogue between the teachers and the students as the programme went along. Quintessentially this was closed-loop control, although the Association's Training Secretary (who had worked out the whole thing one Friday afternoon) would not have recognized the term. There was a Training Committee, but matters were so uncontentious that its meetings were more in the nature of social gatherings, the business quickly over, enjoyable and mildly bibulous. Among the members of the Association all was sweetness and light in the run-up to the launch, and there was no shortage of volunteers to undertake the wholly unspecified teaching. Only the prospective students spoiled things, creating difficulties by adopting the collective view that those who offered a course of training ought to know what they were going to teach and in what order, and making it abundantly clear that they were not about to join a course for which this was not the case. Like the Institute, the Association also found its training programme in crisis, but for quite opposite reasons.

In the end, however unwillingly, both Association and Institute converged towards the same solution. On the open-loop side of things, course descriptions were produced well enough articulated to get the programmes started in the right general direction, to permit selection of teachers who were probably suitably qualified and to enable the students to decide whether, in general terms, this was the course they wanted to study. Subsequently, as errors in the orientation, substance or teaching of the courses showed up, these were corrected by both bodies in an ongoing way under the auspices of the respective Training Committees, who modified course content or changed teachers from time to time as seemed necessary. This was the closed-loop component in the control process.

Both organizations remained for some considerable time dissatisfied with what they had done; the anxious Institute because every closed-loop control action was seen as an indication of failure of the initial planning process, but the easy-going Association also, because for a while they retained the fantasy that if only there could have been no open-loop control at the start something new, strange and altogether wonderful might have emerged. The Association forgot its regrets the quicker of the two, and in any event the students in both organizations prospered in courses which, over the years, came to resemble each other quite closely, as a result of negative feedback operating in the context of closed-loop control from groups of students with essentially similar requirements.

This type of open-loop initial aiming with a closed loop to remove residual errors near the target is a control strategy with much to recommend it, avoiding the pitfalls of overmeticulous bureaucracy on one side and freewheeling chaos on the other. To the extent that we are all the product of the interplay between our genetic endowment and subsequent familial and social conditioning, this is how we all got where we now are. The hybrid of closed- and open-loop control adopted, in the end, by both the Association and the Institute often proves the best available solution. Indeed the pattern of open-loop initial aiming with feedback 'homing' in the terminal phase is in widespread use. Mention has already been made of the use by the military of terminally guided munitions, fired from guns like ordinary shells but flipping out little fins while in flight and steering themselves in closed-loop control once they are near their target. The idea is identical.

Finally, as in the case of the Institute and the Association, it is important not to overlook psychological factors that may affect us when we make a choice of control strategy. From a psychoanalytical standpoint, the preference for open-loop control relates to very early phases in human psychic development, hence the strength of its grip on our thinking. It is fed by the residuals of infantile ideas, such as the omnipotence of thought, a false notion of the relationship of the self to the environment evolved when the self/not-self distinction is still weak and before realistic object relationships have taken hold. By contrast, the infant's first experience of the closed loop is in the relationship with its mother, who gives feedback in accordance with her perceptions of her baby's state, as filtered by the characteristics of her own psyche.

> In recent years experimental psychologists[1] have developed ingenious ways of confirming the chronology of early infant mental development where previously there were only the psychoanalyst's clinical insights as a guide. The two prove not too badly out of line, although the psychologists push phenomena toward somewhat earlier dates in the life of the individual than had been previously assigned. Development of the self/not-self distinction, in particular, appears to come sooner than we thought. It is now beginning to appear that the chronology established by Piaget may be defective also, putting critical developmental stages a little too late. We have consistently underestimated the rate of development of children's reasoning powers and subtlety of response, it seems. No wonder—it is not comfortable to feel the next generation treading on one's heels.

1 Margaret Donaldson, *Human Minds* (1992).

5

Control for action: positive feedback

So far only negative feedback has been considered, but there is more to control theory than that. Returning to my apparent obsession with the temperature of my bath water, there are actually two mutually opposed control strategies that I might adopt to regulate it, although one of them seems quite crazy, at first encounter, and would perhaps only be heard of in an abstract discussion of control. Of course the obvious thing for me to do—the rational strategy—is that if, by testing the temperature, I find the water too cool I should turn off the cold tap a shade and turn on the hot a little also. Similarly, if the water is too warm I should do just the opposite. This is negative feedback, because the controlling action opposes the sense of the error detected. Properly executed it will result in the bath water settling to the temperature I require. As we have already seen, operating in the same way negative feedback is the basis of all those closed-loop controls which aim to bring any aspect of a system close to some specified value. Those who seek a stable and lasting convergence to a preset target, whether in industrial processes, physiology, the economy or the governance of society, even in the temperature of bath water, find negative feedback their most reliable ally.

However, there is the alternative approach. Imagine that while regulating the temperature of my bath I had a brainstorm: suppose I found the water too warm yet instead of doing the sensible thing I perversely increased the flow of hot water and reduced the flow of cold. If I were to persevere in this paradoxical behaviour it is perfectly clear what the outcome would be: before long the hot tap would be full on and the cold turned off. Similarly if I had behaved in this perverse fashion when initially finding the water too cool, quite soon it would be the hot that was off and the cold tap full on. Either way it would give me a very unsatisfactory bath, for the system diverges from the happy mean towards one of only two stable states, either as hot as possible or as cold as possible. It is, in a word, bi-stable. This control strategy is called positive feedback. Controlling for instability not for stability, positive feedback evidently has no sensible place in regulating the temperature of a bath. That is not to say, however, that it is useless—very far from it. It is control for change, not for stasis, the radical not the conservative strategy, and it has a role in life and in the world no less significant than that of its more staid counterpart.

If we look about us there are probably as many examples of positive feedback closed loops to be found as there are of negative feedback. Some are benign, others harmful, some significant, others trivial, but all are characterized by a self-impelled sharp 'switch' or discontinuity between two extreme states. Thus a snap-action electrical wall switch has only two stable conditions—fully on or off. It will hold either of these indefinitely, but it should be impossible to get the switch to settle in any position between these two limiting states, however carefully the switch lever is moved. This action, vital to the safe carrying of significant electrical currents, comes about because the switch is designed with internal mechanical positive feedback.

Sometimes positive feedback, as if taking control, can precipitate disaster. Some years ago the tragic case was reported in the newspapers of a woman involved in a fatal accident while reversing her automatic car from the garage. Her husband was standing in the roadway behind her, ready to wave the car out when there was no passing traffic. Catastrophically, she suddenly reversed out at high speed, hitting and killing the poor man. At the subsequent inquest she could give no coherent explanation of what had happened, stating that she felt as if some outside force had taken control of the car, like a demonic possession.

Early one morning I encountered this same phenomenon myself at second hand when, by arrangement, a very experienced driver came to collect a car from the road outside my house, meaning to take it for a routine service. Suddenly we heard the roar of the engine followed by a heavy impact. My car had been reversed across the road and twenty metres of grass to hit parked cars on the other side of the village green, and the driver, shocked and dazed, could give no explanation at all of what had happened. This car too had automatic transmission. At first we suspected some mechanical defect, but eventually came to realize that this also was automatic reverse runaway.

What happens is simple, and depends on the driver, with the transmission set to reverse, touching the accelerator with the right foot but without (as the car manufacturer's manuals warn drivers to be sure to do) having the left on the brake. In these circumstances the car begins to move backward sharply. If the reverse acceleration is enough it has the effect of causing the driver to press still harder on the accelerator quite involuntarily, as a result of the mechanical inertia of his leg and foot. There is therefore feedback from the accelerator through the car motion and back to the accelerator—a feedback loop—and it is positive in sense. As a result the car has only two stable conditions: stationary with the driver's foot just barely resting on the accelerator, or proceeding in reverse at maximum speed with the foot hard to the floor. For a manual gear-change there is no comparable problem; the left foot is over the clutch and tends to disconnect the engine if there is a violent backward lurch. This is negative feedback, and has the effect of stabilizing the system as a whole.

With the automatic, though, it all develops fast, typically in a few tenths of a second, so that humanly there is no time to react or apply the brake. In fact people who have this experience usually cannot rationalize what has happened, and when it is over will look uncomprehendingly at the damage that they have done. Invariably courts and officials, too, have little understanding of the phenomenon, which happens so much faster and more uncontrollably than common sense would think possible. There may consequently be a search for signs of mechanical failure in the car, or even suspicions of malicious intent by the driver, where neither has the slightest justification. It is positive feedback, and that alone, which has created a potentially deadly trap for the unwary.

> Any reader who feels inclined to try the experiment with an automatic car is strongly advised not to do so; it is more dangerous than may seem possible. Those misguided enough to insist should try it only in a private open space, such as the

> middle of a deserted airfield, wear a seat belt, adjust the steering wheel so that the car will go in a wide turn, and have no spectators within half a kilometre at any point on the circle. Choose a dry day and a non-skid surface. Depending on the power-to-weight ratio of the car, it will be found that there is a critical pressure of foot-dab on the accelerator at which all hell breaks loose. Light or powerful cars are the most susceptible, hence the effect is more common these days, with improved performance.
>
> However, it is only fair to point out that vehicles with automatic transmission, to the convenience of which many of us are so deeply attached, may be reversed in perfect safety if the manufacturers' instructions are followed. Apply the brake firmly with the left foot before engaging reverse gear, press the accelerator slightly, then ease off the brake until the required reverse motion is obtained. The foot on the brake reduces the loop gain of the positive feedback to the accelerator by making the car less responsive and, because it works in opposite sense, also introduces negative feedback, which further stabilizes things.

The characteristic feeling that events are being driven forward by some outside, alien force over which one has no control—typically reported by those who experience the effects of positive feedback—is the key to recognizing this phenomenon. In events as simple as switching on a light, or as complex as starting a war, there is the overwhelming impression that once things have passed a certain point there can be no stopping them. This is not really the case, however strong the subjective sensation, but it is true that to halt the process something pretty unusual would have to happen, breaking the positive feedback loop.

It would be wrong, though, to associate positive feedback too closely with disasters. It is better seen as the control strategy for rapid change, whether for good or ill. Thus, a very different example of positive feedback can arise when a man and a woman meet. If they are attracted each to the other they may smile, talk, join hands, seek out a place where they will not be disturbed, and maybe soon kisses and caresses are being exchanged. Each action by one heightens the excitement of the other, and this again increases the frequency and intensity of the arousal gestures returned. Provided only that the mutual attraction is strong enough, the outcome hardly needs to be spelled out. Such an encounter, an epitome of the effects of positive feedback, creates an interpersonal dynamic which has only two stable states: either the couple are indifferent or maximally aroused. The slightest move away from the first state towards the second triggers a rapid switch; one could say that in their relationship the couple are bi-stable. All the states in the transition between these two limits are transient for as long as the two remain linked in a reciprocally empathetic closed loop. In this case positive feedback has certainly proved of the greatest value; would the human race have survived without it? In a Hollywood movie cliché of the 1940s, when the hero and the heroine were in the process of being swept off their feet by powerful mutual attraction, the dialogue line was 'This thing is bigger than both of us'. Even real-life lovers may have a sensation of being impelled forward in their relationship by a force they cannot control. This supposed external force is precisely that of positive feedback, acting around the closed loop they form with each other, and causing their slightest actions to have consequences far greater than in a normal context.

Regrettably, though, quarrels often come into the same all too passionate category of mutual reinforcement, the provocative act of one party leading to a yet more infuriating riposte. Here too the situation is characterized by just two stable states: mutual indifference or total enmity, its degree and expression limited only by social and legal constraints. Given the mutuality of interaction which constitutes the positive feedback loop, a quarrel can be quickly triggered in this way between people who are on quite civil terms at other times. Notoriously in some cases of wife battering, long periods of mutual amity are interspersed with intervals of mayhem. Often the parties have the sense of being driven to antipathy much against their will by the total and escalating unreasonableness of the other. What they are actually experiencing, both of them, are the consequences of positive feedback, their own actions coming back at them, reflected in the other.

Far grimmer positive feedback effects are implicit in those arms races which lead to wars between nations.[1] Rearmament by one nation can stimulate another to feel threatened and to rearm in turn. This causes

1 Michael Howard, *The Causes of Wars* (1984).

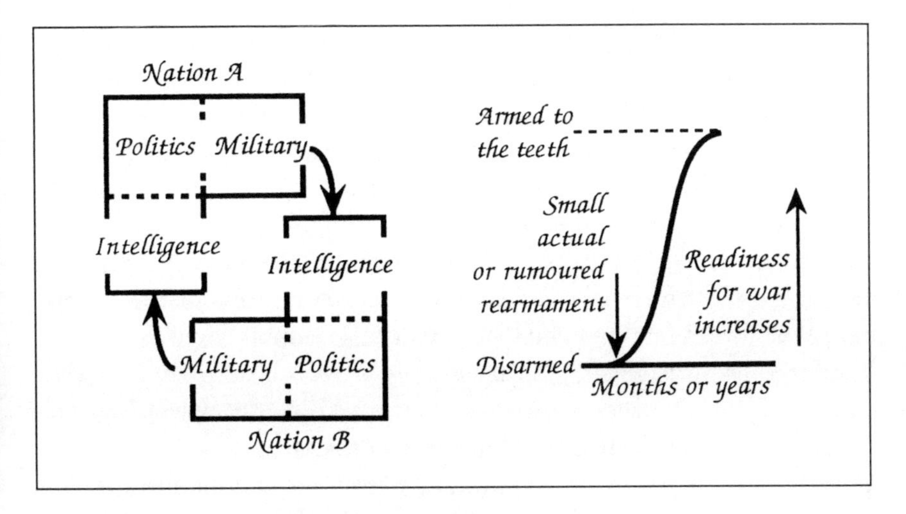

Fig. 3 (a) *above* The arms race feedback loop
(b) *right* An armaments race between two nations

increased fear of the potential enemy's hostile intentions by the first country and hence still more determined effort and expenditure on arms and armies—a closed loop with positive feedback. Provided only that the magnitude of the effect is sufficiently powerful so that the loop gain is greater than one, there will be no stable state short of the absolute maximum level of preparedness for war that each nation can muster. In these cases, as in those before, for the two nations concerned, linked as they are in a deadly positive feedback closed loop, theory predicts that only two states will be stable: complete disarmament or total armament. Starting from an expectation of peace, the slightest perturbation, perhaps some modest re-equipment of an unimportant military unit which poses little actual threat, or indeed even the mere rumour of it, is likely to trigger a rapid switch into the alternative state of total militarization and near-paranoid alarm. The system is bi-stable.

Acute fear of the other in both potential combatants is a feature of the progressive development of the arms race, and each side will be well aware that a high state of mobilization cannot be indefinitely sustained, so actual hostilities are a very likely outcome. Despite this each nation may remain convinced that its own intentions are completely pacific and that it is reacting only to the threat offered by its seemingly bellicose neighbour. Like the driver of the runaway reversing car, politicians on both sides feel that control is out of their hands and that events are driving forward at an accelerating pace, as if impelled by an outside malign influence. Positive feedback effects seem irresistible, but in reality, of course, they can perfectly well be stopped dead (at least in principle) by breaking the feedback loop. However, this is only possible to those who know what is going on, and mostly the people involved do not, at least not until too late.

Note that in all these cases of positive feedback conditions are such that once the 'runaway' begins it will accelerate rapidly for a time. Since the force impelling change is a fed-back proportion of the change itself, the faster it goes the faster it goes. This is absolutely typical of positive feedback processes and is what gives the uncanny feeling of a 'great hand' from outside pushing things forward. That may not, in point of fact, be a good description of what is actually happening, but it certainly feels like it. Later, of course, other forces may come into play, the effect of the feedback loop will diminish, change will slow and the second stable state will be reached.

Thus positive feedback 'runaway' is dramatic and produces great and seemingly irresistible processes of change. It remains true, though, that armaments competition between nations does not always lead to the disaster of war and also prospective lovers do not always end between the sheets. From a control theory point of view, how do we measure if the positive feedback effect is strong enough to produce these most dramatic of results, leading to bi-stable phenomena? As with other closed-loop systems, for a given stimulus it all depends how much feedback is generated, in short on the magnitude of the loop gain, as already defined.

A particularly interesting case arises where the feedback is just equal to the stimulus that caused it, or in other words the loop gain is unity. If the feedback is positive, so that the sense of the feedback is to enhance the stimulus, the effect will be that the feedback generated by the original stimulus is just sufficient to sustain the change which has taken place, even if the stimulus is then taken away. Just as obviously, a gain marginally greater than unity, with positive sense of feedback, will cause the effect of the initial disturbance to more than compensate, indeed to grow. This is the condition for the instability of all intermediate states in a positive feedback closed-loop system. For loop gain greater than unity the system is bi-stable, having two (and only two) extreme conditions in which it is able to rest, but making a rapid transition between them if suitably perturbed. By contrast, if the gain is less than unity the system could rest in any condition between the limits.

Thus, if the two lovers meet and retire to a place of privacy, but the gentleman should happen to be in a melancholy mood, it is not hard to guess the outcome. James Boswell, the celebrated biographer, suffered this misfortune in 1762 at his first intimate assignation with Louisa, an actress. In an unaccountably gloomy mood, his responsiveness to the lady was not sufficient to raise the loop gain of their relationship above unity, no switch between the extremes of amatory states occurred and the result was disappointment for both parties. In these circumstances, not to be able to get one's loop gain up enough to achieve the desired autonomic response is something of a disaster.

> Louisa was actually 'Mrs' Anne Lewis. Mr Lewis had departed before she met James Boswell (1740–95) and the marriage was anyway of doubtful legality. Boswell, then twenty-two, had been consorting with actresses in Edinburgh for three or four years, and had suffered several attacks of gonorrhoea in consequence. Arriving in London he chose Louisa as a permanent mistress, hoping to avoid the risks associated with more casual relationships. Unhappily he began to exhibit the familiar and unwelcome symptoms after just one intimate encounter with the lady. Convinced she must know that she was infected, he broke off the relationship in ill-will. Louisa asserted her innocence, which made him feel bad about it, wondering if he had been unjust. It is now well known that women with chronic gonorrhoeal infection can exhibit no symptoms at all, so she may have been telling the truth even though she was the source of his misfortune. Boswell continued to consort with whores and actresses and had many more bouts of the disease before his death more than thirty years later.

Similarly, but with an altogether happier outcome, if a nation's military reply to its neighbour's first move towards rearmament is not perceived as sufficiently threatening to evoke a certain level of response (of a sufficient magnitude to generate a greater than unity loop gain) no arms race will result. With positive feedback loop gain is all, and the world does not get exciting until it exceeds unity.

To state this result more formally: unity loop gain is a dividing line for positive feedback, between two wholly different modes of behaviour. Above it is the domain of bi-stable systems, below the realm of continuity. By contrast, for negative feedback there is no such sharp division, no discontinuity between two different domains, although loop gain is still very significant. In the case of negative feedback, loop gain can be increased at will, short of the point where the Nyquist criterion is infringed. The larger the negative loop gain (leaving aside the effects of loop delay) the more accurately it performs its task and the more stable the regime it produces. The falcon which responds faster and is more energetic succeeds more certainly in killing her prey, and so she should, because it is a negative feedback system she forms when closing with her quarry and for the lively, aggressive bird loop gain is that much the greater. All of this is in sharp distinction from the effects of varying loop gain in positive feedback.

One of the beliefs said to have been held by witches in former times is that one should always try to pay back whatever one receives from others, whether good or evil, in the same kind but threefold. Whatever worthy intentions may have lurked behind the witches' doctrine of threefold response, its practice would be a disaster. Two people trying to associate and actually pursuing this strategy would have a very tumultuous relationship, since the gain of the feedback loop that they formed, each with the other, would be nine ($= 3 \times 3$) and positive. They would thus hardly ever relate on a normal footing, but instead would trigger on the basis of quite trivial stimuli either into total mutual hatred and contempt or the most blissful love relationship. Real-life couples who behave in such a way are not totally unheard of, but considering how they pass their lives it hardly seems a state of affairs to strive for. In the end simple exhaustion probably reduces their mutual loop gain back below unity.

The alternative Christian doctrine of turning the other cheek aims at achieving loop gain for aggression less than unity from the start, and thus seems to have much to recommend it if conflict is to be reduced. If applied indiscriminately in all interpersonal relationships it is interestingly asymmetrical as between aggression and love, reducing loop gain for the former and enhancing it for the latter, and should thus reduce the incidence of fights but increase the frequency of sexual affairs. This point, which to some might seem to commend the practice, is not made clear in the usual devotional literature.

Present day interest in the witch religion began with Margaret Murray's famous books,[1, 2] not now thought reliable. Since Murray's time there have been innumerable scholarly books on the topic, many sceptical about the whole notion of witchcraft as an organized cult, a few more sympathetic. There are also popular books, the best of which is Paul Huson's, a 'do it yourself' manual of witch-cult practices, and refreshingly down to earth.[3] Sprenger and Kramer's infamous *Malleus Malleficarum* (1486) is a medieval handbook for inquisitors, much taken up with how to identify, interrogate, try and punish witches.[4] It offers little credible about their beliefs. Sifting what seems common in the extensive literature, however, one can assemble some indication of what they believe, despite their understandable secretiveness.

Witches claim to be a pre-Christian cult; their beliefs include reincarnation and the representation at their mysteries of a threefold deity: the White Lady (colour white, the creator), Verdelet (green, the sustainer—'the Green Man') and the Magister (red, the destroyer), their roles enacted by three officers of the coven (itself composed of twelve witches evenly divided between the sexes, plus the Magister). For them all things are cyclic in time, endlessly repeating. This is symbolized by much in everyday life (which thus teaches the cosmic secret) such as the phases of the moon, the rotation of seasons and the cycle of human birth, life, death and rebirth, and acted out in their ring dances. The religious observances (including a ritual meal of mead and honey cake, chants and dancing) aim to promote fertility and the continuance of the world, also to secure that devotees will be reborn in their next incarnation among those they love in this one. It all sounds like an odd variant of Hinduism, in one of its forms (Lady =

1 Margaret Murray, *The Witch Cult in Western Europe* (1921).

2 Margaret Murray, *The God of the Witches* (1931).

3 Paul Huson, *Mastering Witchcraft* (1970).

4 Available in a translation by Montague Summers (1928).

Brahma, Verdelet = Vishnu, Magister = Shiva). The notion of cyclic time is strong in Hindu cosmology and fits this interpretation. Did the Celts bring an early version of Hindu belief to Europe in their migration from India (if indeed that was their place of origin)?

Although everything is possible in corrupted religious forms, the witch cult ought to have no connection with Satanism or the Black Mass. Identifying the Magister of the Witches with the Christian Devil is common but wrong. Satanism is an entirely different belief system,[1] having connections to dualistic religions such as Zoroastrianism. It never attracted much following in the West, where it appeared from the time of the crusades. Twenty years ago there were communities of Satanists in northern Iraq which may yet survive, but their emphasis seemed to be on placating the Devil rather than worshipping him.

So much for bi-stable systems, but for one special and important class among positive feedback systems there is not just one transition but repeated and continually switching to-and-fro between the two limiting states, which are thus neither of them stable any longer. Energy stored at each 'switch' is subsequently used to flip the system back again, and this kind of system is therefore astable. A familiar example is found in a quartz watch, where a positive feedback system is coupled to a quartz crystal, which absorbs and stores energy during a switch. A short time later it delivers a pulse back to promote the reverse switching, doing so at the natural ringing or resonance frequency of the crystal, and thus producing a sustained oscillation somewhat like a musical note, although above the audible range. By electronically counting the regular beats of the crystal, the watch hands can be moved forward every second. This class of positive feedback system is called an oscillator—it is of the greatest practical significance to us because the human heart, though composed of muscle not crystal, is just such a thing, and its oscillations are the very heart beats which keep us alive.

To summarize, when either of two things are observed in the real world it is reasonable to deduce that positive feedback is operating. The first is sustained and continuing oscillation or alternation, and the

1 Paul Carus, *The History of the Devil and the Idea of Evil* (1974).

second a marked and usually rapid 'runaway' as the beginning of the switch between two well-differentiated states. Large or small, trivial or significant, the oscillatory phenomena are everywhere: the swing of the pendulum on the ancient grandfather clock under the gentle 'kick' of the escarpment or the electrically stimulated beat of the crystal in the newest wristwatch, the motion of the piston in the cylinder of a car engine or the throb of the heart of the driver at the wheel—all these are examples of feedback oscillations. That this is a sustained phenomenon is important. Thus, the alternation of day and night is not a feedback phenomenon, but the consequence of a slowly decaying initial rotation of the earth around its axis. Each year the rotation grows a little slower and the day, as a consequence, becomes just measurably longer. By contrast, the beating of a healthy heart continues much the same until it suddenly ends in death, when the source of energy that drives the positive feedback system is at last permanently withdrawn.

As for the positive feedback driven 'switch' between stable states, it is no less universal, found in every kind of sudden or radical transformation: falling in love or having a row, a disastrous run on a failing bank or (no less) the panic to buy shares in a booming stock market, growth in the world computer population, the sudden and unforeseen overthrow of a dictatorial government, the industrial-scientific revolution which has transformed human life, and so many, many more examples. In all of them a swing betwixt the old and the new seems to have a curiously unstoppable quality, with no apparent resting place between. Whenever something of the sort is observed it is always legitimate to suspect that positive feedback is at work. Because this positive feedback switching phenomenon is the principal agent of social change it cries out to be looked at more closely. Understanding it can teach both the businessman how to make a million and the idealist how to change the world. So large a claim demands corroboration: in the following chapters some case histories will be developed in detail.

6

The two William Morrises

Two men called William Morris are associated with the city of Oxford. William Morris (1834–96), educated at the university, was an artist, poet and designer, although he received little formal grounding in any of these professions. He was also a successful businessman, a *mari complaisant* and a communist. William Richard Morris (1877–1963), later Sir William, later Viscount Nuffield, formally educated only to the point of meagre literacy, was a self-taught mechanic who profoundly distrusted engineering science yet played a dominant role in the growth of the British motor car industry, and became extremely rich by it. The two men's lives overlapped in time but took very different courses. They have been compared before, notably by John Betjeman, who called Lord Nuffield 'the second William Morris' and attacked him for his supposed destruction of Oxford, but it is instructive to look at them again from a control theory point of view.

First, the facts of their lives. As a fourteen-year-old school leaver, W. R. Morris took a job as a repairer in an Oxford bicycle shop, learned the rudiments of his trade, then at sixteen branched out on his own, with a total capital of four guineas (£4.20, perhaps equivalent to two or three hundred in mid-1990s currency), first repairing and later making cycles. In a few years, and after painful setbacks and a little success with motorcycles, he began to manufacture cars and soon had a substantial business. Lord Nuffield proved a prodigiously successful businessman, making a personal fortune of some £14 million by the late 1930s, when the currency was worth many times more than it is today. Although in casual encounters an unattractive man, often seeming maladroit and unimpressive, he was nevertheless warmly regarded by his close friends, particularly the directors of his company, who were far and away the majority of all the friends he ever had. To them he was loyal even when they made expensive mistakes.

Once he had become rich and famous, approaches to Nuffield from authors proposing to write a biography were routinely met with threats of legal action, so intense was his regard for his personal privacy. Yet if there were skeletons in his cupboard they have remained well hidden. He married only once, and lived his life without scandal, despite hints that the relationship was less than idyllic.

Nuffield could not write at length, was never an easy speaker and avoided public debate. As a younger man he was reputedly xenophobic and anti-intellectual;[1] he is said to have dismissed senior executives when he discovered they were university graduates and to have addressed French visitors as 'manure' rather than 'm'sieur'. Yet later he was best known as a philanthropist, making charitable donations of some £30 million in all. Throughout his days, though, he remained parsimonious to an extreme in small things, even while generous in large. In his fifth and sixth decades Nuffield, perhaps surprisingly, showed every sign of being particularly sympathetic towards educational causes, endowing a college at Oxford which at first he wished to devote to engineering science. Characteristically for the time, the university talked him out of it, steering his money towards the social sciences instead. Later Nuffield is said to have felt cheated when he discovered that he had endowed a nest of left-wing intellectuals.

The secret of Nuffield's success is very easy to understand, and he was never other than totally open about it. The cars his company sold were not particularly innovative and while fully adequate they were not generally better than competing makes. On the contrary, they were always distinctly conservative in design, perhaps in this reflecting the limitations of his own engineering knowledge. They were, however, cheaper to make. He achieved low factory-gate prices by minimizing the costs of innovation (design, development and tooling) and retaining successful production lines in his factories for long periods, with consequent low defect rates and rework, which also had a favourable impact

1 Robert Jackson, *The Nuffield Story* (1964).

on warranty costs. Manufacturing processes were tightly controlled and any component of the car which proved successful—engine, gearbox, chassis or whatever—was retained for as long as possible in subsequent models. Keeping manufacturing costs at minimal level, his was a good strategy provided only that the technology of the product did not change too fast. On this Nuffield gambled and was proved right, but it is doubtful whether any other strategy was open to him.

Year after year in the 1920s and 1930s he actually reduced the price of his models or introduced new ones for less money. He was able to do this because of the sharply increasing volume of cars bought from him. This numerical increase worked to reduce his costs per unit of production and sales, in a way perfectly familiar to manufacturers. Thus a positive feedback loop was established: by reducing prices he increased sales volume, and was then able further to reduce prices. From the early 1920s his share of the UK market for cars began to increase rapidly, in a typical positive feedback 'switch' between extreme states.

There were, in essence, two parts to the feedback loop. The car market in the UK at that time (which operated behind a protective tariff barrier discouraging to imports) was highly sensitive to price, and marginal price reductions would produce a marked increase in market share and even total volume. This guaranteed a high gain factor between price changes and increase of sales, but that was only one half of the loop. The other half was that, by virtue of the vigour with which Morris Motors Ltd strove to deliver falling prices, Nuffield found a way reliably to translate rising volume into significant reductions. Put these two together and the positive feedback loop which results had a loop gain greater than one. People mostly bought on price, so from the first price cuts in 1921 the switching process began. But where would it all end, when the effects of positive feedback had run their course? What was the extreme state to which the market for cars was moving? Would Lord Nuffield finish up as a monopoly supplier?

In the event, world war forced an artificial end to the situation, but it is intriguing to consider what the outcome would otherwise most likely have been. First, one must recognize that there were parts of the market which were never sufficiently price sensitive to make the Morris cost-cutting tactic work. Luxury cars and high-performance cars are bought on criteria other than price—it is said that those who need to ask the price cannot afford them—so that these market sectors would not have been responsive to the approach which was so successful elsewhere. But even restricting consideration to the market in which the Morris tactic was appropriate, how far would the action of the positive feedback loop have pushed things? The switching action produced by positive feedback arises because any disturbance results in a fed-back stimulus in the same sense and of larger magnitude, provided that the loop gain is greater than one. It will therefore continue until the loop gain falls (for whatever reason) to unity, and then what is fed back will just merely sustain the existing position.

> Business jargon distinguishes between the total available market, TAM, which in this case would have consisted of all those who wished to buy cars, and the served available market, SAM, which was those wanting cars whose needs would have been served by what Morris Motors had to offer. Lord Nuffield tried to widen his SAM by acquiring Wolseley and Riley to supply more luxurious cars and establishing MG to make putative high-performance vehicles. 'For the young Briton who wants a car that looks as if it can go a damned sight faster than it can, the MG is fine,' an official of the Abingdon works once said.

But why should the loop gain fall? One obvious cause is when the market saturates: once everybody who is likely to buy a car has done so, further price reductions will be ineffective. In practice it does not happen quite so suddenly as that bald statement suggests, but as the market approaches saturation the likelihood of more sales resulting from price reductions gets progressively less, so that the loop gain falls smoothly. Another reason for the loop gain to fall would have been if Nuffield had become progressively less able to deliver lower prices despite a growing market, perhaps because the cars were already so cheap that he could find no way to make them cheaper. Either way the falling gain would have progressively decreased the acceleration of sales—the switch between states—until stability of sales numbers was established when the loop gain had dropped to unity.

As already explained, this kind of behaviour is typical of positive feedback loops with more than unity gain. Once triggered by some disturbance, often small, they begin to switch from the one of their two stable states in which they had been resting to the other, doing so at an increasing rate limited only by the ability of the whole system to respond. They continue in that way until they hit some saturating phenomenon which causes the loop gain to throttle back to unity, where they are conditionally stable. Triggering back remains possible, of course. In Morris Motors's case a sudden drop in sales or rise in car prices would most likely have done it.

The Morris Motors experience was, of course, far from unique. Indeed, something similar happens in some industrial sector in most of the major industrial countries every few years. Another classic example was the virtual take-over of the United States computer industry by IBM after 1953, on the back of the evolution of commercially viable mainframe systems. It happened as the result of the establishment of a similar positive feedback loop (although IBM did not use price as their principal mechanism of market capture but instead cleverly exploited particularly close relationships with the customer, crucial in the early days of a technology in which many did not then feel confident).

So much for Nuffield. What of the other William Morris, and what lessons does his life conceal? In this case there is no shortage of biographers.[1-3] His life and times have been extensively studied, even the role of Morris as businessman. He came from a comfortably middle-class background, his father a principal of a successful City firm of discount brokers, and for the earlier part of his life was able to live in a degree of opulence on the proceeds of some inherited mining shares, which his father had acquired in settlement of a debt. These were in a company established in 1844 to mine copper near Tavistock. It prospered, and the shares were soon providing him with an income of some £900 per year, which continued until the mid-1860s and thereafter declined, by which time Morris's business interests had become profitable. To relate this figure to late twentieth-century money is not easy but perhaps the current value was some hundred times greater. William Morris was always a rich man by the standards of his day.

He went up to Oxford in 1853, intending to take Holy Orders and then follow a career in the Anglican Church. By this time Morris

1 J. W. Mackail, *The Life of William Morris* (1901).

2 P. Henderson (ed.), *William Morris, His Life, Work and Friends* (1967).

3 J. Lindsay, *William Morris* (1975).

was High Church, although his family were Evangelicals. (In his last, communist, decade he seems to have become an atheist.) However, his interest in the visual arts began to assert itself, particularly as a result of his relationship with Burne-Jones who went up at the same time, and he revised his plans, aiming instead at a career in architecture. He had quite early decided that he could not assent to the Thirty-Nine Articles of Faith, a major disadvantage for an Anglican cleric but acceptable in an architect. He entered George Edmund Street's office at the end of 1854 and remained with him until late 1856. Street was architect for the Diocese of Oxford, but his practice was not exclusively ecclesiastical. He took a broad view of the role of the architect, believing that it encompassed interior and furniture design, and was a pioneer in the revival of art embroidery. After a couple of years in the architect's office, however, Morris changed his mind again and determined to become an artist. This brief association with Street was his only formal design education.

In 1861 Morris established the firm of Morris, Marshall, Faulkner and Co. (with Marshall, Faulkner, Madox Brown, Rossetti, Burne-Jones and Philip Webb) to make craft objects, glass tiles, jewellery and later wallpaper and textiles, aiming both at church refurbishment, then flourishing, and at the private patron. The business struggled along with some difficulty, Morris being only nominally in charge for much of the time and making many mistakes from lack of business experience. Nevertheless it taught him much which made success possible later. His private income began to decline from 1866, so the firm's profits became more important to him, and in 1874 he reorganized it, as Morris and Co., virtually under his sole control, although still fully supported by Burne-Jones, Faulkner and Webb, who continued in the firm. Crucially, Rossetti had gone, though after much ill-will over the terms of the financial settlement. Morris and Co. grew moderately prosperous thereafter, although with a few difficult times.

Morris's private life was, however, far from happy, ruined by his long relationship with Dante Gabriel Rossetti (1828–82). Others, like Holman-Hunt, suffered at Rossetti's hands but were able to free themselves; poor Morris remained under his spell through it all. Even whilst he was still in Street's office, Morris came under pressure from Rossetti to abandon architecture and become a painter. Considering Morris's genius for design, one cannot but wonder whether we lost a great architect by this. A vastly talented monster, the paranoid son of a persecuted refugee, Rossetti wooed and encouraged Morris in the early phases of their relationship, and thereafter sponged on him for the rest of his life, alienated the affections of Janey Morris (his wife), cuckolded him until impotence made that no longer possible, and did everything in his power to demonstrate his personal superiority in life and art to his long-term benefactor.

Rossetti had a wife of his own, of course; she was Elizabeth Siddal, a one-time shop-girl whom he first encountered in 1849. When she took her own life by an overdose of laudanum in 1862 he consigned manuscripts of unpublished poems to her coffin in a romantic gesture, but in 1869 had her exhumed to get them back. Janey Burden, the seventeen-year-old daughter of an Oxford ostler, had encountered Rossetti (then in his fortieth year) with Morris during a visit to the theatre in 1857. Soon she was modelling for them, and the following summer Morris married her. He always treated both the daughters of the marriage as his own, and was an affectionate father. Fanny Cornforth, a former prostitute and Rossetti's mistress from the year before his wife's suicide, was herself abandoned by him during 1868. Janey had begun to absorb all his interest, and the two certainly became lovers during that year, if indeed they had not been so long before. Rossetti died wretchedly in 1882, an invalid recluse, sunk in paranoia and estranged from Janey. By then it was too late for Morris to reconstruct his relationship with her, although he did his best.

A man of unbounded, if also somewhat unbridled, talent, throughout his life Morris wrote poetry, painted and also both designed and made brilliantly original craft works of many kinds. Thought of by some as more distinguished in his poetry than his prose, Morris's literary output continued to the end of his days, although increasingly a vehicle for social polemic in his last dozen years. He was an effective linguist, making translations from the Icelandic, much admired in their day. Today, however, his reputation rests principally on his talents as a craftsman and designer, and rightly so, for it cannot be doubted that, with Burne-Jones and others, he had a major impact on late nineteenth-century English taste. That he influenced the aesthetics of his day very much to the better is beyond dispute, and in time his work as a designer became widely fashionable. What he achieved in the field of design proved enduring, his influence strong first in the Arts and Crafts movement and later the Art Nouveau and Secessionism.

The last dozen years of Morris's life were dedicated increasingly to far left-wing politics, and were characterized by the fissile and internecine collegiality of that part of the political spectrum. Although undoubtedly well-meaning, perhaps Morris really did not have much talent for politics, as Friedrich Engels stated quite categorically in a letter to Kautsky at the time.

> Friedrich Engels (1820–95) is remembered for his collaboration with Karl Marx. The son of a German textile manufacturer, he was sent to Manchester (1842) to work in his father's business, eventually becoming a partner in the firm. He combined this with journalism, writing for radical newspapers. His *The Condition of the Working Class in England* (1845) described miserable conditions among factory workers. Engels met Marx in Paris (1844), their close relationship lasting until Marx's death forty years later. For much of this time Engels was an important source of income for Marx, who was financially incompetent. In 1848 Engels and Marx issued the *Communist Manifesto*, then seen as a call for revolution but proposing political changes which now seem relatively moderate, so much has the climate of politics evolved. The famous slogan 'Workers of the world, unite! You have nothing to lose but your chains' comes from the *Communist Manifesto*. Over the century and a half since it was written it has consistently failed to convince those to whom it was addressed. Communist revolutions have always been led by people of middle-class origin, like Marx, Engels, Lenin, Trotsky, Mao and Castro. By contrast Benito Mussolini, the fascist leader, was of genuine working-class stock, his father a blacksmith.

Beginning (1883) in the Socialist Democratic Federation (SDF) led by Henry Hyndman, Morris played a leading role in a faction which rejected their leader's willingness to compromise with the parliamentary system. This tendency soon commanded a majority in the SDF but for some unknown reason did not attempt to take that organization over. To Hyndman's infinite relief, it broke away to form the Socialist League at the end of 1884.

> Henry Mayers Hyndman (sometimes Hyndeman) (1842–1921), 'the first English Marxist', was educated at Trinity

College, Cambridge, and converted to Marxism after reading *Das Kapital* in 1880. However, Hyndman's book *England for All*, published in 1881, offended Marx, who thought it did not give him sufficient credit. The relationship between them rapidly deteriorated; given Hyndman's very English background, it may not have helped that Marx rarely washed. Also at this later period of his life Marx's skin was covered with boils, which made him understandably irascible. Soon the great revolutionary and Hyndman were not on speaking terms, the situation made worse because Engels loathed the man and worked to widen the breach. Although little came of his political activities, Hyndman's life was not entirely without achievement; for a few seasons in his earlier years he played cricket for Sussex.

The Socialist League rejected Fabian notions of socialism by reform, but also opposed armed insurrection, a curious compromise which suited Morris, however. After some initial success it too became riven with internal dissension, and soon lost a group of important members who still hankered after parliamentary solutions. As a result of this mass defection by moderates it was progressively taken over by the anarchists, whose enthusiasm mainly centred on guns and dynamite. In 1890 it abolished Morris's post of chairman, and by the end of the year he had departed to his final political resting place in the Hammersmith Socialist Society. In this late political phase the literary quality of Morris's writing became more polemical, but his craft work and design continued at a high level, and if Morris and Co. was somewhat neglected in these years the outcome was not by any means a disaster.

Late in the twentieth century, in the aftermath of 1989 with the exposure of the communist system for the nightmare it was and the apparent vindication of the market economy, it is tempting to see Morris's political activities as the squander of his life on a doomed and misguided cause. Any such judgement would be far too simplistic. In the light of subsequent events, it would be easy but quite unfair to dismiss Morris's socialism as a pathetic error. We now know from bitter experience that the common ownership of the means of production and distribution of wealth, for which he hoped, brings economic and social disaster. Nevertheless, Morris was right in his clear vision of the evils of the capitalist system of his day, and in particular of the fact that the unfettered market was not delivering either an adequate price for labour or acceptable quality of life for most people. Although the solutions he proposed to these social problems may now be obsolete, the criticisms of the failings of his world which he articulated in an original and creative form remain valid, and were rightly influential. His prescription has not stood the test of time, it is true, but his diagnosis was close enough.

But what of the men themselves? How does their reputation stand? Now that both of the William Morrises of Oxford are long gone into history, how does it regard them? Nuffield, the man, is all but forgotten, his name surviving only in the charitable foundation he brought into being and his Oxford College, which diverted his intentions so comprehensively. His great company no longer exists, its identity lost in a long sequence of mergers and de-mergers. Few biographies were written on him and there is little academic interest in the study of his life. He is, in short, well down the road to oblivion

The fate of the other William Morris, the 'real' William Morris many would say, has been quite different. Father of the Arts and Crafts movement,[1] the furniture he made is now honoured in art museums around the world, and eagerly sought by private collectors; one would have to be a Nuffield to afford the best of it. More important than Biedermeier, seen as a precursor to the Art Nouveau and more distantly, through the Secessionists, even of Art Deco, what Morris did is acknowledged as a significant development in the arts. Although now regarded as a writer of barely the second rank, his designs are everywhere, copied and parodied as they were in his own lifetime, and they have become a permanent and consequential part of the Western cultural heritage, featuring in any curriculum on art history or design that aspires to be taken seriously. He has become one of the mighty dead.

Why are these two men valued so differently? Nuffield made much more money than Morris, built a far larger industrial empire, gave employment to many more artisans and a better standard of life to their families. It could plausibly be argued that his cars transformed society more radically than Morris ever managed, either by his art or his politics. Nuffield's expertise and foresight played a useful role in

1 Ray Watkinson, *William Morris as Designer* (1967).

bringing about the defeat of the forces of evil in World War II, and his humanitarian acts were on a truly heroic scale. Yet he is almost forgotten.

Some would attribute this to the characteristically English class-based disdain for trade, which sets literary and scholarly values above those of the market place. However, the story can be paralleled far beyond England's borders. Alfred P. Sloan, Nuffield's greater United States counterpart, the founder of General Motors, has fallen into a similar obscurity, his name recalled (if at all) only through such things as the Sloan Foundation, the Sloan-Kettering Institute for Cancer Research and a building on the Massachusetts Institute of Technology campus. But John Sloan (1871–1951), an artist for whom first-rank status can hardly be claimed, finds a place in all serious United States art histories and dictionaries of biography. A social realist, Sloan painted New York in a naturalistic style and with his wife Helen Farr wrote *The Gist of Art* (1939), a book once influential but now forgotten.

However, from a control theory point of view there is indeed a radical difference between Morris and Nuffield, and the widely divergent recognition they are accorded can be explained in these terms. Lord Nuffield was, from the beginning, an actor in a closed-loop system. It was one, as we have seen, with positive feedback sufficient to promote a characteristic fast transition from the earlier state of a small, low-volume car industry characterized by hand work, to a new one of high volume, mass production and low product cost. Nuffield succeeded because he was a sensitive responder to the demands of the market and could organize his factory (often under negative feedback internal controls) to provide what the people would buy. To achieve growth his task was simply to maintain the gain above unity of the loop formed by his business and the market, and that he did.

By contrast, creative artists are little affected by any control loop with its components in the outside world; what they do comes from within them. When Sandro Botticelli painted his incomparable 'Primavera', an audacious manifestation of the Renaissance spirit and arguably one of the truly great paintings of the Western tradition, it was a monumental achievement in its own right, and could not conceivably be seen as no more than just a well-executed and sympathetic response to a commission. Artists may or may not receive the approbation of others but either way such feedback seems to have little impact on their work, which comes rather from their own inner compulsions and aesthetic values. Often those later most admired are little valued in their own times—J. S. Bach thought less able than Diderik Buxtehude, the Impressionist painters (whose works now sell for millions) in their own time considered inept—but it does not seem to affect the course of their artistic development much.

Though it cannot be denied that all artists of genius are influenced by the world around them, the difference between their case and the businessman is clear. When we stand before Botticelli's great masterpiece certainly we are amazed, moved, elated, inwardly changed by a perception of the courage and virtuosity of doing what he has done, and for those reasons we give the work our recognition. If it influences its contemporaries or those who follow later it is solely because, like us, they recognize its almost superhuman quality: incomparable work, no tentative, hopping or precursory flight, but a great soaring cruise of the human spirit. In music, literature, the arts generally, we value cultural achievements for themselves, not merely for the precision of their response to the world into which they come. In brief, creative people are deeply committed to open-loop control of their output, seeing fidelity to that as the necessary truth to their own inner perceptions. The most the artist will concede is to seek material support from a sympathetic quarter, yet granting only a little in style or content even to the most generous patron. Their work launched into the world for those who receive to make of it what they will, hoping for approval no doubt but not dependent on it, the truly creative are more likely to damn the critics if praise is not forthcoming than to modify in the least their compulsive loyalty to their own vision.

Do we not admire the painter, the novelist, the composer so much more than the businessman for just this reason? Is our preference not one more manifestation of our compulsive adulation for virtuosity in open-loop control? It seems suspiciously like it. Though scholarly studies of Morris's business methods and his commercial success or failure have been researched and written, everybody knows very well that nothing of his business life would interest most of us in the least if the man had not achieved what he did in the realm of design and the creation of a new and different vision. What he did when he was driven by his demon is what justifies him; his conduct as a person or as a trader is incidental. In sharp contrast is the way we judge the useful and productive in commerce or administration, the worthy creators of wealth, the dedicated public servants and all those others who hold together the fabric of the world in which we live. They may indeed be well-rewarded in their day, one way or another, yet for all the brouhaha in the financial newspapers they are not really heroic in our eyes and certainly are soon forgotten.

Is this irrational? In the past it has led to acts of political folly, that disastrous failure of the critical faculties which gives us a fatal predilection for the charismatic leader, represented in David's romantic image of Bonaparte on his charger—the man of destiny who forces his own vision on the world. The consequences of that choice have often been tragic and just occasionally downright absurd. It is the proclivity which tempts us to neglect or pass over the more mundane virtues of William Pitt—'that damned Billy Pitt' as G. M. Trevelyan, the Whig historian, called him—who responded with remarkable assurance (and in a closed-loop fashion) to things as they actually were. It was he who, with Burke and others, painstakingly built the political structures that were to bring Napoleon down in the end, a decade after he himself was dead.

> Edmund Burke, in a remarkable example of political prescience, correctly predicted the course of the French Revolution within a few months of the formation of the National Assembly, including in his prognostication the killing of Louis XVI, the Terror and the ultimate transition to military dictatorship, and this at a time when even the majority of those participating in the events in Paris were convinced that the outcome could be nothing other than a constitutional monarchy. The magnificent biography of Burke by Conor Cruise O'Brien tells the fascinating story.[1]

The roots of our preference for the virtuoso of the open loop, our conviction that this is a more admirable, a better way to control things, go far back into the childhood psychodynamics of the individual and no less to the heroic legends, the odysseys and quests upon which all our culture rests. No doubt it is unjust to be so unappreciative as we are of the means by which the world of everyday life is kept in good order and to hanker, as we do, for the great romantic gesture. Even so,

1 Conor Cruise O'Brien, *The Great Melody* (1992).

there is more than a spark of reason in it. If Botticelli had died in infancy, as doubtless many others who might have been great painters did in his day, it is more than likely that the walls of the galleries would not have been any less well-populated today. There are other painters of the period whose work is also admirable. Similarly, if there had not been William Morris there would still have been John Ruskin, Ford Madox Brown, Edward Burne-Jones, Philip Webb, even Rossetti. Later it would have been the turn of Charles Rennie Mackintosh, C. F. A. Voysey, Arthur H. Mackmurdo and, in the United States, Louis Sullivan. Yet can we say that without Morris, or for that matter without Botticelli, something crucially important would not have been lost? Indeed it would: for we should lack precisely the creations that they left to us.

By contrast, had there been no William Richard Morris, no Lord Nuffield, it cannot be said that the motor car industry would have been so very much different, but only that some other man would have captained it. There were many others available indeed. In England, Herbert Austin was almost as successful as Morris; in America Olds, Ford and Sloan built a vigorous industry, as did Citroën in France and Opel in Germany. Had Morris not lived some of those business competitors in England whom in the event he destroyed might have flourished instead of him, the Clyno car perhaps taking the lion's share of the market, instead of the Morris. The Clyno might even have looked much like the Morris, for that would have depended principally on the designers, not the entrepreneurs. If Morris Motors had gone down, those who designed for them would assuredly have migrated to a more successful manufacturer.

Nuffield merely responded, though deftly it cannot be denied, as a component in a closed-loop control system. In a deep sense he contributed little but a quick and perceptive reaction to the demands and pressures placed on him by the market. Indeed, had Nuffield's personal qualities been more firmly fixed, less adaptable than they were, his personal vision clearer, he would have found it hard to respond as flexibly as he did to the prompting of the closed loop. Had it been so, the loop gain of the positive feedback which was to create his company might have remained less than unity and in that case the Morris Motors revolution would never have happened. In the event, he was of a type indispensable to any successful free market economy, the perceptive, energetic and single-minded responder to outside forces. It follows that Nuffield himself, as an individual, may have been entirely dispensable, not even truly unique but merely a particularly competent example drawn from a very necessary class of persons. At best, such people—the entrepreneurs—are doomed to make a great and notable mark for a day, perhaps to see it well rewarded, but then quite certainly to have it washed away by the tide of subsequent events. For good or ill, Nuffield's were qualities harder to admire than those that marked his now more illustrious namesake.

Just as Isaac Newton was said to value his writing on theological topics above his scientific work, William Morris thought his communism the most important thing that he could do to form the shape of society in the years to come. Both were wrong in their judgements: in the event Newton relaunched the physical sciences on a new and for centuries more profitable line, while Morris changed the aesthetics of the age that followed him. Both, in their influence, are with us still. Once the creative act is made there follows a discontinuity in human affairs: something irreversible has happened, a birth. There has been a change, perhaps forever, in the way we see things.

The action of the market–industry closed loop is quite different. Having flipped in one direction, it will often remain capable, given a suitable trigger, of flipping back again (but not always, although this is a subtlety not to be pursued at this point). Whom the operation of market forces make they may also break, when circumstances change. Great industrial enterprises, which seem for a time impregnable in their power, are capable of collapsing as fast as they rose. Morris Motors, even at the peak of its success, could at any time have fallen back into relative obscurity had the market demanded of it a strategy which, for one reason or another, it was not able to pursue. Such extinction of companies, even the greatest, is a commonplace of capitalist societies. Sometimes the familiar name itself may be seen as being of residual commercial value and becomes associated with a new activity. In effect the old activity dies and a new enterprise is created under an old banner, but in the case of Morris Motors Ltd this did not happen. The company name was lost in mergers, and although it lingered on some cars for a decade or two it eventually gave way to Rover, thought more prestigious because it had historical connections to a more up-market class of car than Morris aspired to produce. (At the time of writing, it seems likely that the Rover name will survive the take-over by BMW, itself a highly esteemed German marque, and will not sink beneath the waters of international conglomeration.)

Contrast the products of the open loop: new ideas, images, insights, once widely disseminated are notoriously tenacious of life, and even the most vigorous attempts to suppress them are but rarely successful. In truth, it was the open-loop invention of the motor car (in fact a complex synthesis of many interrelated inventions and discoveries) which changed our civilization, and at the most generous estimate Nuffield was no more than a midwife to a birth. In sharp distinction, for the development of the arts and crafts in the late nineteenth and twentieth centuries, Morris was a parent, the child of his thinking still with us. The closed loop may be practically effective, and certainly it alone gets run-of-the-mill things done efficiently and well, but the open loop more easily commands our emotions and our respect, for we are more impressed by the activity which we believe shows us, for the first time, the way to the future, or a possible future.

Yet that is not quite the end of the story. Curiously, it could be argued that the actions of the entrepreneur are undervalued in part because the closed loop has unconscious gender connotations. Our first experience of closed-loop interactions is the nurturing relationship between mother and baby. If in consequence the closed loop has female associations, however deeply buried in the psyche, then in our current society it would most likely be taken for granted and undervalued. To the extent that the manager spends his time sustaining his business through negative feedback, by adjusting its performance to meet desired goals, it is plausible to see his as a nurturing function, and the mothering association deserves consideration, even if at first sight bizarre. However, company growing—the positive feedback closed loop—sits less easily in this context. Truth to tell it is wholly wrong to think of control strategies as gender-specific, and much harm comes from our habit of doing so.

Which leaves one last difficult question still to be answered. Why do people like Lord Nuffield do it, why do they lead this entrepreneurial life, since the public esteem that they attract is so much less than they might enjoy in other callings? 'I wouldn't like to have it all to do again' was WR's sad verdict on his own life, delivered near its end. Why do it in the first place? The conventional answers are that the entrepreneurs work for the rewards of money and power, but these explanations, though universally accepted, are not adequate looked at more closely.

> People know less about their own motivations than a bystander, and often much less. Useless to ask a millionaire the secret of becoming rich; such a person never understands which of their actions were indispensable to their achievement and which were not. The answer, even if given in the greatest good faith, will most likely be entirely useless.
>
> Years ago the creator of a large and thriving computer company explained his success to me as solely and exclusively due to every physical dimension in his business being strictly a multiple or submultiple of 25 cm. Not only the distances between holes on his circuit boards and sizes of the boards themselves (where it might perhaps have made good sense), but also the size of the factory buildings, of the rooms, the workbenches, the chairs, bays in the car park and even seats in the lavatories—all were said to be 25 cm multiplied or divided by a whole number. That was his only secret, he assured me, and anybody who did likewise would prosper similarly.
>
> Of course it was all nonsense; a banker told me his real gift was that he was remarkably shrewd, habitually making excellent guesses about business trends, while hardly noticing he was doing it.

An entrepreneur may begin life in poverty, as W. R. Morris did, and in such cases the need to make money is a plausible motive for getting started. However, it is also true that such people, if they succeed, not infrequently continue in their efforts long after they have become so rich that the need to acquire more money is not a faintly plausible motivation (although it may still be one they themselves give when asked). Compulsively working long hours under severe stress at great cost to private happiness, health and even life itself, often the large fortunes they accumulate are left to unappreciative heirs and charitable foundations or spent, in part at least, on ruinously expensive hobbies like race-horses, ocean-going yachts or divorce.

> Georges Pompidou, once President of France, is reputed to have said, 'There are three good ways of losing money: women are the most agreeable, gambling the quickest, technology the most certain.'

Money cannot be their prime motivation, if only because they acquire too much of it and too soon for such a thing to be remotely plausible, while the love of power is disqualified as their driving force for quite the opposite reason. Characteristically, chief executives of the largest industrial companies do not, in their inner hearts, see themselves as men of power, indeed they feel almost powerless in the grip of the market, dominated rather than dominating. (I assume the male gender here as a matter of regrettable probability amounting to near-certainty.) Every day a tide of events washes over their desks, most of it bad news. They hear of contracts lost, an overrun of costs, a crisis in production or new sales opportunities emerging which a competitor threatens to take, and the consequences of all of these must be addressed at once, given immediate management attention. This process will involve interviews, exchanges of opinion, persuasion or exhortation, either face-to-face or by telephone. Over a large part of every month crucial documents will be in preparation for presentation to the board of directors at their regular meetings, particularly the profit and loss account, with its chilling comparisons with budget figures agreed at the beginning of the year and its doom-laden out-turn forecasts for the year end. Almost always, response in the form of corrective management action is needed to bring things back on course, if indeed that proves possible.

At the same time there is the Stock Exchange to worry about, and the risk of bids from potential predators. Are competitors stealing a march, with new technology, perhaps, or by seducing away the best managers? A retired army general who had taken a job in industry once remarked to me that what he found hardest to come to terms with was the junior officers forever deserting to the enemy. But there are yet more threats to be worried about, nearer home. Is the board hatching a conspiracy to replace its chief executive? Under fire from every side, not even confident of the loyalty of all but a very few subordinates, heads of great companies are forever wondering whom they can trust. Although they may at first have been impelled by a hankering after power and independence of action, few chief executives will think they have achieved it.

There is a sense, of course, in which the reality is that it is they themselves who are the threat, and the consequences of their own actions reflected in the outside world are what comes back to plague them. Thus the chief executive who achieves cost reductions will soon find that his competitors, feeling threatened by him, have done the same, and perhaps even surpassed him. He is therefore challenged to find yet further means to reduce his own cost base. It feels like pressure from outside, but can better be seen as the consequence of his own actions, coming back at him around the closed control loop. Yet even if he understood this (and abstract intellectual analysis is unlikely to be a mode of behaviour with which he is at all happy) it would give the chief executive no power to stop the never-ending pressures he feels himself under, for he would have no strategy open to him but to continue.

So if not for money nor yet for power, why do they do it? Close observation suggests that they go on because they cannot bring themselves to give it up. The practice of business is like a serial game: a sequence of challenges each well enough defined to be attacked alone, with a clear indication later whether success or failure has been the outcome. From whatever quarter, suddenly the challenge comes, and if it is successfully met there are the plaudits of colleagues, perhaps a mention in the financial press, but above all the favourable outcome on the profit and loss account, all of which makes life seem good. If things go less well it hurts a little, naturally, but the setback gives an opportunity to demonstrate the heroic virtues of courage and steadfastness in the face of adversity, and makes the motivation to win the next round all the stronger. Anyway, since invariably many problems will be running side by side, by the time the worst is known the next challenge will already have arrived, deflecting attention from the failure.

Danger, challenge, the exercise of skills, rewards which are largely symbolic—all these compose the entrepreneur's life. For an animal which evolved as the carnivorous hunter and scavenger of the plains it is a life style which could hardly be bettered, except maybe for the lack of exercise. Even for that there are the options of a game of golf, the company gym or perhaps a demanding mistress.

> Among male European or American managers the golf course is a special area for business negotiation, where an

accord can be reached in a relaxed atmosphere and what is said is off-the-record. Because of shortage of land for golf courses, Japanese use bars for similar purposes; this has led them to adopt the useful social convention that what is said while intoxicated does not signify.

7

But is it science?

The theory of control can illuminate many things, it seems, but is it really science? Certainly it seems very different from many things that go under that label. How do we recognize a science when we see one? Until the nineteenth century the dominant ideology of scientific investigation was reductionism. Its practitioners sought to understand all manner of phenomena by looking ever closer at the fine detail of what was happening, convinced that all things ultimately become simple, or at least comprehensible, when examined under a sufficient degree of magnification, actual or conceptual. Some people still believe this to be the scientific archetype.

If you take to such a view wholeheartedly then all sciences necessarily find their place in a kind of hierarchy. Thus zoology, concerned with multicellular animals, is dependent on cytology, the study of the individual living cell, the latter being in some sense more 'basic' than the former. Cytology in turn draws upon biochemistry, more 'basic' still, and itself the child of chemistry, which in turn derives its legitimacy from physics, in this interpretation the most 'basic' science of them all. Yet even within physics the larger-scale phenomena are further explained by the properties of atoms and radiation, and these in turn by subatomic 'fundamental' particles and quanta. If only everything could be understood at this level it would be possible to build back up to classical physics, then to chemistry and so on further up, in an unbreakable logical chain with everything on an unshakable foundation. It is a fantasy of perfect understanding, and its realization is neither always possible nor even desirable, and for more than one reason.

The most superficial objection to such a science world-view is that, at least for the moment, it seems that there are no fundamental particles. The atoms of matter are not fundamental, as they were once thought to be, because we know that they are built up of hadrons (things like protons and neutrons) and leptons (such as electrons). But hadrons and leptons are not the last word, because they themselves are composed of quarks and gauge bosons (so-called 'gluons' because they stick the quarks together). However, there is a significant faction among physicists who say that these cannot be fundamental either, because there are too many kinds of them and they do not reconcile enough of known physical laws, so there must be building bricks within them, smaller still.[1] Opinion among physicists is fluid just now.

Postmodern physics looks for the yet smaller building elements. Perhaps they are the superstrings, smaller in size than the atoms in about the same ratio as the atoms are smaller than us, or perhaps twistors (which may or may not be much the same) or maybe something else again. In any event they are very odd things, entirely remote from our experience, and we are never likely to make experimental observations on them because there seems no way to detect them with anything that we could manipulate—it would be like trying to use the solar system to detect a flea. So when we go in search of the 'fundamental' it recedes from us in what seems like an infinite regression, and we find ourselves dealing with entities with no evident existence outside our mathematics, having properties which cannot be directly observed but must be inferred from things that are less 'fundamental'.

Even more important than this objection, however, is the more practical one that the bottom-up approach to science rapidly leads to intractable and useless complexity. It might perhaps be in some sense true that physics is more 'basic' than chemistry, but understanding a complex chemical reaction is difficult enough as things are. To seek to do so in terms of what happens to the fundamental particles involved, even if successful, would add nothing at all in terms of what the chemical understanding is needed for, such as to design chemical reactions that work. Still less would it be possible or useful to describe the functioning

1 David Peat, *Superstrings and the Search for the Theory of Everything* (1988).

of a living cell in particle physics terms. Thus each scientific discipline defines its own 'basics', below which by convention it does not choose to venture, and the particular choice of these 'basics', along with the selection of the questions that it tries to answer, gives each subject its unique identity. For physics the 'basics' might indeed be superstrings someday, for chemistry they have long been the properties of the known chemical elements and for, say, structural engineering they are the properties of materials. Only in this way can the explanations that a discipline gives, and the paradigms it uses, be of tractable complexity and predictive value. Of course it is essential that the basic assumptions of the different disciplines are compatible with each other, that, for example, the basics of chemistry do not break the laws of physics, but that is all. Thus there is a necessary limit to reductionism, even in those areas of study where it is the mode.

The point deserves to be pushed a little further. Consider a computer running a program: it could be argued that what is really going on is that a series of electrical charges are being transferred between certain locations on one or more silicon chips. Using instruments like the scanning electron microscope it would be possible, at any rate in principle, to identify all the electrical currents and voltages in the chip at any instant of time, and so to create a complete representation at the physical level of the computational procedure. An avid reductionist could argue that only this would be a truly basic description of computer function, but in fact it would be a very poor way indeed of trying to understand what the computer was doing, difficult or impossible to interpret in any useful way.

Instead, when using a computer attention is normally concentrated on the software, specifically the various steps of the program, described in terms of abstract 'software objects' and the operations carried out on them. Whilst it is necessarily true that these software objects must be represented somewhere in the works of the computer by patterns of electrical charges, this is a matter of complete indifference to the user provided that the machine continues to function satisfactorily. What the user is concerned with is the software objects, which are themselves pure packages of information, perhaps representing things in the real world that are to be understood, modelled or controlled. For this purpose to talk about electrical voltages and currents in the chip is not wrong but also not helpful; it is a description at too low a level of abstraction to be of use. The higher level description in software language is both simpler and more serviceable, and in fact there is nothing less 'real' about it than what is going on in the chip. They are both aspects of the same phenomena, both valid representations but at different levels, and it is sensible to choose the more appropriate to the task in hand. When using the computer in normal functioning it is the software descriptions which are primary; only to repair the machine when it malfunctions, or perhaps to design another, will it be important also to consider the hardware in detail.

In much the same way, whilst it may be perfectly true that mental functions are properties of the brain and all mental states can, in principle, be mapped onto corresponding neurological events, nevertheless to hope that the workings of the mind can one day be described entirely in terms of brain physics and chemistry, thus making psychology redundant, is equally misguided. Even if such a thing could be done it would lead to immense descriptive complexity and would not be tractable to those who wanted to make statements about sophisticated processes of thought. It is thus an inappropriate mode of description except, doubtless, in those important situations where brain chemistry or structure becomes subject to temporary or permanent malfunction. The brain too has its hardware and software; neurologists are concerned with the former, psychologists with the latter. Which of the two groups has the more useful knowledge depends on the problems being addressed, and it is naive to suppose that one discipline is more basic or fundamental than the other; they merely describe at different levels of abstraction. Their work is complementary and it is much more constructive to ascribe legitimacy to both than to try to subsume one in the other.

Finally, reductionism in science has run into a critical philosophical difficulty at the end of the twentieth century, one which derives from the study of the phenomena of chaos. At the heart of the reductionist approach is the belief that all things get simpler when they are examined sufficiently closely. Thus a complicated squiggle drawn on paper—a signature perhaps—will resolve itself on close examination into relatively simple curves joined together, and what is more every tiny segment of each such a curve approximates ever more closely to a straight line as its length gets shorter. In mathematics this was the basis of the calculus, invented independently by both Newton and Leibniz, which is still the principal tool of contemporary science and engineering.

Gottfried Wilhelm von Leibniz (1646–1716), an inappropriately educated isolate who remade science, was the son of a professor of moral philosophy at Leipzig. He is said to have taught himself Latin and Greek in order to read his father's books. He studied law and held a doctorate in jurisprudence. Sent to Paris in 1672 on a diplomatic mission by the Elector-Archbishop of Mainz, Leibniz remained there until 1676, practising law. Christian Huygens directed his interests towards science during this period. Thereafter until his death Leibniz lived in Hanover and served the Guelph family as judge and minister to the Duchy of Brunswick (Braunschweig), his scientific interests never more than secondary to this, his 'real' profession. Yet for all that Leibniz is regarded as a founder of modern science. He expounded a theory of substance based on monads, seen as a forerunner of the atomic theory, and also invented the calculus[1] independently of Newton[2], with a superior notation including the still-current symbols for integration and differentiation. When the Royal Society (partisan to Newton) charged him with plagiarism he defended himself vigorously, and in the final debate advanced the modern-sounding argument that all space, time and motion are relative. Leibniz also made contributions to philosophy and psychology, opposing John Locke's theory that the mind is a *tabula rasa* at birth.

However, it has long been known to mathematicians that, although plausible enough in many contexts to be useful, the assumption that simplicity progressively emerges at the level of finer and finer detail is simply not universally true. In recent years there has been much interest in Mandelbrot sets, complex fern-like patterns which have the curious property that any part, closely examined, is just as complex as the whole, and this goes on being true to any possible degree of magnification.[3] This much alone is enough to prove that it is by no means

1 In 1675, published 1684.

2 In 1666, published 1687.

3 Benoît Mandelbrot, *The Fractal Geometry of Nature* (1982).

a universal truth that things get simpler the closer one looks at them. Indeed, the signature considered above may be approximately resolvable, looked at closely, into a series of almost straight segments, but if it is examined closer still this apparent simplicity will break down. Under a microscope the paper surface will appear as a jungle of fibres and the ink line as a series of discrete dried blobs, all trace of neat, straight segments having vanished. In fact once these ideas are current it comes to seem rather obvious that the reductionist principle is more like a special case rather than the general rule. But this is nonsense, some will say. Suppose the paper to be perfectly smooth, the ink perfectly continuous, the line itself of negligible width, and at once the straight line segments will be reinstated. Perhaps, but it will then no longer be a real signature on real paper, or indeed anything at all that exists outside the human mind. We have long deceived ourselves in order to rescue the dream of reductionism from its failures; now at last we have woken up.

To have reached the conclusion that reductionism has its limits and can at times lead us far astray is by no means radical, although one still comes across a few in the scientific world who seem disoriented by it, having led untypical sheltered lives. In truth, the nonreductionist sciences have been with us for a very long time indeed; thermodynamics is the archetype of a holistic scientific approach. Thomas Newcomen's steam engine of 1713 (not the first in history but the earliest to achieve widespread use) was a development made by an engineer with little science basis to his understanding, beyond what had already passed into common knowledge. At first the problems perceived surrounding its use were the many practical ones which had to be solved to permit construction of working engines at an acceptable cost, using the limited machine-shop skills of his day. The question of their efficiency in converting the heat energy from burning coal into mechanical energy for pumping water seemed less important at first than the advantages they brought in draining flooded mine workings.

> Newcomen invented a beam engine, exclusively used for pumping water. His design was slow acting, completing only a few strokes per minute. Able to generate large forces and hence lift a big volume of water by means of a pump on the end of the beam opposite the steam cylinder, it was too slow to be successful in rotative versions. Pioneers of the steam-

driven factory were consequently obliged to derive rotary power from a water-wheel, as in times gone by, using their Newcomen engine solely to pump water back from the lower to the upper mill pond.

Later, however, the very high fuel consumption of the Newcomen design began to attract attention and Sadi Carnot, using essentially thermodynamic reasoning, published his *Discours sur la puissance motrice de feu* (1824) which related the efficiency of the engine to its operating temperatures.

The Carnots were quite a family. Sadi Carnot (1796–1832) was the eldest son of Lazare Carnot (1752–1823) 'organizer of victory' during the French Revolution. A military engineer, Lazare was elected to both the Legislative Assembly and National Convention, from 1793 serving as the military expert of the Committee of Public Safety. After the fall of Robespierre (which he helped bring about) Carnot joined the Directory but was ousted in the coup d'état of 1797, only to be recalled to government by Napoleon when First Consul. A later Sadi Carnot (1837–94), the assassinated fourth president of the Third Republic, was the grandson of Lazare and nephew of the first Sadi. His father, Hypolite, was a poet.

This was a turning point in science, although not many realized as much at the time. The new approach that Carnot pioneered was rigorous but quite unlike most of the scientific reasoning of his day in its style. He began a wholly new discipline which, although it started with the most mundane consideration of the essentially technological problem of trying to get a little more efficiency out of Newcomen's steam engine, was to grow into something of awesome power and generality with things to say about matters as varied as chemical reactions and the nature of information. Today it is commonplace to see thermodynamics as of universal significance and to encapsulate the foundations of the subject in its three great laws.

The first law of thermodynamics, based on the work of Count Rumford (1753–1814) and James Joule (1818–89), was stated by Rudolf Clausius (1822–88) as 'In any process, energy can be changed from one form to another (including heat and work), but it is never created or destroyed'. This is the principle of conservation of energy, modified later by Einstein's epoch-making discovery that matter could be transformed into energy and conversely; we would now say that it is matter and energy together which are jointly conserved. Perpetual motion machines, which create energy out of nothing, would violate the first law of thermodynamics and are therefore considered impossible.

The second law of thermodynamics derives from Sadi Carnot's work. It has been stated in a confusingly large number of apparently different ways, but the simplest is due to Lord Kelvin (1824–1907), who said, 'It is impossible. . .to take heat. . .and convert it into work without, in the same operation, transferring heat from a hot to a cold reservoir'. This seemingly innocent observation, amounting to only a little more than that heat will not flow unaided from a colder body to a hotter, leads to many surprising conclusions, including the famous formulation that the disorder of a closed system tends always to increase. Disorder in a system is measured by its entropy which J. Willard Gibbs (1839–1903), a great thermodynamicist, described as a measure of its 'mixed-upedness'. Because information corresponds to the selection and ordering of strings of symbols (such as the letters of the alphabet or the sounds of speech) it is possible to build a bridge between entropy and information (equated to negative entropy). The information theory version of the second law is that information in a closed system will always tend to be corrupted and hence to decrease. However, the equation of information with negative entropy, although often illuminating, contains some hidden pitfalls.

The third law of thermodynamics considers perfect order, and states that the lowest temperature conceivable is that at which disorder in a perfect crystal completely disappears (so its entropy is zero). Heat equates to disorder in this view; perfect order cannot be bettered and nothing stands beyond it, so it corresponds to the lowest conceivable heat state. This leads to the idea of an absolute zero on the temperature scale, which, it turns out, corresponds to – 273.15° Celsius, temperatures below which have literally no meaning. A temperature as low as absolute zero can never actually be achieved, since strictly perfect order is impossible in the real world, but it has been approached in the laboratory to within one thousandth of a degree. Even at temperatures within a few degrees of absolute zero very strange things happen: liquid flows uphill (superfluidity) and certain materials lose all resistance to electric currents (superconductivity), so a current started in a wire loop could go on circulating forever. The absolute scale of temperature, much used in science, has its zero at absolute zero but degrees the same size as Celsius ones; temperatures are quoted in degrees K (for Kelvin). Thus the freezing point of water is 0°C or 273.15°K.

Thermodynamics grew out of attempts to relate mechanical work and heat in the eighteenth and nineteenth centuries, but over the years it has progressively spread its influence to embrace ever-wider questions in physics, chemistry, biology and engineering. We have been used to partitioning the whole domain of science into disciplines descended from those established in the seventeenth century, namely physics, chemistry, biology, the subdivisions into which these three may be broken, and below them the subdivisions of the subdivisions, forming a tree of ever finer distinctions. It comes as a shock to see things sliced in a very different way, to recognize new sciences in process of definition, not so much transcending former boundaries as setting new ones, running at right angles to the old, and so claiming to have something to say in all their fields.

The interesting point about thermodynamics, for present purposes, is that it is certainly scientific but not at all reductionist. Sadi Carnot did not proceed (and could not have done) by considering the impact of every molecule of steam on the piston of the Newcomen engine, but rather looked at the operation of the heat engine as a whole. To be sure, he simplified his problem by idealizing it to a high degree, suppressing many detailed complexities of real heat engines in the interest of putting matters into an intellectually tractable form, but his argument related to an engine as such, not the parts of which it was composed. In consequence there were some in the last century who even argued that thermodynamics was not actually a science at all, or more plausibly that it should be regarded as a purely interim theoretical 'fix' until the reductionist detail could be worked out 'properly'. All such ideas would now be regarded as absurd. Thermodynamics explains

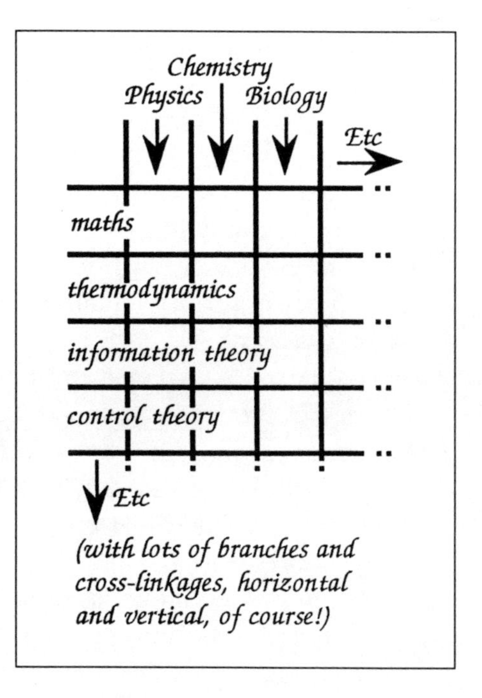

Fig. 4 Could science be something like this?

very well what it sets out to tackle, and is confirmed up to the hilt by a wealth of experimental evidence; nothing could be more scientific.

Now, in the twentieth century, some of the most exciting developments in science are in the nonreductionist areas, and the study of control is among them. Control science is a discipline growing from its own intellectual roots, quite independent of engineering, physiology or economics, about all of which it nevertheless has things to say. Not widely perceived as a unified entity until the late 1930s, it encompasses problems of control wherever they may occur, a range of competence which extends from the setting of my bath taps, through the sophisticated program of the computer controlling a chemical plant, to the workings of the economy and even the great complexities which regulate the conduct of a human life. It is, however, unashamedly holistic in its approach, for it makes no sense to talk about a feedback loop without taking it as a whole; break the loop into its parts and its unique characteristics are destroyed. Similar things could be said about a weather system, a computer, a human mind, an ecology or a human society. The study of any of these has been cried down from time to time as not being capable of being really scientific, but that attitude stems from the fallacy of equating reductionism with the very nature of science itself, a vulgar error which should have been laid to rest a hundred years ago.

None of this should be taken as meaning that reductionism is wrong in principle, however, for where it fits it is triumphantly successful, but rather it leaves it as a valuable scientific tool, yet only one among others. A reductionist approach works well where it works at all, but nevertheless has important limitations. It is certainly not of the very essence of the scientific method, as it may once have seemed to be; there are areas where it prevails but others where it has nothing to say. In short, reductionism and holism are mutually supportive and complementary ways of studying the world; science has shown that it can use both and that neither has uniquely the mandate of heaven.

For psychodynamic reasons the reductionist style has a powerful appeal to people of schizoid temperament, however, and so survives tenuously where quite inappropriate, and recently has afflicted those philosophers who try to say things about the nature of science.[1] It is hardly surprising, since philosophy is the spiritual home of the schizoid, just as rock music and the rag trade are for a hysteric, or hard work and duty to the depressive.[2] Curiously, a belief in reductionism as being of the essence of science was also common a generation ago in some of the newer, so-called 'soft', sciences, perhaps as part of a hankering after some notion of 'respectability'. As a result some practitioners, particularly in the human and social sciences, made a misguided attempt to tackle their subject in a pseudo-reductionist style. This explains the one-time modishness of behaviourism in psychology, but the ploy is easy to see through and 'hard' scientists remained unimpressed. Actually the one reliable distinguishing mark of the practice of a truly scientific method of investigation is the cycle of 'normal science' and revolution, with its characteristic deployment of different control modes at different times in the cycle, and it is to this complex of ideas that we now turn.

1 John R. Searle, *The Rediscovery of Mind* (1992), particularly pp. 86–8.

2 Frank Lake, *Clinical Theology* (1966), the clearest exposition of the psychoanalytical theory of personality types I know. The author adds a theological commentary.

8

The mighty dead

Who are the mighty dead, those overpowering human entities from the past who still exert their influence from beyond the grave and whose presence we shall never escape? They are the great names; we read their thoughts, carefully recorded and stored up for us, we study their books, look at their creative works, wonder at their great deeds of courage, intellect or virtue, or the social movements they founded, and we consider their achievements, pondering the light they cast on the questions that puzzle and plague us. To those mighty dead most recent in time we have a matter-of-fact approach, but as they become more distant from us they take on an increasingly mythical character, so that, as with Taliesin, the supposed historical person is almost submerged in legend, or like Homer or King Arthur we cannot be sure that in reality they ever lived at all.

> Taliesin is the semimythical author of surviving Welsh language verse dating from before the sixth century. It is mostly flattering stuff about bardic patrons; that was how bards made a living in those days.[1] Welsh literature contains much fine poetry, from Taliesin to the present time, and in particular Dafydd ap Gwilym (1320–80) was a truly great poet.[2] At Strata Florida, a beautiful remote ruined abbey in central Wales, he lies buried under a memorial stone inscribed in Welsh and

1 Robert Graves, *The White Goddess* (1961).

2 Rachel Bromwich (tr.), *Selected Poems of Dafydd ap Gwilym* (1982).

Latin, English being thought out of place there. English translations of early Welsh verse are available, however.[1]

It has been claimed that 'Homer' was actually the name of an ancient Greek publishing house, but this is a tale believed only by publishers.

There are those among us today whom we feel confident must take their places among the mighty dead when the time comes. Some, like the popes, have every chance of getting there almost ex officio, others do so only by their achievements, real or supposed, yet others because they embody an important myth. While they live, however, we can never be quite certain they will make it, for history could arrive at a judgement different from ours, with the advantage of hindsight seeing significance hidden from us or downgrading once fashionable artists or thinkers. Nevertheless after a while, when the dust has settled, a list emerges in every field of human activity by a kind of consensus, a roll of known names subject only to occasional and slight revision. Attempts forcefully to change the received view rarely succeed. Thus Leningrad has now reverted to being called St Petersburg as it was before the Bolsheviks; is this not because it is widely felt that St Peter is surely one of the mighty dead but Lenin is not, despite all of the posthumous boosting?

So what are the qualifications that take a person's memory into this distinguished but very mixed company, which in the arts includes personalities as different as Cimabue and Ingres, Chaucer and Dostoevsky, Palestrina and Elgar, which in politics takes in 'Billy' Pitt, Lincoln, both the Roosevelts and Winston Churchill, and in science runs in direct line from Alhazen to Newton to Turing, and Copernicus to Einstein—to quote just a few names pulled from the air.

Why do we in the West still call the Arab physicist Ibn al-Haytham (965–1039) 'Alhazen' or for that matter the physician Ibn Sina (980–1037) 'Avicenna'? Have we something against Arab names?

To answer in generality would be diffuse; it will be convenient to make things more concrete by concentrating on science. To do so, it will be necessary first to look at how the scientific community proceeds, and it is Thomas Kuhn's model that seems persuasive. Kuhn modified

1 Joseph P. Clancy (tr.), *Medieval Welsh Lyrics* (1965).

his thinking over the years, but the bones of his case survive unbroken, while his clarity of thought and elegance of style remain enviable. (His book is exciting to read, but best look at the postscript first.[1]) Kuhn believes that science proceeds through a series of paradigms, that is to say accepted descriptions, models and explanations of a closely related group of natural happenings. More precisely, Kuhn later came to say that the paradigm could be seen as the concrete solution to scientific problems which, acting as an exemplar, could replace explicit rules as the basis for solving further problems in the relevant area of science.

Thus, the modern explanation of burning as a process of oxidation is a paradigm in Kuhn's sense, and it replaced an earlier paradigm which saw burning as the release of a supposed substance called phlogiston from whatever it was that burned. The name 'phlogiston' was invented by Georg Stahl (1660–1734) of Halle, chemist and personal physician to Frederick I of Prussia. The theory, which probably originated about a century earlier, held that (together with a residue) all combustible substances contained phlogiston, a 'principle of fire' liberated by burning. This line of thought died between 1770 and 1790, replaced by the new oxidation theory of Antoine Lavoisier, the father of modern chemistry.

> Attacked by Marat, Antoine Lavoisier (1743–94) was arrested during the Terror and ten months later guillotined.[2,3] His offences were that he had taken a leading part in the Royal gunpowder business; also objection was taken to his activities as a banker and his membership of the Ferme Général, a Royal agency for collecting indirect taxes. Legend has it that just before his decapitation Lavoisier protested that as a man of science he was wrongly condemned, only to be told by the executioner, 'La République n'a pas besoin des savants.'[4] Lavoisier was being disingenuous—understandably in the circumstances. His position at the time was more like somebody today who had been chief of ICI or Dupont, a director of a big bank and helped run a scandalously lucrative

1 Thomas S. Kuhn, *The Structure of Scientific Revolutions*, 2nd edn (1970).

2 Norman Hampson, *The First European Revolution* (1970).

3 William Doyle, *The Oxford History of the French Revolution* (1989).

4 'The Republic can get along without intellectuals.'

government contract on the side. Three months later Robespierre had fallen and the Terror was over. As for Charles Sanson, the executioner, his reply seems unfeeling but he was, after all, paid on heads removed.

Jean Paul Marat (1743–93) was a French Revolutionary journalist. Charlotte Corday stabbed him to death in his bath in July 1793. Marat took frequent medicated baths for a disfiguring skin disease, possibly psoriasis. The killing was opportune for Robespierre: it eliminated a potential rival, propelled him onto the Committee of Public Safety (in effect the war government of Revolutionary France) and was a pretext for the Terror. An interesting historical parallel is the murder of Sergei Kirov in St Petersburg (1934), which gave Joseph Stalin the pretext for a Terror in the Soviet Union; however, there is an important difference. Stalin contrived Kirov's murder, but few seriously blame Marat's death on Robespierre; Corday was just a lady possessed.

Maximilien Robespierre (1758–94) was old-fashioned and unimpressive to look at, but a shrewd politician. An early moderate and opponent of the death penalty, he grew ever more radical, seizing power through his oratory in the Convention and the Jacobin club, and also (from mid-1793) the Committee of Public Safety. However, his use of the Terror to liquidate opposition both from his left (Jacques Hébert) and right (Georges Danton)—all in the name of Virtue—did not endear him to potential future victims, and opposition was hastily organized. On 26 July 1794, after several weeks of an illness which may well have been a psychotic breakdown, he made a long and very threatening speech to the Convention, which then turned decisively against him. After a coup, he was tried next day under his own law which allowed accused neither counsel nor defence witnesses. Hardly able to speak because of a jaw injury from a bungled suicide attempt,[1] his trial was a farce. Along with two other Committee members, Louis de St-Just and Georges Couthon, he was

1 Charles-André Merda claimed to have shot him during his arrest, but it seems doubtful. See Christopher Hibbert, *The Days of the French Revolution* (1989).

> executed that evening (followed subsequently by eighty of their supporters, guillotined at a rate of forty per hour). The law which condemned them was then repealed. Naturally, surviving Committee members did their best to blame the three for everything unpleasant that had happened.
>
> After the Terror was safely over the social life of Paris flourished once again. It was soon all the rage for the ladies to wear a scarlet ribbon tied round their necks in a pretty bow, to signify their sympathy with the victims, while for the same reason the gentlemen had their hair cut short at the back, as one did in preparation for the guillotine—a fashion which survives to this day.

Progress in science, Kuhn argues, comes in two distinct ways. Within a good existing and (for the time being) accepted paradigm, there is the attempt to relate more and more of what can be observed to the ideas which the paradigm promotes. Kuhn calls 'normal science' this process of articulation and elaboration of the explanation of what happens in the world in terms of the current paradigm. It is essentially a phase of problem solving and most of what scientists do in their working lives, in fact the overwhelming part of all scientific activity, is of precisely this kind. The outcome of their work is evaluated, tested and rewarded primarily by a community of fellow scientists working in the same field of study, who hold the same paradigm (or paradigms) in common.

There can be good paradigms and not so good. The former identify challenging scientific puzzles, supply clues to their solution and give hope that clever practitioners will succeed. Good or bad, every paradigm has a limited life span and a typical history. At first it explains things well—that, after all, is why it has gained acceptance. However, after a while problems begin to emerge; there are undoubted facts that the paradigm does not fit and certain puzzles it will not solve. At first an answer is sought in 'stretching' the paradigm and for a time this may succeed well enough.

> The first blow to the phlogiston theory of combustion was that, after the phlogiston supposedly came out of what was being burnt, the remains were actually heavier than at the outset—no problem for the oxidation theory, where the increase in weight is explained as that of oxygen now combined

with the original material. This difficulty was met by phlogiston supporters arguing that phlogiston did not have weight but, instead, the property of 'levity' which was the opposite (negative weight, in modern terms). This saved the phlogiston theory for a time but met with little enthusiasm, while other problems began to multiply as combustion was more closely studied.

The notion of 'levity' encouraged some early aviators, who thought that their hot-air balloons were catching phlogiston given off by burning, and that the 'levity' of this carried the balloon aloft. Others, like the Montgolfier brothers, were more prosaic: they thought it was smoke that did the lifting, and put wool and damp straw on the balloon's fire to make sure there was plenty of it.

Finally, however, the contradictions facing the established paradigm become just too great to bear. A crisis then ensues, in which other paradigms, often more than one, are proposed. In time one of the new paradigms ousts the old and establishes itself; this process Kuhn calls a scientific revolution, and the period of change between two paradigms may fairly be described as abnormal science. Note how different the normal and abnormal activities of science are. The normal phase consists of extensive problem solving based on a 'standard' paradigm widely accepted within the scientific interest group concerned. This small community of scientists with like concerns is, for as long as the normal phase endures, a highly conformist one, governed by a set of unwritten yet well-understood rules, infraction of which will lead ultimately to exclusion of the guilty party.

There has been much study of the sociology of the scientific community since Kuhn wrote, which clarifies, reinforces and in some ways modifies Kuhn's perceptions. For example Collins emphasizes the social character of scientific knowledge (and of course not only scientific knowledge).[1] It is a deception to claim, as was at one time widespread, that either the understanding or the practice of science (and still more of technology) can be wholly rationalized. Much of what we know we do not know we know, as Polanyi pointed out in the case of a

1 Harry M. Collins, *Computers and the Sociology of Scientific Knowledge* (1989).

person riding a bicycle (who does it but cannot articulate how).[1] It must be assumed that it is so with scientific and technological knowledge as much as with any other.

The trouble is that, in the past, and for reasons which must be sought in the psychodynamics of those engaged in the scientific activity, many commentators on science have been motivated to ascribe a superior order of rationality to it, and have therefore tried to play down the importance of implicit knowledge. This reduces the anxiety that scientists feel facing the unknown, because the subliminal message is that everything will make sense in the end, and that the answers can be reached by a wholly rational process. It is evidently not true, but it is comforting to believe. Even those who have worked in science (or technology), therefore, and should know from personal experience that the pretence of total rationality is a hopeless illusion, have often been, in effect, brain-washed into denying their own experience. Science needs the myth of rationality to sustain its proponents through the pressures of creative work.

> An interesting issue is raised by the occasional falsification of experimental results. Any suggestion that this happens scandalizes the scientific community but nevertheless it certainly does, and not all that infrequently. Furthermore, the border between interpretation and downright falsification is notoriously hazy. It is commonplace to exclude a few 'rogue' results which do not fit a hypothesis, for example, and experimental science would otherwise be intractable. Holton touches on this in his highly relevant account of the experimental determination of the charge on the electron by Robert Millikan (1868–1953).[2]
>
> Then again, the most brilliant scientific minds 'know' what the outcome of an experiment must be and will generally see what they expect. That being so it may soon become irksome to have to do the work at all. For Isaac Newton actually to conduct experiments, the results of which he knew very well in advance, could have seemed tedious in the extreme, and it appears certain that in some cases he took short cuts. It is,

1 Michael Polanyi, *Personal Knowledge* (1958).

2 G. Holton, *The Scientific Imagination* (1978).

though, a dangerous doctrine for lesser mortals.

Alternative interpretations of the scientific process are perceived as threatening, because the pressure to conform in the scientific community is great (as it genuinely needs to be if science is to be successful in its normal phase). Suggestions of that kind are just as unwelcome as alternative paradigms would be for interpreting ongoing scientific observations (that is, until the accepted paradigm breaks down and the phase of revolution begins). The whole point of normal science is to play the game strictly according to the rules, and it is unpopular to claim that the rules are not exhaustive and not well-articulated, even though every practitioner who summons up the courage to consider the matter dispassionately will find this to be true.

The community of science is thus one which does not achieve its ends by deep self-knowledge but rather by acting in accordance with a set of firm rules, established empirically as a result of past scientific tradition. What are these rules? The first is that the working community of scientists is 'all-informed', that is to say that (so far as practicable) what is known of the subject by one is communicated to all. In the very early days of science this was done by means of books, aimed at least notionally at the general reader. Newton still published his results partly in this way, but by the late seventeenth century to do so was becoming dated, because by then scientific journals had begun to make their appearance.

Sir Isaac Newton (1643–1727) is one of the greatest of all the mighty dead in science, a towering figure whose laws of motion stood unchanged as the ruling paradigm of mechanics for nearly three centuries.[1,2] His insights in optics created new paradigms which were crucial to the future of the subject. Yet he was a difficult person, with clear paranoid traits, and supported his published theories with experimental observations some of which he probably fabricated. John Flamsteed (1646–1719), when Astronomer Royal, lost his friendship by declining to undertake certain observations for him, the favourable outcome of which the great man had already published.

1 John Fauvel, Raymond Flood, Michael Shortland and Robin Wilson (eds), *Let Newton Be!* (1988).

2 See 'Isaac Newton', in Anthony Storr, *Churchill's Black Dog and Other Phenomena of the Human Mind* (1989).

Fond of his cat and the reputed inventor of the cat-flap, Newton was for a time Controller of the Royal Mint (after brief mental illness—a psychotic interlude—ended his scientific work in 1693) and made a fortune from the South Sea Bubble of 1720. Near the end of his life and after his death he became a kind of 'saint' of science, seen as almost superhuman. This adulation may have been inspired by Church politics; outwardly a Low-Church Anglican, Newton was annexed by that party to buttress their cause.[1] It is now certain that in private he was unorthodox, a heretic by the standards of the time, probably an Arian. It was for this reason that he never took Holy Orders, as was the custom for academics in his day, escaping by royal dispensation although under pressure to do so.

It was Newton's influence which gave the *Philosophical Transactions* of the Royal Society status as one of the first three or four true scientific journals of the modern type. These journals are periodical publications aimed solely at the scientific community and therefore able to assume a detailed knowledge of the current paradigms. In the eighteenth century they quickly became the dominant means of passing on scientific knowledge to fellow professionals, and largely remain so to this day, a powerful instrument for the enforcement of scientific orthodoxy as well as effective bulwarks against error or charlatanism. Contributions are published in the 'respectable' journals only after being reviewed and accepted, with modifications if need be, by two or three (anonymous) scientists senior in the field, who will normally ensure that nothing reaches print which does not conform to the currently accepted paradigm and against whose judgements there is, in practice, no effective appeal. Attempts at scientific publication which have not passed through this process are simply not trusted by other scientists. To be perceived as legitimate, first publication must always be through the 'good' journals.

> An example of irregular scientific publication and its consequences is the claim for cold nuclear fusion by Pons and Fleischmann widely publicized in 1989. It shook the scientific community at the time but did not gain acceptance. It is widely believed in the scientific community that a paper to a learned journal describing the work would not have survived the

1 Margaret C. Jacob, *The Newtonians and the English Revolution 1689–1720* (1976).

refereeing process, further experimental confirmation being requested. By choosing to publish through press and television rather than the journals, Pons and Fleischmann broke the rules; the widespread disapproval and rejection this attracted among scientists was a predictable consequence.

Another important rule is that of affiliation. Those who wish to undertake research are expected to have undergone a period of apprenticeship in an established group working in the field, and will find it difficult to get acknowledged, or to have their papers published, if they neglect to do so. This is a way of ensuring a minimum standard of knowledge of the accepted paradigm and of demonstrated competence in its application.

Finally, it is the custom of normal science that only those scientific problems will be tackled which are comprehensible and seem to promise solution in terms of the current paradigm, whilst those that do not, if perceived at all, will not be allowed to distract the attention of research workers or their supervisors for long from their 'proper' concerns. More commonly problems that the dominant paradigm does not address are dismissed for as long as possible as being of, at most, marginal importance and little scientific interest. This is essential if the normal science phase is not to be disrupted.

These rules may appear rigid to the point of authoritarianism and are sometimes resented by younger research workers, but they have the virtue of concentrating all attention on problem solving using the accepted paradigm. The research community is regulated by negative feedback closed-loop control, powerfully steering research toward this one central purpose. As a result, the dominant paradigm is progressively exercised to the limit in all possible directions. Sooner or later, needless to say, tested in this ruthless fashion it must fail. Once its weaknesses become apparent, as the inability to offer the possibility of solutions to real and evident problems, a period of crisis ensues.

Emphasis on the attempt at falsification of hypotheses (and hence paradigms) as a crucial element in scientific thinking long predates Kuhn, and was tellingly urged by Karl Popper.[1]

Sometimes the problem goes away because it becomes clear that the difficulty has arisen solely through lack of sufficient skill in applying

1 Karl Popper, *Conjectures and Refutations* (1963).

received ideas; by a renewed effort the old paradigm, perhaps with some insignificant modification, is made to work once more and normal science can resume its course. That, of course, is what everybody very much wants to happen, and for this reason the scientific community will sometimes try to delude itself that the old approach still works after the evidence is already quite clear that it has irretrievably broken down.

> This is what happened with the phlogiston theory; people just about got used to the implausible idea that it had 'levity', not weight, when further experiments showed that when something burns in an enclosed space the volume of air over it decreases. No problem for the oxidation theory; oxygen in the air has gone into the burned substance. Phlogiston believers were reduced to claiming that when this remarkable substance was released it decreased the air's 'springiness' so the volume went down, a hypothesis which was not at all easy to accept. The old theory was running out of credibility fast.

More commonly, however, it becomes apparent that no amount of ingenuity will help the old paradigm out, and science moves into its second mode of growth—revolution. At this point old problems with the established paradigm, which had previously been marginalized, are remembered and restated. Soon an alternative paradigm is proposed, sometimes more than one. If, after an initial period of uncertainty, the new paradigm shows that it can do all or most of what the old one did, and in addition that it can tackle problems in the face of which the previous orthodoxy found itself powerless, the new model will attract a growing number of adherents.

The phase of transition between old and new paradigms is by no means orderly. The two are so different that their proponents may describe things in quite a different language, so that attempts by each side to persuade the other can resemble a dialogue of the deaf, with much emotion bolstered by undignified and ineffective polemic. In those branches of science where paradigm changes are infrequent things go worst, because the participants are likely never to have experienced such a thing before and may find it profoundly unsettling. All they have known is normal science, and attempts to propose an alternative paradigm will therefore perplex them and may even be seen as in some way 'unscientific'. Yet the old paradigm is no longer fully

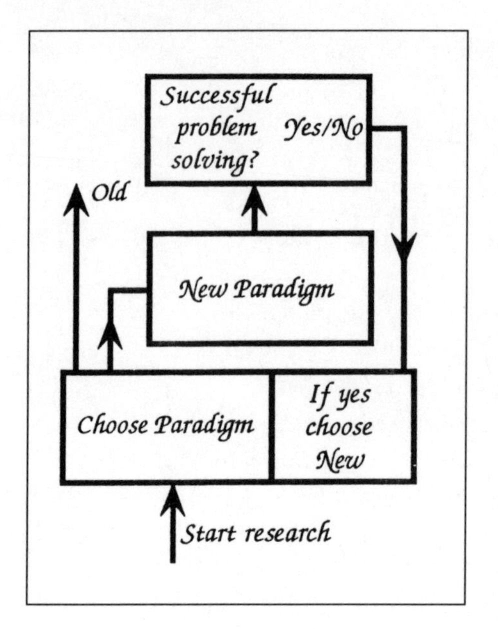

Fig. 5 Provided that the new paradigm is capable of giving solutions to problems, the more it is used the more it is used—positive feedback.

trusted—an unfamiliar and uneasy state of affairs—therefore every success for the new results in an increasing tendency for it to be preferred in the solution of future problems, making it more widely attractive. Once the point is reached that every problem solved in the new way results in more than one further problem being tackled using the new paradigm, the loop gain has gone over unity and the system will switch, resulting in a rapid and complete elimination of the use of the old version.

By this time the outcome is not in question; the change must take place and it surely will, if only because the new entrants to science opt overwhelmingly in one direction, and either peer pressure or the consequences of mortality may be relied upon to complete the transition from a scientific orthodoxy based on the old paradigm to one based on the new. As the ranks of the new paradigm's supporters swell, the scientific journals, hitherto a bastion of the old pattern of thought, will begin to be more sympathetic to publishing contributions based on the new line, if only because there is by then a fair chance that new-thinkers will be numbered among the referees of the papers submitted. Before long, the new paradigm will completely replace the old, now seen as 'a special case', oversimplified or just plain wrong. The new paradigm becomes the new orthodoxy, as rigorously enforced during a renewed phase of normal science as its predecessor once had been. At this point the probability that the scientific journals will accept a contribution based on the old paradigm quickly tails away to nothing, and there is no longer any alternative for active scientists but to think in terms of the new.

The switch between two states, new and old, is a positive feedback phenomenon. However, the positive feedback loop which has been described (and is shown in the diagram), although the most important, is not the only one operating. Another, which is also significant, depends on the fact that the more a paradigm is used the more people become experienced in using it successfully, which in turn makes it easier to get good results from, hence leading to it being used still more. Yet another relates to training of research workers: the more widely the new paradigm is adopted, the more likely it is to be taught, hence used and hence adopted. All of these work, however, only if the new paradigm is a good one—if it can identify challenging scientific puzzles, supply clues to their solution and give hope that clever practitioners will succeed—and also has another positive quality, difficult to describe, which amounts to being intellectually economical and aesthetically pleasing. One could say that for the scientific community a paradigm with all these qualities has 'charm', and is likely to be taken up quickly.

Thus scientific research is controlled during the phase of normal science by negative feedback, which promotes quite a strict orthodoxy, but by positive feedback with consequent radical change during the abnormal period of revolution. It is this relatively orderly alternation of phases of positive and negative feedback which enables science to achieve the paradoxical combination of seemingly well-disciplined and concentrated attack on problems with at the same time a capacity for remarkable flexibility of thinking and rapid change. If there is a 'secret' at the heart of the scientific method this is it. Yet to have said so much is by no means in itself to explain all, because there still remains the question of how the process of alternation between the two forms of feedback occurs, in short why and when the change-over takes place.

The reasserting of stabilizing negative feedback at the end of a 'revolution' can be dismissed easily. The mechanisms of regulation are in place throughout the epoch of change, but in temporary abeyance, because the feedback loop gain falls to a low value. Referees of papers submitted to the science journals, for example, do not know any more what is the received paradigm, or are mixed or muddled in their opinions. In consequence, not knowing towards which target to shoot, they do not let their arrows fly. Similarly, when the community is rent between alternative allegiances it is hard to say what constitutes a 'good' team in which a research worker may serve his apprenticeship. However, once the positive feedback has done its work, the change of paradigm is nearing completion (at which point, saturation effects having set in, the loop gain of the positive feedback is falling) and the wholeness of the community is recovering, these problems all vanish, new criteria of 'soundness' for papers and people are thankfully asserted and the gain of the negative feedback quickly recovers to its 'normal science' value.

More mysterious is the reverse process, by which, at the end of a period of normal science, perhaps an extended one, suddenly positive feedback effects begin to appear. At this stage what happens is that, although not yet by any means wholly discredited in the minds of those using it, the accepted paradigm on which scientific activity has for long been based is increasingly seen to suffer from more or less severe inability to provide solutions to currently important problems. Disconcertingly, the difficulty proves impossible to resolve despite a great application of human ingenuity and perhaps some marginal changes and revisions in the paradigm itself. As a result the paradigm begins to lose its charm, and in consequence becomes vulnerable.

Among the research community at such a time there is a general awareness that things are somehow awry, a growing sense of dissatisfaction with the state of understanding and often an almost doom-laden feeling of the inevitability of impending change. Even so, nothing much alters in the day-to-day conduct of scientific affairs, if only because there is no sense of the direction in which change should proceed. The old orthodoxy remains in place.

> The concerns that senior research workers feel at these times of crisis are not usually expressed to students, who still learn the old paradigm as if it were unchallenged, at least until close to the start of their own research. The problems are then presented as indicating a fruitful area in which research may be undertaken, but only in the sense of trying to patch or

> stretch the old paradigm. Implicit is the assumption that new researchers can only succeed in normal science and that constructive participation in revolution is beyond them. History shows this to be flat wrong. I suspect that the established research workers are unwisely trying to protect their young colleagues from a concern they could not in fact share, namely the fear that the pillars of the established temple are about to be pulled down.

Indeed, the only thing which could have the capacity to change this decaying 'normal' situation is the appearance of a new paradigm with a certain minimum claim to the succession. This is the crucial event which alone has the power to vivify the processes of positive feedback, and hence of the necessary rapid change. So how does it come into being, the new paradigm? In a word, it does so through an act of creation, and almost always in the mind of a single person, working alone. Schumpeter was quite clear about what he called a 'Vision', 'the pre-analytic cognitive act that supplies the raw material for the analytic effort'. This new insight was something, he argued, 'of which the source is not to be found in the facts, methods and results of the pre-existing state of science.'[1]

Just how wholly new solutions to problems are found is an issue of great interest to psychologists, and there are purported answers which go back to the time of Plato.[2] What is beyond doubt is that the process is largely unconscious. Karl Duncker suggested that solutions are obtained by repeated reformulation of the original problem, and introduced the term 'functional fixedness' to describe a difficulty frequently encountered in problem solving.[3] A fixation on the common perception and usage of some concept or object may prevent progress if the solution requires that it be pressed into service in an unfamiliar way. Thus too confident an awareness of current ideas inhibits the necessary fresh view, which explains why newcomers to a subject often do best. Liam Hudson pursued this idea from a different standpoint with his descriptions (based on a study of English schoolboys) of convergent

1 The quotation appears in Robert Skidelsky, *John Maynard Keynes* (1992), p. 539.

2 E. F. O'Doherty, 'Psychological aspects of the creative act', in J. Christopher Jones and Derek Thornley (eds), *Conference on Design Methods* (1963).

3 Karl Duncker, *On Problem Solving* (1945).

and divergent thinkers, the latter being those who are particularly well able to avoid Duncker's functional fixedness.[1] Hudson sees thinking in the Arts as essentially divergent and in the sciences as convergent. This could only be true for science in its normal, nonrevolutionary, phase (which, of course, is most of it). Gyorgy Polya sought general methods, which he termed heuristics, for solving problems.[2] His stimulating book is well worth reading, but the three or four principal methods he proposes either verge on common sense or else do not seem to work particularly well. The central mystery remains unexplained.

Sadly, sociologists of science have little to say about scientific revolutionaries. One can sympathize; the phenomenon is both rare and difficult to identify until well after the event—at the time it can look like charlatanism, under which label perhaps half the scientific community will stigmatize it. Perhaps the historians have more chance of success; if it were the case that a key to the puzzle could be obtained by a close look at the circumstances in which new paradigms were created it should prove relatively easy to resolve, because the lives of great scientific innovators are well recorded.

So then: Isaac Newton, perhaps the greatest of them all despite his oddities, was the posthumous child of a yeoman farmer, brought up from the age of three by a grandmother, his mother having remarried and left him. She was widowed again when he was eleven, and promptly returned with three children of the second marriage. All too soon after that she sent him away from her once more, to the King's School at Grantham, where he boarded in the house of an apothecary. He remained at school until seventeen years old, when he was called back to work on his mother's estates. Perhaps not surprisingly he showed little inclination toward the task, being more interested in books and the construction of mechanical models, so her plans for him to take charge of her business affairs were frustrated. His uncle intervened, with the support of Newton's schoolmaster, and as a result he entered Trinity College, Cambridge, in June 1661, aged eighteen. While there, he was not regarded as a particularly promising student, but he received his BA in 1665.

Although Cambridge was then still dominated by Aristotelian think-

1 Liam Hudson, *Contrary Imaginations* (1966).

2 Gyorgy Polya, *How to Solve It* (1945).

ing, Newton took the opportunity to read extensively in the scientific literature of his day, principally mechanics, mathematics and astronomy. Consequently in everything that mattered subsequently he was substantially self-taught. In the summer of 1665, an outbreak of plague in London reached Cambridge, producing understandable panic, and Newton returned home to Lincolnshire in order to avoid the infection.

> Terror of the disease was well justified. Bubonic plague is caused by *Yersinia pestis*, a bacterium transmitted to people by fleas that feed on infected rats. Symptoms appear in about a week, with temperatures up to 40° Celsius. Lymph nodes become inflamed, and these swellings are called buboes (hence 'bubonic'). Extremely unpleasant symptoms multiply, and up to ninety per cent of untreated cases die within a few days.
>
> Past epidemics of plague cut a swathe across entire continents; the fourteenth-century 'Black Death' killed about one in three of the population of Europe, about the same proportion as could be expected to die in a modern nuclear war. The English children's rhyme
>
> Ring a ring o' roses,
> A pocket full of posies.
> Atishoo! Atishoo!
> We all fall down.
>
> relates to the Black Death. The 'ring o' roses' is a rash that appears early in the disease, posies of flowers were (wrongly) thought to give protection, the sneezing is characteristic of a later stage (spreading plague in its even more deadly pneumonic form, with no known case of untreated recovery), while the last line speaks for itself.
>
> Small outbreaks of plague still happen in a few parts of the world, due to persistence of the disease in wild rodents, but it can now be cured by timely administration of antibiotics such as streptomycin.

Distant now from the scholarly community, Newton began to think along new lines and within a couple of years had created all of the original scientific paradigms associated with his name, in mechanics, optics, gravitation and calculus. He was then not quite twenty-five years old, and scientifically the rest of his life was no more than commentary on that early work. 'All this was in the two plague years of 1665 and 1666,' he later said, 'for in those days I was in the prime of my age for invention, and minded Mathematicks and Philosophy more than at any time since.'[1]

It is interesting to compare his story with that of Einstein, one of the mighty dead from our own century and a great maker and breaker of paradigms.[2] Albert Einstein (1879–1955) was born in Ulm. After the failure of their electrical manufacturing business (1894), his family moved to Milan. Shortly afterwards, when he was sixteen, he sat an examination for entry to an electrical engineering course at the Zurich Polytechnic, but failed. After some further coaching at the cantonal secondary school however, he gained entry to the Zurich Polytechnic in 1896, but qualified (1900) only as a secondary school teacher of mathematics and physics.

With little gift for teaching, for two years he was unemployed, but in the end found a job at the Swiss patent office in Berne, where he remained for seven years. During this period, working in his spare time and without much contact with any centre of learning or with other researchers, he wrote a series of scientific papers which changed the face of contemporary physics. In 1908, on the basis of his publications, he became a lecturer at the University of Berne, moving to a professorial appointment at the University of Zurich in the following year. He was then thirty.

The similarities to Newton's case are striking. Both men had an inadequate scientific education and were largely self-taught, both became creative in a situation of isolation from the scientific community of their day, and both laid the foundations of their major work when they were in their twenties. The pattern is oft repeated, a notable case being that of Charles Darwin, the propounder of the theory of evolution, with its vital paradigm of the natural selection process, and the father of modern biology.[3]

1 J. W. N. Sullivan, *Isaac Newton 1642–1727* (1938).

2 Ronald Clark, *Einstein: the Life and Times* (1972).

3 Gavin de Beer, *Charles Darwin: A Scientific Biography* (1965).

Charles Darwin (1809–82) was the son of a physician and the grandson of Erasmus Darwin, poet, philosopher and naturalist. He was educated at Shrewsbury School without achieving much distinction and read medicine at Edinburgh University, but went down after only two years, unnerved by witnessing operations performed without anaesthesia. He then read for Holy Orders at Christ's College, Cambridge, but with little enthusiasm, showing more interest in natural history. After graduating in 1831, he took an unpaid post as naturalist on a scientific expedition, the five-year voyage on the H.M.S. *Beagle*. She set sail on 27 December 1831, her mission to study coastal areas of South America and the Pacific. Darwin's duties were to research the geology and biology of their landfalls.

It was as a result of what he learned during these years, in his mid-twenties, that his evolutionary biological paradigm came into being, but he waited for many years before publishing. After 1842 Darwin lived as a semi-invalid at his home in Downe, Kent. Some thought him a hypochondriac, but opinion now inclines to the view that at some time during his voyage, maybe when in Argentina, he was bitten by insects carrying *Trypanosoma cruzi*, the protozoon which causes Chagas' disease. In its chronic form it gives rise to symptoms similar to those of which he complained.

Once again in Darwin we have the spectacle of a person who did not receive a proper educational grounding in the subjects (geology and biology) to which he ultimately brought so much distinction, who formed his most important and original ideas while still in his twenties, and did so on his own, remote from the scientific community upon whom he was later to have so great an impact. Similar examples from among the mighty dead could be multiplied to the point of tedium.

In the twentieth century the pattern changes a little, because the extent of scientific knowledge is so great that it becomes more difficult for scientific innovators to appear entirely self-taught, although it remains true that they are often isolates and frequently do not come from the most distinguished stables. Paradoxically though, to be irrelevantly educated for future research interests is even easier today than it was in the past. The increasing subdivision of the sciences into ever narrower specialities is the cause, and it now limits even the coverage of undergraduate curricula and graduate training, so that a couple of excellent degrees from a good school are no guarantee that one will have any qualification but that of self-education in a subsequent area of research activity.

Alan Turing,[1] who established the basis of computer theory, was self-taught in science at school and an isolate most of his life, largely because of his homosexuality, which was of a pro-active kind many of his contemporaries found difficult to accept. He created the theoretical basis of computer science when twenty-four years old, without much help from colleagues, who were uncomprehending and sceptical, thinking his approach eccentric.

Alan Mathison Turing (1912–54), son of an Indian Civil Servant of Scots descent, was born in England but at fifteen months his mother left him to return to India and he was brought up by a retired army couple, the regime reputedly spartan. At Sherborne School, Turing did not shine, interested only in chemistry and mathematics in which he was substantially self-taught. He fell in love with a fellow student whose death at nineteen (from tuberculosis) emotionally wounded Turing for life. Twice failing a scholarship to Trinity, he finally managed one to King's (Cambridge), read mathematics under G. H. Hardy, and in 1935 was elected Fellow. His paper on computable numbers, written in his mid-twenties on wholly original lines, laid the foundations of computer science. Published in 1937, it was far from the main area of contemporary mathematical interest and made little impression. In World War II he played an indispensable part leading military code breaking at Bletchley Park. Here T. H. Flowers built *Colossus*, the first electronic digital computer (1943). Later Turing worked on computers, initially at the National Physical Laboratory, where he came to feel inadequately supported, and then with Frank Williams and Tom Kilburne at Manchester University, then one of the world's leading centres for computer technology.

However, he was still actively homosexual, and at that time English law and public opinion were very cruel to men of his orientation. Turing suffered repeated persecution and died in most odd circumstances, found in bed with an apple by his hand from which he had taken a single bite. Cyanide poisoning killed him and it was presumed that the apple was smeared with it, although apparently this theory was not tested. The death was judged a bizarre suicide, but some believed

1 Andrew Hodges, *Alan Turing: the Enigma* (1983).

it an accident and others thought murder not impossible.

> There seems to be very little common pattern in the sex lives of the paradigm innovators. Turing was actively homosexual, while Newton, by his own account, had no sexual experience of any kind, his warmer feelings lavished entirely on his cat.
>
> At the other extreme, Paul Langevin (1872–1946), who originated the modern theory of magnetism, is alleged in French scientific circles to have fathered forty-two children (by various ladies), twenty-eight of whom subsequently became university professors. Contrary to hitherto accepted opinion, stories of a highly coloured emotional life are also beginning to be told about Einstein;[1] if they are true one can only say that, like a good Swiss (if only by adoption), he kept it well hidden.
>
> By contrast Darwin led a life of tranquil sexual conventionality, as befitted an English clergyman *manqué*. Perhaps Chagas' disease left him little option, but one would prefer to think that Emma Wedgwood made him very happy. Freud would not have found it at all surprising if she did: after all Darwin's mother was a Wedgwood too.

The personal histories of none of these people need be surprising, but they are instructive. An eccentric or defective scientific education may be a positive advantage for the paradigm innovator because too perfect a grounding in the currently received paradigms is inhibiting to thought about alternatives. But why is isolation significant? Being alone means that whatever is done by way of shaping a new paradigm is necessarily an open-loop control activity so far as the innovator is concerned, forced into that mode because there is no source of feedback from colleagues or the scientific community at large. As with the tennis player, the choice of the shot made is open-loop, the product of will in its direction and thrust, without benefit of feedback. The detailed mechanics of putting new ideas into viable form, like those of actually making the tennis shot, may be assisted by closed-loop controls within the individual concerned, but closing the loop to the rest of the scientific community would be positively undesirable. If there were feedback

1 Roger Highfield and Paul Carter, *The Private Lives of Albert Einstein* (1993).

from that quarter it would necessarily be negative, reinforcing adherence to the old paradigm (because that is what normal science is quite rightly all about) and thus assuredly inhibiting the creation of a new. Also paradigm makers are necessarily paradigm breakers, since the new can only rise on the ruins of the old. Personalities vary; some paradigm makers seem motivated quite as much by the desire to tear down the old as by the promotion of the new. The misanthropy born of isolation, a little paranoia, do these perhaps enhance the impulse to supplant the ideas cherished by others?

> Another curious characteristic of the paradigm innovators is that they are often quite superstitious, Einstein notoriously so. It is told of Niels Bohr (1885–1962), one of the founders of quantum mechanics, that a friend noticed he had a horseshoe nailed up over his door.
>
> 'Surely you don't believe in that sort of thing?' the friend enquired.
>
> Bohr looked uncomfortable. 'No,' he replied, 'of course not, but I'm told it brings good luck whether you believe in it or not.'
>
> To be a paradigm innovator it is necessary to have habitual processes of thought distinct from those of the generality. Being overtly superstitious amongst the rational pretensions of the twentieth-century scientific community is perhaps one small indicator of that difference, as maybe also was Newton's heretical Arianism, in his day.

A pattern is now emerging for the evolution of scientific ideas. In the mode of normal science everything proceeds under negative feedback closed-loop control, which focuses effort on the ever more rigorous exploitation of the established paradigm. This continues until its inadequacies are revealed by persistent failure. A new paradigm (or more than one) is created by an innovator who forms and articulates it working open-loop, often in isolation. If this new paradigm has the right characteristics, in short if it has charm, it can be depended upon rapidly to displace the old version in a scientific revolution, the process being driven forward by positive feedback. When this reaches saturation, in practice by the total defeat of the old paradigm, the positive feedback loop gain falls below unity and the negative feedback regime of normal science can reassert itself. From a control theory point of view we thus see a complex story: closed-loop control is always present, but the feedback switches between negative in the normal science phase and positive during revolution, the change-over being initiated by the open-loop control actions of paradigm innovators, ending the life of the old and starting that of the new.

Create, sustain, destroy—the first by the open-loop initiative of the paradigm innovator, the second by closed-loop negative feedback in the regime of normal science, the third by positive feedback in a revolutionary phase of science—this is the life history of a scientific paradigm. In the most esoteric Hindu theology it is also far more: an endless cycle of creation, sustaining and destruction are the pattern and model of the universe itself, the cosmic drama in the mind of the One, the unnamed great and incomprehensible, of whom all the gods of the Hindu panoply are themselves but manifestations.

Be that as it may, the life cycle of the scientific paradigm evidently calls on every facet of control, although it is the paradigm innovator who necessarily sets the whole cycle in motion. And here is the paradox, for it is just these same paradigm innovators—Newton, Darwin, Einstein, Turing—whom we revere as the mighty dead. The ninety-nine per cent of scientists who devote themselves to normal science go uncelebrated all, even though these are the very ones who diligently exercise the paradigms to the point of failure and therefore prepare the scene in which the next wave of paradigm makers will enact their memorable deeds. To be sure, the scientists of the normal phase may receive modest honours in their lifetime—the medals and prizes of their learned societies, and perhaps an honorary degree or two if they do particularly well. When they are gone doubtless they will be remembered for a while by colleagues, and possibly may rate brief entries in the textbooks, but nevertheless oblivion is their inescapable fate, their papers mouldering unread in scientific journals long forgotten.

Once again, as with the two William Morrises, as with the artist over against the businessman, it is the successful practitioners of the open-loop control who receive our admiration and the diligent participants in the closed-loop phase of science whom we take for granted. We do so for similar reasons in all these cases. The paradigm makers and breakers bring something wholly new to history, while the closed-loop operators, by contrast, just seem to crank the handle of time, however skilfully. If they were lost to the world they could quickly be replaced by others like them. How different from the case of the paradigm makers: they are the ones who set a path for the future and they do it alone. It is the singers of new songs, therefore, who become the mighty dead.

Yet there is a contradiction, for these very people whom we venerate as the truly great of the scientific community are the least well-suited to be role models for the majority of those who choose to make science their lives. Temperamentally, in their manner of working, and certainly in their education, there is nothing about the mighty dead that would suit them to careers in normal science. As exemplars for the young, therefore, they could hardly be less well-chosen, and there is an awkward tension between the people they actually were and the values of the normal science community which regards them as its saints. Not even the assiduous hagiography they are subjected to, once safely dead, can entirely disguise that.

And there is more. To be assured of its own survival, in each generation the scientific community must throw up a clutch of young people who are equipped, by their intelligence, personalities and background, to be paradigm innovators. Most of them will never get the chance to demonstrate their potential, though, because their scientific careers will be passed entirely in periods of successful normal science, when there is no place for paradigm creation. So what becomes of them, born out of their time as they are? Some drift away from science altogether, to become teachers, writers, maybe even patent examiners, while others pursue normal science careers but most probably without great success, because their education, and still more their renegade temperament, is less than ideal for it. They, alas, will never make their names, never achieve distinction. For paradigm innovators it is not only necessary to be the right kind of person, it is also essential to be born in the right epoch, when normal science drifts towards crisis. Valued only in such times of desperate need, they are the scientists of last resort, ill-socialized and eccentrically equipped, but they have it in them to become the mighty dead.

9

Great sea-changes

'Well,' said the Technical Director, 'what do you think of it?'

I looked down at the artefact in my hand, sturdily made in metal and finished in shiny chromium plate and black. It was as sweet a piece of mechanical engineering in small as I had seen, and I marvelled that they could make and sell it for the extremely reasonable price he had quoted.

> Nontechnical people sometimes give too little weight to the aesthetic pleasure engineers derive from their creations, which can seduce them to persevere with a product even when the rational case for doing so has gone away. This has ruined many an entrepreneur, led astray by the belief that technologists are uniformly guided by science and reason. Not so, for engineering is quite as much heart as head.

'Very pretty,' I answered. 'Still...what about the competition?' I turned it in my hand again. 'But it is very nice,' I added.

He knew what I meant about competition, but merely shrugged. 'I've told you our price—it's comfortably below theirs. And to be honest—not for publication, mind—we could get down a bit lower and still make some kind of profit. Besides, look at the opposition, just look at their product! Those things are rubbishy: flimsy plastic mouldings, not a quality product to last a lifetime like ours. No, they don't worry me; they're bound to take a bit of the market, particularly with people who like novelties, but when things have settled down I doubt they can really hurt us.' I nodded politely, uneasy yet not feeling sure enough of my ground to argue, as so often. Was he attributing his own professional aesthetic to the customer, a common but deadly mistake? 'Now let me show you our five year business plan,' he went on. 'We intend to grow quite a bit, I can tell you.'

A couple of summers had come and gone before I drove that way again. By then the factory was dark and silent, because nobody was buying mechanical calculators any more. The electronic alternative offered greater capability for much less money than my friend the former Technical Director would have dreamed possible, and he himself had been glad to find a job in a quite different industry. After some tribulation, he went into expensive mechanical watches, bought by the rich as display items. The accuracy of a quartz watch, which can easily be under a second per day, is more than most people need, which explains why there is this small market, still remaining even now, for almost hand-made mechanical watches at ridiculous prices. Less precise than quartz but accurate enough for all practical purposes, they are possessed as a status symbol rather than merely to tell the time by, an example of what Thorstein Veblen described as 'conspicuous consumption'.[1]

The fact of the matter is that when something can be done by electronics rather than using mechanical devices it is invariably far cheaper that way, in a few cases by as much as a thousand times. This is just an inherent difference of characteristics between the two technologies; electronics is much less costly. In consequence, contemporary automobile engineering, for example, is greatly concerned with finding ways of replacing mechanics with electronics to achieve cost reductions (or performance improvements for no greater cost, which amounts to a similar thing). For the same reason electronic clocks and watches, telephones, cheap musical instruments and typewriters, as well as calculators, have pushed out their mechanical counterparts. So a great sea-change came over the calculator industry, due to the replacement of mechanical technology by electronics, based on the microelectronic silicon chip. A well-established, settled and progressive business sector, exploiting fine mechanical engineering skills, was hurried to extinction, and another, chaotic and inexperienced, took its place.

1 Thorstein B. Veblen, *The Theory of the Leisure Class* (1899).

This was a particularly dramatic example, but many others are all too familiar. Something similar was happening to watch-making at about the same time, thanks to the introduction of the quartz watch, which offered a hundred times the accuracy of its mechanical predecessor at a fraction of the price. In Switzerland so rapid was the change that some sixty per cent of mechanical watch operatives were thrown out of employment for a time. This trend to electronics will certainly continue, although user preference can be a partial check on it. The digital watch did not succeed in supplanting analogue watches, in which the display is mechanical—hands on a dial, perhaps even with Roman numerals—even although the 'movement' is now electronic. There also remains a predilection for musical instruments to avoid using electronics (at least where 'serious' music is concerned); in the Anglican Church, for example, parishes wishing to replace pipe organs by cheaper electronic instruments are currently unlikely to get permission to do so, even though the sound generated by the best modern examples of each is almost indistinguishable.

> Some notes on terminology: the chips are of silicon (the crystalline element) not silicone (the car polish), and they are called chips or microcircuits but not microchips, which is nonsense. The chip is not microscopic, only the electronic circuits built on it.

Both the calculator and the watch stories were spectacular, and to many of those involved must have seemed cataclysmic indeed, but they leave us unsurprised because we have seen it all many times before, and so, for that matter, did our parents and grandparents before us. Look back a century to 1887, for example; in a German laboratory, a spark jumped across the gap between two metal spheres even although they were not directly connected to any visible source of electrical power. Heinrich Hertz had succeeded in demonstrating for the first time the existence of electromagnetic (radio) waves, already predicted on grounds of theory by James Clerk Maxwell. Just a few years later on the eastern seaboard of the United States a kite lifted a wire into the air, to act as the antenna for the first detectable radio signals from Europe. Not much later, the Russian army began the military use of radio telegraphy in their war with Japan, and the exploitation of maritime radio started to transform the life of the seafarer. But what of it? Dramatic technical innovation is so much part of the fabric of our lives that it has long since ceased to evoke either surprise or wonder. Nor is there any sign of a slackening of the pace of change; it was out of the invention of radio that, in turn, the electronics revolution of the twentieth century first grew, an innovatory process that went on to metamorphose not only communications but virtually all aspects of everyday life.

To look at a small corner will serve to illuminate the whole: just consider what has happened to music. Until a little over a century ago, to hear music it was necessary to be in the company of musicians and except for church music the opportunities were few and the quality of performance often low.

> It might be argued that this is not entirely true, because chiming clocks, musical boxes and other musical automata have been around for a long time, the barrel organ being used in English churches from the beginning of the eighteenth century. The player piano (or pianola) continued this tradition, gaining great popularity from the middle of the nineteenth century.[1] Moderately successful attempts were made to build automatic orchestras, but they were impossibly expensive. Nothing could be done to reproduce a singer's voice in this way, although a few tried. Thus the music offered by automata was both costly and limited in scope, so this approach finally proved a dead end, despite its encouraging start.

Mechanical methods of recording and playing back sound waves that could be of any kind at all—voice, instrumental or whatever—were described as early as 1877 by Charles Cros, but it was Thomas Edison (1847–1931) who turned the idea into a practical working model. In the Edison 'phonograph' a sheet of tinfoil was wrapped around a grooved metal cylinder, which was turned slowly by hand. The user spoke into a conical horn and the concentrated sound waves at its point caused a thin diaphragm to move in sympathy. A blunt needle fixed to the diaphragm inscribed these movements as vertical 'hill and dale' indentations in the foil. To play the recording back a larger horn was used to improve the audibility of the weak vibrations picked up by the needle. By this primitive means permanent records of sounds were achieved, although the quality was barely good enough to reproduce

1 Harvey N. Roehl, *Player Piano Treasury* (1973).

intelligible speech. Later it was improved through replacing the foil by hard wax, in which the vibrating stylus engraved grooves of varying depth (hill and dale recording). Within a few years, production of record cylinders and players had become substantial, yet that was no more than the first beginnings of the story of recorded music.

In 1888 Emile Berliner demonstrated his disc 'gramophone' and the Victor Talking Machine Company, which he formed in 1901, quickly went on to achieve world dominance for the disc format. Berliner's alternative approach was to engrave the waves in a spiral groove on the surface of a flat disc, the stylus moving from side to side rather than up and down. During the ten years that followed, Berliner improved the sound quality, evolved techniques for mass-producing records at low cost using metal moulds, and began to manufacture record players driven by spring-wound motors. The acoustic gramophone soon reached great heights of popularity, despite its limitations, so that when the greatly improved electrical recordings were issued in 1925, exploiting electronics technology, they were launched into a prepared and eager market.

> It may be that sound was being inadvertently recorded centuries before either Edison or Berliner, however. Microscopic examination of old oil paintings sometimes shows surface striation of the paint, consistent with the possibility that the canvas was vibrating as the stroke was made. This could be because the painter was speaking at the time. In principle, therefore, the striations could be measured and the sound that made them reconstructed, but so far attempts at recapturing the voices of the old masters from their paintings have not produced anything intelligible.

World War II cut off the supply of shellac from the Pacific basin, so record manufacturers were driven to use vinyl for discs instead. Somewhat unexpectedly, this proved a breakthrough: vinyl's reduced surface noise led to the development (1948) of the long-playing record (LP). In 1957 the record industry adopted the present system of compatible single-groove stereo, based on a 1936 invention by Alan Blumlein at the EMI laboratories near London. This, combined with long play, full frequency range recording and the quiet vinyl disc, launched an era in which any sound could be reproduced with plausible authenticity in the living room. So impressive were the results that Herbert

Marcuse, the neo-Marxist philosopher, was once moved to assert that LP records were the only thing from twentieth-century technology worth having.

Meanwhile an altogether different recording technique was developing in parallel. A magnetic recorder using steel wire was patented in 1898 by Valdemar Poulsen, who also made notable contributions to the early development of radio. In 1928 a better recording medium appeared—paper (later plastic) tape coated with iron powder—and in 1939 it was discovered that radically improved sound quality was obtained by adding an inaudible ultrasonic tone to the signal while recording. These advances were the key to high-fidelity magnetic recording. In 1946 recorders were produced by the Ampex Corporation using tape moving at 76.2 cm per second. Later 'ampex' entered the Russian language for a while as the word for video tape recorder. With progressively improved tape, speeds were repeatedly halved, down to the present standard of 4.76 cm per second. In 1964 the Compact Cassette was introduced by Philips, the great Dutch manufacturers, who had the foresight to give free licence to use the system to anybody who was prepared to adhere strictly to the established standard. The cassette consisted of a small plastic box containing both of the two reels and the tape; it made loading a recorder foolproof, and after 1983 became the general medium of choice for magnetic recording.

By this time there had been three successive formats for records—78 r.p.m. disc, LP disc and cassette—each achieving wide acceptance in turn. Cassettes and LPs gave superior sound quality and this might logically have been the end of the road, but in the event it was not to be, for both were based on analogue technology and the digital age was already dawning. Digital recording became practicable around 1975 with the arrival of sufficiently sophisticated microelectronics to allow the very complex circuits required to be fabricated at low cost in small size on a silicon chip.

In the analogue sound technology a representation of the sound wave is stored directly in the recording medium, for example the undulations of the groove on the surface of a disc recording, themselves exactly replicating the continuous fluctuations of air pressure (or velocity) which constitute the sound wave. Such a representation is vulnerable to spurious noise, wear and damage. Digital recordings, by contrast, store

> a description of the sound wave expressed as a string of numbers, each representing in correct sequence an instantaneous numerical measure of the pressure of the sound wave. By choosing a suitable mathematical format, once in numerical form the digits of the numbers can be made highly resistant to corruption by accidental circumstances.

The compact disc (CD) system, using optics-based digital recording, was soon developed, Philips and Sony playing leading roles. Storing up to 74 minutes of music in digital form, CDs first appeared on the market in 1983.

CDs are 12 cm in diameter and the digital code is cut in an aluminium film on the disc as a string of microscopic pits along a spiral track, beginning near the centre and continuing to the edge. The pits are 0.5 microns (millionths of a metre) wide, with 1.6 micron spacing between tracks. (For comparison, a human hair is 100 to 200 microns thick.) For playback a laser is focused on to the pits through the rear of the disc, and the disc plays from the centre out, slowing from 500 r.p.m. to 200 r.p.m. as the playing head approaches the rim, so that the pits will pass through the laser beam at a constant speed. A photocell detects the strong and weak reflections from the undisturbed and pitted metal film, yielding a two-state signal. This binary digital code, representing a sequence of numbers giving the instantaneous magnitude of the sound wave, is fed to converters and wave filters to recreate the original audio waveform in each channel.

Soon the CD was adopted as an international standard. During the 1980s, as listeners turned to the cassette tape and the all-digital CD, vinyl LP sales declined sharply and by the early 1990s the older format had become obsolete.

> There remain, of course, some people even yet who would dispute that the old vinyl disc analogue recording system truly is obsolete. This is a psychosocial rather than a technical phenomenon, well reviewed by Joseph O'Connell.[1] It has close analogies with the continuing small market (see above) for prestige mechanical (as against quartz) watches despite the high accuracy and far lower cost of the latter, indeed precisely

1 Joseph O'Connell, 'High end audio and the evolutionary model of technology', *Technology and Culture* 33, no. 1 (January 1992).

> because of their lower cost, which does not satisfy the purchaser's need to feel unique, a member of an elite.

The short history of recorded music has been one of change and change again, not just one single technical revolution but several, coming hard on each other's heels, a period of unceasing development and upheaval by no means at an end as yet. In this it is a technology typical of our age; one of many depending on the advances in electronics which have driven forward everything from communications and computers to calculators and watches, as well as the recording of sound.

It would be absurd, though, to imagine that only in information technology, with its electronics base, have we been witnessing revolutionary engineering advances. The whole thing is much wider than that, in fact constituting a unique historic transformation of every aspect of industry and the economy. For the last two centuries great sea-changes have been the rule rather than the exception in every area of technology. The advances in materials are a good example. During 1854, in a small factory near Paris, Henri Sainte-Claire Deville produced the first commercial quantities of aluminium. Various objects made of the metal were shown at the Paris Exposition in 1855, and an aluminium dinner service was made for Emperor Napoleon III. When first completed it was probably the most costly service of its kind in the world. Thirty years later the modern process for smelting aluminium was in place, so that by today the metal has become so cheap that it is used for making beer cans. What was precious not long ago is now the stuff of everyday life. If it were not so, indeed, the revolution in air transportation, which has depended on aluminium alloys, might have been badly held back.

Deville's process was an improvement on an earlier method proposed by Friedrich Wöhler in 1845. The metal had been discovered in 1825 by Hans Christian Oersted, who was also the first to observe experimentally the connection between electricity and magnetism. From this latter observation the work of Michael Faraday and hence, through him, all of modern electrical engineering stems. Later it was the availability of cheap electricity which made modern low-cost aluminium smelting a practicable proposition, a curious example of interlocking developments involving surprisingly few people.

Progress in materials technology also impacts, if it does not dictate, the built environment in which we pass our lives. For centuries the only structural materials available were wood, brick and stone, with occasionally a little wrought iron in particularly critical locations. Then, a revolution began: cast iron was introduced as a primary structural material in the late eighteenth century. In no small part this was as a result of the efforts of the three generations of an English Quaker family of iron manufacturers, the three Abraham Darbys. Abraham Darby I (1677–1717) built a blast furnace at Coalbrookdale, Shropshire, in 1709, and was among the first to substitute coke for charcoal in iron-smelting. His son, Abraham Darby II (1711–63) established coke-smelting as the preferred technique for making cast iron. Abraham Darby III (1750–91) built the first cast-iron bridge (across the River Severn), its design a parody of earlier wooden bridges.

Textile mills with interior columns and floor beams of iron were built in England before 1800, and other kinds of buildings supported by iron frames appeared in London and Paris within the next decade. In America, James Bogardus carried this form of construction to its limit. Having built several buildings partly in iron, in 1849 he proposed the exclusive use of cast iron in construction: external walls of ironwork and floors of iron plates carried on an iron frame supported by iron columns. In England, Sir Joseph Paxton's spectacular Crystal Palace, built for the Great Exhibition of 1851, was a triumphant example of the same direction of evolution, though using glass to in-fill. But was a new technique of building firmly established, the structural revolution secure and complete? Not at all, for after 1880 the popularity of cast iron declined rapidly in the face of newer techniques.

Sir Henry Bessemer revolutionized the production of steel in the 1850s and in the last half of the nineteenth century suddenly this 'new' material, with its superior structural properties, became available in quantity at low cost. Skeleton steel construction evolved in Chicago in the 1880s and 1890s and continues to be one of the most important techniques used in the construction of tall buildings. A skeleton steel frame consists of a framework of columns and beams connected by bolts, rivets or electric welding. This steel skeleton supports all the floors and walls. Neither the exterior curtain walls, hung from the steel framework, nor the interior partitions add to the rigidity or strength of the building. Yet the steel frame, too, ultimately proved insecure in its hold, increasingly challenged by reinforced concrete. Thus the history both of materials and of building is one of constant flux, great sea-changes following one upon another.

No less have the last few generations seen a revolution in transportation. A quarter of a century after Hertz's experiments gave birth to radio yet another revolutionary act of invention occurred in a quite different technical area. At Kitty Hawk, North Carolina, in 1903 an engine roared, a fragile fabric-covered wing lifted into the air, and Orville Wright had made the first self-propelled heavier-than-air flight. The Wright brothers also demonstrated by that flight the utility of the wind tunnel they had used for planning their machine, with the result that this device became the mainstay of the systematic design of aircraft, only in very recent years being partly replaced by highly sophisticated computational techniques.

Thereafter development was rapid. In little more than a decade flying machines fought the first air battles above the trenches of Europe at war. On 25 August 1919, a de Havilland DH 4A owned by Aircraft Transport and Travel Ltd flew from London to Paris with one passenger and a little cargo, initiating the world's first daily international civil airline service. Indeed, so dynamic were the consequences of that event at Kitty Hawk that within a human life-span supersonic aircraft were to carry passengers on regular schedules across the Atlantic in only three and a half hours, travelling in great comfort. Today, a visitor to the magnificent Sydney harbour will find row after row of extensive and well-appointed ship berths and landing stages, where once the great ocean liners docked to disembark passengers from around the world, but with very few ships to be seen, except perhaps for freighters or a cruise liner on a pleasure voyage. In Australia, as in every other country, intercontinental passenger movements are now entirely at the airports. Little but freight travels by ship today, and not even all of that. A transportation revolution has passed through, and neither the Sydney docks nor yet the world will ever be the same again.

To go on reviewing all the dramatic changes in every aspect of human life over the last two or three centuries must become tedious, not least because they follow such a similar pattern. Something new appears, either doing better what was already done or doing something entirely different. At first it is expensive and perhaps does not work very well either, but soon the price begins to fall and the specification improves. The new technology begins inexorably to sweep out the old. So powerful is the sense of an irresistible movement in technology, a kind of current that carries all before it, that many have imagined that some sort of technological determinism must be acting, as if once a new technical solution appears it is inevitable that it must be used, and nothing that society can do, no conceivable political response, can avert the predetermined outcome. This idea is quite wrong, however, contradicted by many historical examples where new and superior technologies were introduced and yet did not succeed in ousting the old. The most impressive of these is perhaps the suppression of firearms in Japan, by successive Tokugawa shoguns, from the seventeenth to the nineteenth centuries. It was done out of a belief, doubtless an entirely correct one, that the traditional Japanese social order could not survive the eclipse of the art of swordsmanship on which so many social distinctions were based. This example is but the most dramatic of many demonstrating that human beings are not merely the pawns of an unfolding technology but can still control the world in which they live if they are sufficiently determined. The power of technical innovations is so great, though, that it does not always feel that way.

Make the experiment of asking the average educated person what is the outstanding feature of the last few hundred years of European history and the industrial revolution or the advances of science are likely to figure very often among the answers received (particularly now that Marxism is receding into history). Indeed some will be shrewd enough to speak of the industrial-scientific revolution, recognizing both changes to be aspects of a common social phenomenon.

> Professional historians might have a different characteristic pattern of reactions. Among scholars of economic and social history there is a whole faction which devotes itself exclusively to the industrial revolution. The first topic of debate among them, curiously enough to the layman, is whether it ever happened at all. To understand what lies behind this bizarre undertaking, it must be appreciated that academic reputations are frequently made by denying the obvious, and although most of the time this is pure folly, it has to be admitted that just occasionally it leads to new and valuable insights. Anyway, for all kinds of reasons connected with tenure of posts and advancement to higher academic rank, it is worth a try. Besides, as Robert Skidelsky observed, 'Cut off from direct

> responsibility for practical affairs, the intellectual's main chance to assert himself lies in his actual or potential nuisance value.'[1]

So much change, then, and in so short a time, all with the common characteristic that once set in motion these transitions appear almost incapable of being stopped. Given the benefit of hindsight, it all seems to have a certain inevitability: a series of revolutions in a wide variety of areas of technology and economic life which join together to create the transformation in human affairs which has characterized the last three hundred years, the industrial and scientific revolution. Is there a pattern in these innovative transitions, a common model for all of them, and if so does it have a lesson to teach?

In fact they follow, more or less, an archetype suggested a generation ago by Derek de Solla Price, who noted how many processes of technological growth and change followed a pattern he described as the 'natural growth curve'.[2] Others have called it the normal curve or the sigmoidal curve (meaning S-shaped). Long recognized as a mathematical description of the growth of many plants and animals, it also fits a wide variety (but not quite all) of social and technical change processes. There is a perfectly good and well-understood reason why it should be so commonplace, but of that more later.

To plot a growth curve it is necessary to take some numerical measure of the progress of growth. For a bean shoot or a person that measure might be height, while for a process of technical change more appropriate measures might be, perhaps, things like the tonnage of mechanically propelled ships in commercial trade at sea (which was once zero and is now large) or the maximum number of electronic devices that can be fabricated on a silicon chip (which was once just one but is now tens of millions). Looking at all the change processes about us, they can mostly be fitted to one of two categories.

In some cases the growth pattern appears disordered or to follow a somewhat random course. This is likely when the measure of growth concerned is under direct control from somewhere extraneous to the system, maybe under political or administrative regulation or maybe manipulated by an industrial manager. This is a classical open-loop

1 Robert Skidelsky, 'Philosophers can't teach us morals', *The Independent* (24 March 1993).

2 Derek J. de Solla Price, *Little Science, Big Science* (1963).

control and the measure of growth can follow any pattern the controller pleases. The number of soldiers in the army, or the investment an industrial corporation decides to make in a particular year, are both of them like this. About such cases there is not much more to be said than has been presented already; open-loop control is just that, with all its strengths and weaknesses.

More interesting are the surprisingly large group of changes which follow, with some precision, a well-defined common pattern. The first thing that may be noticed is that the pattern of change is continuous in the mathematical sense. As it happens, it is also at all points differentiable, indeed it is what is called a 'well-behaved' function. To put it another way, the chosen measure does not jump from one value to another instantaneously, so that the process of transition has about it the feel of organic growth. It starts very slowly, to the extent that it may be difficult or impossible to decide the exact moment at which it began. Thereafter change progresses, at first very slowly but gathering speed.

After some time this steady development of the rate of advance will have been sufficient to produce change which is rapid, perhaps very rapid, a phase often called exponential growth, something already encountered in an earlier chapter and in quite a different context, that of positive feedback. When positive feedback exists and the loop gain exceeds unity a system can easily be made to 'trigger' out of its existing stable state into another (usually in some sense at the other extreme) and no state in between these two is stable or can endure. Indeed, immediately after the initial triggering process a positive feedback system is subject to progressively increasing acceleration—'the faster it goes, the faster it goes'—generating a process of change which approximates closely to exponential growth. So are the man-made exponential growth processes, so commonly observed in a phase of technical innovation, also due to positive feedback? It is a point to which we will return.

What exponential growth actually means is that the growth parameter successively doubles in equal intervals of time. Thus if, for example, the measure of growth is looked at every year end and shows a pattern of the form 1, 2, 4, 8, 16, 32...(that is, doubles between each year end and the next) it would be in exponential growth. The numbers get very large quite quickly, in the example quoted exceeding a million

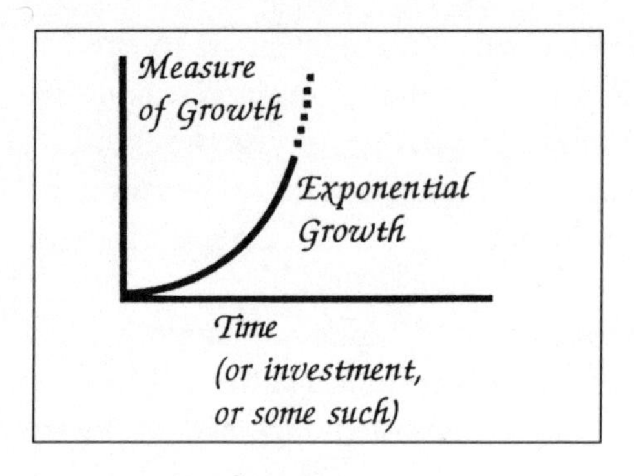

Fig. 6 Exponential growth

in twenty years. The doubling time is often taken as a measure of the speed of exponential growth (in this example one year).

Alarming predictions are often based on forward projection of exponential growth, making the assumption that it will continue without limit. Thus, taking the present nearly exponential growth of human population, scenarios have been created (often, needless to say, with political intent) of universal want and devastation only decades ahead. Indeed, it has been calculated that just a few hundred years hence the surface of the earth will be entirely covered by human beings. Such scare stories ignore the fact that the very circumstances they describe would rein back the rate of reproduction and increase the death rate so as to falsify the predictions long before the disasters they foretell had fully unfolded.

There are many other examples of the absurdity of exponential extrapolation, such as the prediction made in the 1880s that horse droppings would be uniformly knee deep in the streets of London by the 1920s. In the event motor cars were invented, postponing anxieties about waste product pollution by half a century. Another absurdity is based on the observation that, while both the population of the United States and the number of scientists and engineers who live there are in exponential growth, the latter has a much shorter doubling time than the former. According to a misguided interpretation of these trends, the growth of the latter will overtake that of the population as a whole at some date not far into the next century, so that everybody in the United States will then be a scientist or an engineer. But of course nothing of the kind will happen, if only because many do not care for that way of life, and others who could be interested do not have the specific talents it requires. Indeed, arguments of a similar nature can be developed to 'prove' that at about the same time citizens of the United States will every one of them be working for the government, living in California and suffering from AIDS. All such predictions are nonsense, of course. Nothing grows exponentially forever. Instead, sooner or later a slowing of growth begins, identified by many as a 'saturation' process. Exponential growth may endure (approximately) for a while, but it must decelerate before long, just as world population growth has for some years. Toward the end growth comes very slowly, proceeding so gradually at the last that it is hard to say it has not stopped altogether. A more or less steady state is reached.

If a graph were made of the growth process, by plotting the selected measure of growth as the vertical axis and time as the horizontal, the resulting curve would look like a very flattened S: almost horizontal on the zero line at first, curving gently but increasingly upward until in the middle region it rises quite fast, but then decelerating again, the curve turning over progressively, until once more the line becomes almost horizontal. On the basis of control theory it is now possible to see how the famous 'natural growth curve' comes about.

We begin with the early stages, when the curve, though initially very low, trends steadily upward, the growth ever faster in the early stages of an exponential pattern. What is happening here is the birth of an innovation, the introduction of new goods or services, or of new ways of doing things, either of which will leave the world not quite as it was before. Obviously to any process of change this birth phase is crucial,

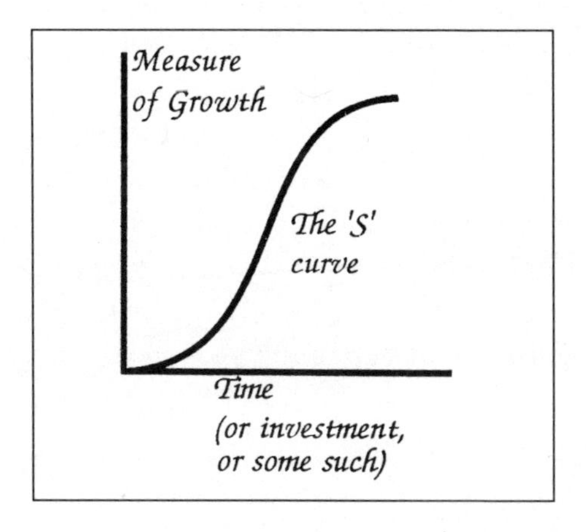

Fig. 7 The 'S' curve

and a favourable outcome is by no means assured. Sometimes the introduction of the new technology succeeds rapidly and without much apparent faltering, as when the steam train swept its earlier competitors into oblivion or the cellular radio-telephone burst onto the developed world in the mid-1980s. By contrast, at other times the birth is never really completed and the promise of innovation is cut short, as with the disaster-prone steam-powered British fleet submarines of World War I or the great airships of the 1920s and 1930s, which began with a bright promise of worldwide air travel and ended in spectacular crashes.

Sometimes, again, the innovation occurs, only to be overtaken by another before it can properly establish itself, just as Berliner's disc recordings quickly ousted Edison's cylinders, or Isaac Shoenberg's electronic television system eclipsed Baird's mechanical version in a very few years during the early 1930s.

> All great inventions are the subject of nationalistic attempts at 'take-over', so it may be as well to get the record straight where television is concerned. Shoenberg led the team at EMI which developed fully electronic television, the basis of the BBC's world-first scheduled transmissions from 1936. Electronic TV was proposed by A. A. Campbell-Swinton in 1906 but its implementation was largely by Russians, of whom Shoenberg was but one. Constantin Perski invented the name 'television' at the St Petersburg Artillery School in 1901, and much early research was undertaken there by Boris Rosing in the years following. Shoenberg studied under him, while Vladimir Zworykin, another of his students, emigrated to the United States, pioneering the evolution of television there. David Sarnoff, also a Russian émigré, became head of the Radio Corporation of America (formed from the United States end of the Marconi company), and played a leading entrepreneurial role in establishing TV.[1] From 1910 to 1930 there was widespread enthusiasm for television in the technical community, so that most developed countries can claim their own 'inventor of television': René Barthélemy in France (with

1 Some say that Sarnoff was Rosing's student, but others, who knew him in his early days with Marconi, think not (private communication).

> his assistant Dimitri Strelkoff, another Rosing student), August Karolus and Manfred von Ardenne in Germany, Denes von Mihaly in Hungary, John Logie Baird in Britain and Philo Farnsworth, Herbert E. Ives or Charles Francis Jenkins in the United States. Although these are all honourable names, and all invented a kind of television, they were not the direct progenitors of what we have now. It was mostly Russians—particularly Rosing and his students—who created television as we know it, whether on their own turf or as refugees in other lands.

However, whilst the natural history and growth of particular innovations is a varied and complex story, one thing they all have in common. For almost every invention of modern times it is possible to find in the historical record the moment of its beginning and an inventor or inventors. Sometimes the issue is not quite clear-cut, since simultaneous invention in different parts of the world is fairly commonplace, as if time had worn out its pregnancy and was ready to be delivered, it matters not by whom. Sometimes too an invention does not first appear in quite its modern form, so it becomes possible to dispute which particular point of origin is the true root of what followed.

Nevertheless, and despite these caveats, there can be no doubt of the fact of invention: that before a certain time there was nothing and afterwards something new had come into being. This starting point and the process of bringing it about is self-evidently critical for the evolution of a technological society and has rightly been the object of scholarly study. Because the birth of innovations, which begins the upward movement of the 'S' curve, is a process so central to technological and economic development it will be necessary to take a closer look at it.[1] Only then will the near-universality of that curve of growth be fully explained.

1 William Gosling, *The Kingdom of Sand* (1977).

10

Getting off the ground

Inventions are the backdrop to our lives; all around us are collected artefacts of varying degrees of usefulness which were unavailable, perhaps inconceivable, to our grandparents. How did they come into being? Today we might be inclined to say that they did so through research and development, whether in industry or the laboratories of research centres or universities, but in greatgrandfather's day research and development seemed of little importance. Not much was done anyway, and it did not then appear by any means vital to industrial success. Even highly technical companies of that period simply went on making the same thing with minor improvements for decades. Founded to make a product innovative at the time, something which was usually the brain-child of a lone inventor, when the next major advance came along they often went into decline and perhaps out of business.

One of the influences that broke the mould was the growth of the great industrial research laboratories. In the electrical industry the critical step forward came in the United States when that bizarre original Charles Steinmetz founded the General Electric research centre at Schenectady in 1901 and recruited Willis Whitney from MIT to run it.[1] This was the laboratory which, early in its existence, developed the process for making ductile tungsten on which all filament electric lamps depend, giving GE a dominant position in the lighting

1 George Wise, *Willis R. Whitney, General Electric, and the origins of US Industrial Research* (1985).

industry for a generation. As a result of this and similar experiences, particularly in the electrical and chemical industries, companies sought to grow strong by spending heavily on research and development, hoping to establish dominant market positions with a sequence of new and innovative products or processes. The days of the lone inventor seemed numbered then, but contrary to widespread expectations such people never quite disappeared and they still make important contributions from time to time.

So what was actually happening here? Was it the coexistence of two distinct patterns of innovation, or, as many believe, the supplanting of an old style of invention by a new corporate form? These questions can only be answered through a deeper insight into the innovative process. What are the forces which start innovations going and propel them forward? In particular, can we come to understand them by applying ideas drawn from control theory? In the published literature of technological history there are two principal explanatory myths for the emergence of new ideas in technology, incompatible and mutually exclusive: that of the heroic inventor, or the alternative of the blind force of economic determinism. This word 'myth' is not used in a pejorative sense, but rather to imply a complete and self-consistent pattern of explanation, without judgement as to its truth. In this case both myths contain part of the explanation but the whole story appears rather more complex than either of them.

The hypothesis of the heroic inventor is romantic in cast and, naturally, beloved by inventors themselves, and indeed by engineers generally, for we too need our great exemplars. In strong contrast, the stance of those who commit themselves to economic determinism, which has been described as the 'necessity is the mother of invention' school of thought, is to assert that (in some unspecified and fundamentally unimportant way) it is the workings of the economy—'market pull'—which calls innovations into being, the actual inventors being no more than almost casual midwives to an inevitable birth. As might be expected, this hypothesis principally appeals to economists and political scientists and is incomprehensible to engineers. The literature of technical development rings with the sound of battle between these two factions, and many thousands of scholarly words have been written on the topic.

The best of this debate goes far beyond mere polemic, though.

Jacob Schmookler, for example, in a now-famous book, reported some painstaking research on the United States patent records relevant to capital goods industries which seemed to give support to the view that new technology arises in response to market needs.[1] First, he found no conclusive relationship between the development of scientific knowledge and the volume of related patents, suggesting that growth in science was not the principal spur to invention. Secondly, Schmookler found little evidence that earlier inventions stimulated later ones. Finally, and perhaps most tellingly of all, he believed he could demonstrate that variations of capital goods investment preceded similar variations in the rate of patenting inventions. Thus, if the money available for investment increased, growth in the flow of inventions would follow with a short time-lag, which seemed to confirm that invention depended on economic demand. Yet although persuasive at first reading, Schmookler's evidence in favour of economic determinism as the motive force of invention proves not conclusive for a number of reasons.

George Basalla points to many shortcomings in Schmookler's analysis, of which the most obvious are: the concentration on capital goods to the exclusion of the arguably more important consumer goods, the use of patents as an index of inventions (faulty because many inventions are never patented, many patents never exploited and some patents are taken out for reasons of industrial competitive tactics rather than because of the perceived merits of the invention) and the implicit assumption that all patents are of equal value, so that the volume of significant invention could be arrived at simply by counting them.[2] Europeans would also perhaps be inclined to argue that patenting practices within industry and research centres are very different in the United States, which Schmookler exclusively studied, from those in most of the rest of the world, not least because of certain unique features in United States patent law. Anyway, strict economic determinism as the source of invention is mocked by the number of highly desirable and commercial innovations, with attractive marketing possibilities obvious to the most superficial consideration, which are not in fact evoked by economic forces. These range from pollution-free motor

1 Jacob Schmookler, *Invention and Economic Growth* (1966).

2 George Basalla, *The Evolution of Technology* (1988), Chapter IV.

vehicles, through computers with common sense, to a drug to cure AIDS or halt the processes of human ageing. The dedicated supporter of economic determinism might argue that market forces will work one day in these areas too, if they are but given time enough. Of such is the miracle of faith, but the fact is that it has not happened yet, so a simple deterministic model is inadequate.

Some authors have tried to show that shortage of labour is the principal spur to innovation.[1] There is no need to give separate consideration to any such possibility, because it is just a variant of the economic determinism argument, seeking to show that one particular economic motivation (high labour cost) is the principal generator of market pull. So also is Marx's characteristic argument that the chief spur to technical developments is the desire of capitalists to use them as weapons in their struggle against the proletariat (yet another manifestation of the class war, in short). In his view this explains why such innovations have a positive market value, but Marx still assumes that, if they have, then they will necessarily appear. This too is just economic determinism, though wrapped in a red flag.

Those who make the case against the exclusively market pull, or the unabated 'necessity is the mother of invention', view of the origins of technological innovations emphasize that the way in which an invention is made, where and by whom, are often crucial factors determining its subsequent history. Thus one of the critical technical advances which shaped the twentieth century was the invention of the transistor—an electronic device able to work entirely in the solid state, as distinct from the high-vacuum radio valve ('tube' to Americans) which preceded it. This made possible the whole of modern computer and telecommunications technology, and thus defined the form of the contemporary world. Yet in fact it was invented not once but many times, over a period of more than twenty years. For various reasons the earlier processes of invention did not 'stick'.

The creation of a working transistor by Shockley, Bardeen and Brattain in 1947 is now known to have been at least the eighth time such a device was proposed (although each 'invention' seems entirely independent of those that preceded it).[2] The first inventor was Julius

1 For example, Sir John Hicks, *Capital and Growth* (1965).

2 William Gosling, W. Godfrey Townsend and Joseph Watson, *Field Effect Electronics* (1971).

Lillienfeld, professor of physics at Leipzig, who later emigrated to Canada. Between 1925 and 1928 he patented the three basic types of transistor (a junction gate FET,[1] a bipolar transistor and an insulated gate FET). The transistor was subsequently reinvented in varying forms by Weber (1930), Heil (1934), Holst and van Geel (1936), Hilsch and Pohl (1938), Glaser, Koch and Voigt (1939) and van Geel again (1943, 1945) as well as by Shockley, Bardeen and Brattain (1947). (Shockley had been working unsuccessfully on precursors to the transistor since the late 1930s.) Probably the earlier inventors achieved little in practical results, although Lillienfeld's ideas might have worked. However, Julius Lillienfeld did not have the opportunity to persevere until his devices could challenge the performance of the valves then available, while the next wave of inventors of the late 1930s and early 1940s were overwhelmed by the European political chaos and World War II, so only when the devices emerged yet again in the Bell Laboratories in the late 1940s did the invention get a fair wind. Today it is Shockley, Bardeen and Brattain who are generally regarded as the 'true' inventors because it was from the genuinely functional devices they built that all subsequent development stems, and they jointly received the Nobel prize for their achievement.

> Geoffrey Gaut, formerly Research Director of the Plessey Company, spoke of employing Julius Lillienfeld in the 1930s as a consultant on the manufacture of electrolytic capacitors, then one of the company's most important products.[2] Lillienfeld sought an opportunity to describe his amplifying device (transistor), but was not encouraged. With the infinite good manners so characteristic of him, Gaut invited Lillienfeld to concentrate his attention on the problems for the solution of which he had been hired. In later years Gaut was haunted by the thought that he had turned down for Plessey the opportunity represented by the transistor, and wondered what other inventions of world-challenging significance he might have encountered unawares during a lifetime spent in the management of research.

Still more seriously, economic determinism could only be plausible

1 FET = field effect transistor.

2 Geoffrey Gaut (private communication).

if there was a very different economic out-turn dependent upon which evolutionary path technology took. Since no differential pull could be exerted if, as between two possibilities, the outcome was indifferent in its economic consequences. The point is important, because it has been persuasively argued that the evolution of technology might have been quite different from what actually did take place without much affecting economic activity. If such a view were accepted it must follow that the unfolding of technological history is a far from deterministic process. The question was thrown wide open by a study of the significance of the evolution of rail transportation in the development of the United States economy.

It was regarded as axiomatic until quite recently that the introduction of railways was a crucial factor in economic development worldwide, and that without them the modern world could hardly have come into being. In 1964 Robert Fogel challenged that view, building an economic model of the United States in the nineteenth century as it could have been without railways, their function being largely taken over by canals.[1] His persuasive arguments suggest that the difference to the American economy if railways had not been introduced might have been as little as one per cent of gross national product even as late as 1890. Yet Fogel's analysis could plausibly be regarded as too conservative. Steam-powered road vehicles were taken quite seriously up to 1830 and only thereafter eclipsed by the railroads, until their return as the steam cars of the turn of the century. They then had a successful run of over ten years before giving way to road vehicles driven by petrol engines, for reasons that in retrospect seem less than overwhelming. It is quite possible, therefore, to envisage a scenario for nineteenth-century technological evolution in which railways do not appear at all but are substituted by a combination of canals and steam road vehicles, avoiding any negative economic impact.

If Fogel's argument is accepted, it imposes the view that in such cases economic forces alone are powerless to determine which route is actually taken in the evolution of technology because no purely economic mechanism could distinguish between them, the consequences being so similar. Other similar examples of alternative economically indistinguishable possible paths for technology are legion. In conse-

1 R. W. Fogel, *Railroads and American Economic Growth* (1964).

quence a more plausible model for the evolution of technology envisages a series of 'evolutionary niches' being available at any time for innovative products or services, niches which are generated by economic and social needs and wants. These niches can often successfully be filled by a number of alternative inventions. The possible candidates for the niche are in competition to occupy it, and the particular path history subsequently takes may be determined by the circumstances in which competing inventions come to birth or by the vigour of their exploitation, rather than by any simple economic mechanism of market pull.

What is also manifestly true is that when one invention, meeting a social want or need, becomes established by joining up with a market opportunity, it will begin to draw more and more of the available resources to itself by a positive feedback process, making it difficult or impossible for an alternative solution to take hold. An analogy is the cuckoo chick in the nest of another species of bird; the nest parasite hatches quickly and then ensures, by pushing them out, that other eggs never come to maturity. Which of the possible inventions gets into the field first (and thus kills off the others) may depend on many things—chance alone, perhaps, or political factors, or simply on emulation of what has happened elsewhere. A complicated story indeed! The problem raises issues which can be clarified, however, once the existence of two quite different but complementary driving forces to innovation is recognized, namely market pull and technology push.

In the case of market pull inventions, a new product, process or service arises because a potential purchaser asks for it and can afford to pay the price. For example, a large organization may issue specifications and invite tenders for the supply of some new product—this is the approach typical of military and utility procurement. Less formally, the marketing people in a company may become aware that a new product or service would find buyers if it had specified characteristics and could be offered below a certain price. Either way, the effect is as if an order had been placed on the engineering and manufacturing functions in the company, charging them to design a product compliant with the desired specification yet able to be made to sell for a competitive figure. The new product appears in consequence of the pull force exerted by a perceived customer requirement: it is entirely a market pull development. In control theory, innovations of this kind are shaped by a closed loop, in which the degree of user satisfaction with existing products (or the reverse) drives the process of adaptation and innovation in the new one, so that a negative feedback control loop is formed between users and designers. If left to itself, this will tend to make the product approximate ever more closely to the users' wishes.

Quite different developments are those driven forward by technology alone, which therefore do not appear in response to demands of customers at all. They are born as the result of a bright idea by research engineers or inventors, either within industry or working independently, perhaps in a university. Some technical expert in a laboratory somewhere becomes aware of a major potential for technical advance in what he is doing. The sequel depends critically on how much 'push' the idea generates, which settles whether anything further happens or the idea is simply forgotten again.

Technology push has more than one component. Part of it, and the most crucial, is something very like the 'charm' already mentioned in connection with scientific paradigms. In a technical invention, charm is the quality of intellectual seductiveness, the ability that the idea has to capture the hearts and minds of engineers and technologists, making them believe that there is some mysterious 'rightness' about it, a kind of inner logic sometimes hard to put into words, which powerfully conveys the certitude that this is the best and most elegant way in which the desired ends can be achieved. A good example of an idea of great charm is that of the transistor, which turned into a real and successful innovation and replaced the thermionic valve (or tube) as the central element of electronics in the 1960s. The idea as originally conceived was of a solid-state device which would work with low electrical supply voltages, would be long-lasting and (because it did not need an internal heater element) would consume much less energy than the valve. To any engineer with experience of the power hunger, fragility and high voltage operation of valves, the notion of the transistor was an idea with great charm, enhanced by the awareness that some (though much simpler) solid-state electronic devices were already in successful use. In the event the realized device had all the desirable properties envisaged but also others, notably the possibility of manufacture in very small, indeed microscopic, sizes which in turn led to the next idea of great charm—the chip or microcircuit.

Sometimes, though, charm is a deceiver in the conception of a new invention. Many technological ideas of the past with great intrinsic charm proved ultimately to lead only to dead ends. A telling example of an idea of great charm which came to nothing was the one which inspired the experiments on colour photography, now almost forgotten, which were carried out by Sir John Herschel in the 1840s.[1] His central idea came from the observation that certain natural vegetable dyes were sensitive to light, changing colour on exposure. What was more, their sensitivity proved to be exclusively to light of a certain colour—red, green, blue and so on, depending on the dye chosen—so that if only he could find dyes which changed to the colour to which they were sensitive, coating a paper with them would produce a photographic material which would register colours directly. It was an idea with great intrinsic charm. Herschel spent much time searching for the dyes which would do this but never found them; they always changed to the wrong colour and their photographic sensitivity was phenomenally poor—he actually used exposures to sunlight of several weeks. Despite the charm of the idea it came to nothing, nor is this the basis of any subsequent process of colour photography.

Innovative ideas with great charm can be a dangerous commodity for engineers; it is hard at first to know whether they are the harbour lights of a significant destination or whether they will lead to the rocks. Perhaps the difference between an ordinary engineer and an innovator of genius is the ability to detect the wrong ones early. Even so, although charm may sometimes be deceptive it is always essential if a new idea is to be taken up, and one entirely without charm has no hope at all. However, whilst charm alone would be enough in itself to recommend a new paradigm to the scientific research community, the world of technological innovation demands more before technology push is generated.

For significant technology push, charm is certainly one vital ingredient, but there are two others, also important. One of them is feasibility: whether or not there is the reasonable possibility of successfully manufacturing the new product, within the capabilities of contemporary industry, and with the resources likely to be available. Lillienfeld's transistors invented in the 1920s failed on this score, and in consequence they did not generate technology push. The issue of feasibility

1 Larry J. Schaaf, *Out of the Shadows: Herschel, Talbot and the Invention of Photography* (1992).

is more complex than it may seem. It is entirely possible, perhaps commonplace, to make mistakes here. Many new products prove far more difficult to manufacture than had been foreseen, of which a good example is the Wankel rotary car engine which promised much in the late 1970s but proved very difficult to make at that time. Perhaps the same could be said of airships in the 1920s.

Finally, as the third necessary factor for technology push to develop, there must also be the belief, which again will not necessarily be rational or well founded, that a market exists for the proposed new product. It is possibly in this area that more mistakes are made than in any other, indeed a degree of overoptimism about markets must probably be regarded as the norm, and perhaps few innovations would get started without it.

So then, whether wisely or foolishly, with good reason or irrationally, if all three of these components—charm, feasibility and market—can be attached to a new idea, then it is safe to say that the invention will generate technology push. If so, in due course a new product will be created having radically different characteristics from anything seen before. Then the troubles really start. By definition this is a development nobody asked for and therefore its design has been entirely open-loop. The inventor may be optimistic about his brain-child, but the people who have to bring it to market will soon realize that there is no ready-made slot for it to drop into. It can all too easily end as nobody's baby: born at great expense only to languish from inattention, never living up to its early promise.

Indeed, technology push inventions of this kind are so hard to establish in the market place that some think them scarcely worth the risk—why not just stay in the market pull domain and make products that people know they need? Whether consciously or not, some companies do precisely that. One firm comes to mind that has not introduced a technology push product for twenty years—launching their first, on which the company was founded, proved so painful that the management vowed never to repeat the experience. In the end, though, industries which ignore technology push pay a high price, because the successfully launched push invention of today is the ancestor of a new world to come. It finds a few users at first, prepared to put up with its early disadvantages in return for the new features that it has to offer, and this gives rise to market pull opportunities tomorrow. So entrepreneurs dare not ignore such things, and must try to find a way to use both push and pull forces to carry innovation forward.

The overall picture of how new products and services are evolved is at last beginning to become apparent, and case studies show that it always advances in much the same sequence with only minor variations. At first investment goes into the research and development (R&D) programme, but little measurable improvement in the product takes place. The only force impelling the work forward is technology push, and the investment is primarily into improving understanding of the technical aspects, but hardly contributes at all in creating a viable product. Within an industrial company neither the marketing department, manufacturing or indeed any but the R&D staff can give much input to this process.

This is the first, slow-growth phase of the 'S' curve, at such a low level that it is often hardly perceptible. There may be weak positive feedback because technical successes with the early developments may increase the confidence of the innovators in the technical approach being adopted, so increasing the technology push by which in this first phase the research workers are propelled. However, technology push is a promiscuous thing and can push in many directions, not all of them to the advantage of the company which is sponsoring the work. A few years ago, a major European electronics company found that it had developed a new class of internal combustion engine in its laboratories, without any obvious path for the company to exploit the idea profitably. This kind of thing all too easily happens in the technology push

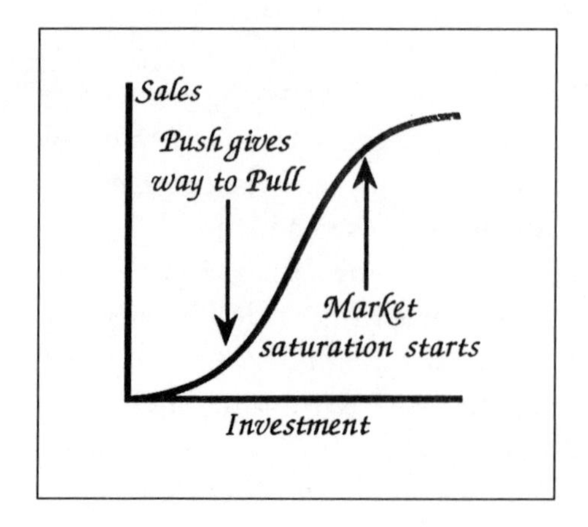

Fig. 8 The life history of an innovation (the 'S' curve yet again)

environment, and one of the prime tasks of those charged with the management of research programmes is stopping thrusts in directions which cannot lead to profitable exploitation, although such discontinued programmes may have a market value if they have generated intellectual property useful to another industry.

In this first phase of research, communications addressed to the innovators from the sponsoring company's marketing or manufacturing people are not important, and it is possible for the work to be done successfully outside the company, for example in a university. Otherwise it is usually the province of a central research laboratory within some large organization. Because at this stage the work is very far from the market place, those companies which try to charge all their research back to operating divisions (i.e. those semi-autonomous parts of a large industrial group which have the task of making a specific product and selling it) invariably underinvest in this area. Central funding of precompetitive research is one solution, but not much liked by chief executives because it is hard to control. A possible answer is for the central research laboratory to make a profit on late-stage research, performed for operating divisions, and to devote this income to funding work still concerned with the infancy of new ideas.

Because at this stage the work is precompetitive, cooperative arrangements with the research departments of other industrial companies are both possible and effective. Government funding is often available for programmes in this category, and this is a very important way in which public money contributes to technological development in some countries. People who do early-stage research are often PhDs or the like; they need excellent scientific qualifications and innovative minds, but long experience in the field concerned is found to be a positive disadvantage, inhibiting new thinking. In short, this is particularly a young person's world, and industrial laboratories dedicated to this class of work commonly make provision to move most people out after a few years, into later-phase research or operating divisions.

In a favourable case, after a time the product (or service) begins to improve noticeably, it becomes possible to persuade people to buy it, and a population of customers starts to grow, exerting the first beginnings of market pull on the innovators. At this point the positive loop gain of the control process increases rapidly, and with luck it soon climbs to greater than unity. For developments which start from technology, this transition from push to pull demonstrates when the new product has been successfully launched. The loop gain will then be sufficient for the exponential growth process to begin. This middle phase of the R&D, typically also carried on in central research laboratories of companies but to a lesser extent in operating divisions, is quite different in character from that earlier on. It requires the fullest dialogue with the marketing staff of the company, and increasingly with manufacturing experts also, at least towards the end of the phase. Good R&D managers monitor such communication continually and ensure that it is satisfactory. Funding of this mid-phase work is best arranged by direct contracts from the operating divisions of the company concerned, which are already beginning to exploit the new product in the market place. Mid-phase people still need a good scientific foundation, but it is also important for them to be able to communicate with nonscientists in other business functions. Knowledge of the product area, including competitor offerings, gives them credibility, and in consequence this work is better suited to those with a few years of experience behind them.

Of course, the path does not always run so smoothly. There are some inventions which have tremendous initial technology push, but sufficient market pull never subsequently develops, so they do not achieve a self-sustaining market position. Airships were a good example, promising much at first but achieving little as a route to practical air transportation in the out-turn. Luftschiffbau Zeppelin ran successful air transportation services in Germany before World War I, using their airships. At that time heavier-than-air craft did not have the carrying capacity required for commercial services, and therefore had less technology push. During the war, however, heavy bombers were developed, rendering the concept of commercial transport aircraft plausible. Services using converted bombers soon began to develop a little market pull, and the days of the slow, weather-sensitive airship were numbered, although they still retain a few proponents.

The airship idea had great charm, in part because the analogy with sea ships made them easy to understand, in part because a large enough size and carrying capacity seemed likely to be achieved with relatively primitive technology. Airships also seemed just about feasible with the resources then available, and appeared to have a market. All of this was enough to generate very significant technology push. It all proved a blind alley, however, because for airships large enough to be commercial the problems of structural design within the weight limitations proved to be intractable and because the altitude and speed which were practicable for airships were both well below the ideal for commercial air transport services. Perhaps it was all for the best; the noise nuisance caused by present-day jet aircraft would be as nothing compared with an airship with fifty thousand horsepower diesel engines passing slowly overhead at a thousand metres.

Fortunately not all inventions go the way of the airship, which in the end had little more than charm to recommend it, the two other necessary components of technology push—feasibility and market—having proved illusory. Other classes of new artefact, such as the hovercraft, may have to struggle hard for a time to establish themselves yet be sustained by technology push for long enough ultimately to generate a level of market pull sufficient for them to continue in existence. Yet others—the lucky ones—quickly develop strong market pull and never look back. Cellular mobile telephones are in this happy class.

This, then, is the model of the birth of new technical products. It is very simplified, needless to say, and although the general conclusions are valid there are also many complicating factors which need to be borne in mind. First, it is obvious that a new product is rarely launched into a market not already being served in some way. It therefore has to establish itself in the face of an existing product, which may be at any stage of development, a situation modelled by two 'S' curves. The curve for the new product must rise more sharply and intersect that

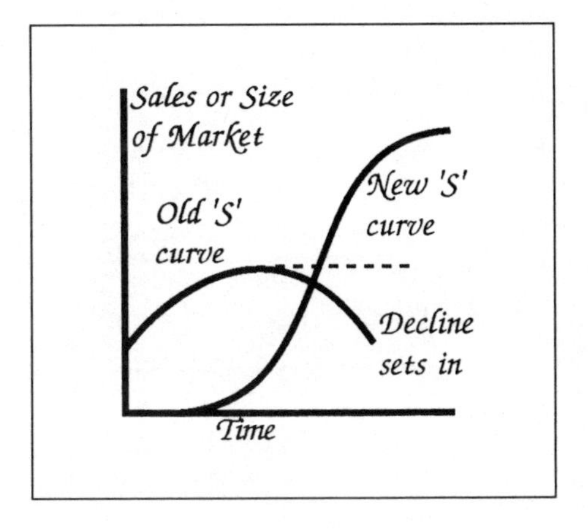

Fig. 9 A new product displaces an old one

for the old if it is to be supplanted. A consequence of this more complicated situation is to delay the point at which the new product no longer has to depend on technology push to keep it moving along, and hence to increase the investment necessary before it is profitably established. The level top of the 'S' curve, too, may be somewhat notional and never seen in practice, for in some markets products never mature, but appear in rapid and never-ending succession. In this case their sigmoidal curves overlap to give the appearance of continuous explosive growth—a classic example being the silicon chip industry.

All of this assumes that the appearance of a new product has little or no impact on the characteristics of the old. This, too, is not really the case, for often a phenomenon known as 'sailing-ship effect' is seen.[1] When a new technical solution to a requirement appears, bidding to replace an existing one, it is often found that the older puts on a new burst of technical growth. This is particularly likely when the old product has long been mature, in the late, flat phase of the 'S' curve. As the new product threatens to take over, the old one begins renewed development, improving its characteristics once again. Thus for thirty years from about 1860, when steam ships threatened to take over from sail, the sailing ships began a new phase of development, becoming faster—as much as thirty per cent—and needing less labour to run them, down to a quarter. For a time it looked to some as if sail might head off the challenge, but in the end the sailing ship was rendered obsolete nevertheless.

Sailing-ship effect happens because the product development is moved out of the hands of people who depend more on experience of custom and practice than on deeper technical or scientific understanding, and is instead given to others with qualifications more suited to the early phases of the life cycle of an invention, who typically have a more recent science base and are not too much impressed by the traditional approaches. Almost always the sailing-ship effect is transient, but it can be useful, giving the proprietors and employees of an old technology time to adapt to the new, provided that they have the will. However, it can also be dangerous, since it may lead people to think that an old technology can go on forever, leaving them with a delusion of security against the challenge.

1 This expression has been around for at least a decade, but its source is unknown to me.

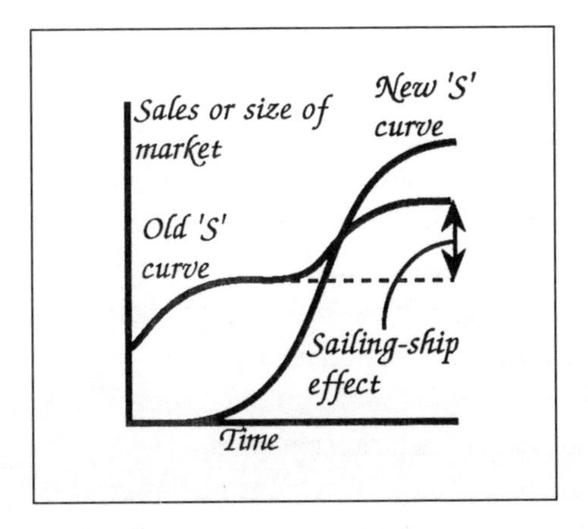

Fig. 10 A new product evokes 'sailing-ship effect' in an old one

Struggles for dominance between new and old products along with the sailing-ship effect are but two examples of the interaction between competing products. Often much more important is the mutual reinforcement that technological innovations may give each other. This is effective at two levels: the operational and the social. At the operational level, some inventions actually fit together so that one supplies the needs of the other. To understand this more clearly it will be convenient to look at what has happened in the realm of microelectronics and computers over the last few decades.

The general advance in electronics dates from the introduction of a transistor in 1947 by John Bardeen, Walter Brattain and William Shockley. Quickly leading to the invention of the silicon chip (by Kabowiak, Atalla, Noyce and many others) this triggered the biggest technological change recorded in human history, still continuing today.

After their Nobel prize (1956) the subsequent history of the three inventors was very different. Walter Brattain (1902–87) stayed in the Bell Laboratories and served them well, but never again reached the greatest heights. He retired in 1967, a much respected man.

John Bardeen (1909–91) had a career of the utmost distinction in science, and was awarded a second Nobel prize (1972) (jointly with Leon Cooper and John Schreiffer) for a theoretical explanation of superconductivity, the loss of all electrical resistance by certain metals at temperatures near absolute zero. He died full of years and honour, admired by all who ever worked with him.

In the greatest contrast to his collaborators, a dozen years after his triumph William Shockley (1910–89) was leading a wretched existence. As a result of some painful personal experiences, he came to espouse certain theories about intrinsic differences of intelligence between groups of human beings of different skin colour, which understandably alienated him from liberal opinion in the United States. Worse still, he did so at a time of great militancy on the university campuses, when the response to his views was more extreme than it might have been at other periods. Among students his image was rapidly demonized, and before long it was hardly possible for him to speak in public, even on engineering, without provoking a near riot.

It is difficult to know whether it was his enemies or the friends he picked up from the far right of the political spectrum who served Shockley worse. A man who fatally combined simplistic social views with stubbornness, he never understood the source of the troubles he had stirred up, saw the whole thing as a conspiracy against him, and became increasingly paranoid. When last I met him, shortly before his death, he brought along a tape recorder with which he recorded every conversation, however trivial, out of a fear of misrepresentation.

One of his less endearing traits was that he carried his Nobel medal in his pocket (actually a replica, I think). When in danger of being worsted in argument, he had the habit of pulling the medal out, throwing it onto the table and saying, 'When you have one of these you can argue with me!' He tried this ploy once with a New York bartender, who picked the medal up, turned it over in his hand, threw it down again and replied 'So what!'

So ill-understood is the magnitude and pace of the microelectronics revolution that it helps to compare it with other processes of change. Consider transportation: a transformation in travel has happened over the last couple of hundred years. Then ten passengers on a stage coach might hope to reach ten miles per hour, but now a complement of 350 travels at 500 miles per hour on a Jumbo jet, so 100 passenger-miles per hour has evolved into 175,000—an increase of just over three orders of magnitude, in scientific parlance. (An order of magnitude is the same thing as a factor of ten, thus three orders of magnitude is a factor equal to three tens multiplied together, or one thousand.)

By contrast, from the first commercial transistors in 1951 to the present day the number of electronic devices fabricated on a single semiconductor chip has increased from one to ten million (and passed the density of packing of nerve cells in the human brain in 1974) while at the same time their speed has increased a thousand times, giving a total increase in the product of speed and numbers by ten billion times or ten orders of magnitude, and this in a mere forty years. While transportation has developed at the rate of an order of magnitude every fifty years, microelectronics has progressed more than twelve times faster, with an order every four years. History has never seen anything remotely comparable. This amazing electronics revolution is properly seen as a one-off, a freak of nature, the consequence of a chance coming together of uniquely favourable scientific, industrial and market factors, and is not likely ever to be repeated, certainly not in our lifetimes.

The rapid evolution of silicon chips had a major impact on the life history of computers, making possible the economic manufacture of progressively smaller yet faster and more powerful machines. As a consequence from 1970 to 1990 the cost of executing a million instructions per second in the most cost-effective computer available at the

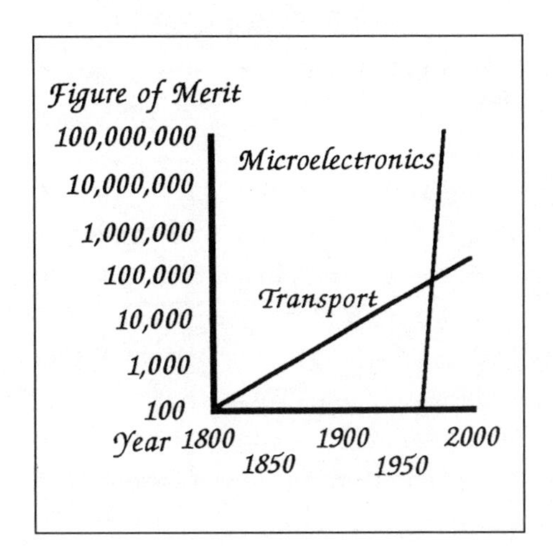

Fig. 11 Technological evolution of transport and microelectronics compared

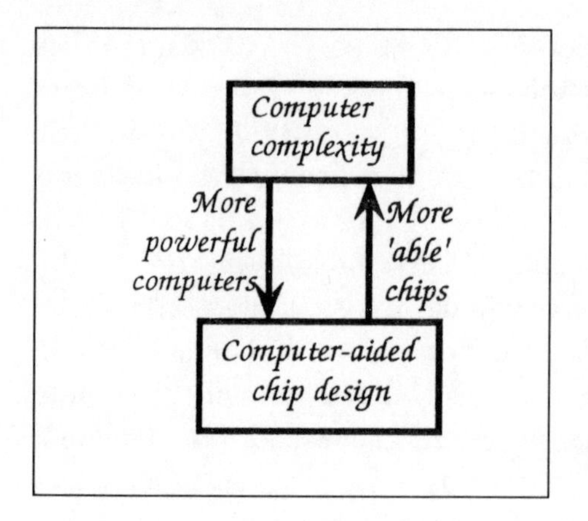

Fig. 12 The positive feedback loop that promotes exponential growth in chip complexity and computer power

relevant time fell from around £800,000 to under £600, and is still dropping at least as fast. In the light of this dramatic story, it is not unreasonable to say that the present standing of computer technology is solely a product of the innovation process in chips. However, the matter is more complex than this, for there is also help flowing in the other direction. Since the middle of the 1970s the design of chips has been performed exclusively on computers, which in turn has made it possible to design quickly and economically structures far too complicated for manual techniques—'more than a head full' as people in the industry have been in the habit of saying. This computer-aided design of chips is one of the factors which has made possible the growth in chip complexity and therefore in cost-effective computer performance. What this amounts to, in control theory terms, is that the computer and the chip have between them created a positive feedback closed-loop system, in this case with a loop gain evidently greater than one.

The consequence is that both the measures of chip complexity and computer performance have 'run away' into exponential growth, increasing ever faster. This will continue until some limiting saturation process sets in. The limit could be of two quite different kinds: either the technology might hit some physical limit, such as the inability further to reduce the size of devices on the chip, making further increase of complexity impossible, or alternatively it might come up against a stop determined by the market, if ever the time came that there was no further consumer demand for an increase in chip functionality. At the time of writing (1993) there seems no prospect of either.

In short, a typical positive feedback phenomenon has occurred: the system of chip fabrication is making a rapid transition between its initial stable state of low computer performance and chip complexity towards a new stable state, as yet in the future, where chip complexity has saturated at a new high level. At the same time the performance of computers is growing in a way to parallel this explosive development. Plotted as graphs against time, these technical characteristics both of chips and computers would show the typical 'S' curve of growth that is so widely distributed. Note that, unlike some positive feedback systems, considered earlier, this one cannot switch back from the high-technology state to low. The system has a much higher loop gain for changes in the sense of increasing technology than in the opposite direction. Thus the loop gain is greater than unity for advances, but much less than unity for technology collapse.

This is a classical example of mutual reinforcement at the operational level between two processes of innovation happening at the same time. Others abound, from the mutual reinforcement of the development of gas turbine engines and the new metallic alloys needed to build them to the evolution of optical fibre communications and the advances in the solid-state lasers (which are the pulsed light sources on which they depend). In each case a positive feedback loop is established, although it does not always follow that, as in the examples quoted, the loop gain is always large enough to cause state switching; sometimes it may not be and the results in such cases would be undramatic but for some other source of positive feedback acting at the same time.

Often this is provided by a different kind of reinforcement, this time at the social level. New inventions are born and effectively exploited if somebody has the inclination to make them, in the sense of thinking about doing things in a way unknown before, but also, and most importantly, if the inventor or some contact has access to the resources, often considerable, to prove the idea and launch the product. This will involve supporting it until enough market pull develops for it to have a self-sustained existence. Naturally, such things are far more likely to happen in a conducive environment, one in which conduct of that kind attracts significant rewards. Any society has more probability of creating continuing successful innovation if it is one in which invention is prized and the launching of new products or services treated as a valued and prestigious activity, to be well rewarded. Rewards are not, of course, necessarily monetary. They may include such things as professional standing, membership of exclusive honour groups, the award of titles and public honours and attention by the media. Needless to say, people in different occupations tend to be rewarded in different ways. Thus in Britain inventors have a moderately high probability of becoming Fellows of the Royal Society and holding professorial titles but a very low probability of being multimillionaires, whereas for entrepreneurs these probabilities are exactly reversed.

This supportive atmosphere for industrial development may well itself have been generated, and is certainly intensified, by the prior successful examples of highly publicized and well-rewarded innovation. Another positive feedback loop is at work here: success for technical innovation is conducive both to yet further invention and to investment in new products or technology, and therefore tends to create more successful innovation, in turn further strengthening the sentiment from which it derives. As might be expected, a few failures along the way hardly seem to matter once the feedback loop is switching, the tide flowing.

The invention of the Bessemer converter process for making steel (1855) resulted in a business which paid its shareholders one hundred per cent dividend on investment every year for a decade.

> The inventor and industrialist Sir Henry Bessemer (1813–98) developed a process for low-cost, high-quality steel manufacture. An established industrial inventor, he began work on improving iron used for casting cannon during the Crimean War (1853–6). His process involved blowing a blast of air through molten pig iron to oxidize its impurities. The heat of the oxidation raised the temperature of the iron, saving fuel and hence cost. The process is a sight not to be missed: an awe-inspiring 'fireworks display' which can verge on the alarming to those who witness it for the first time.

Bessemer's Sheffield steel works exported successfully throughout the world, and the availability of good, cheap steel had a reinforcement effect on many other innovative processes then current, particularly the development of railways and of steel-framed building construction. A return on investment of the magnitude that Bessemer achieved (along with similar if less dramatic stories) evoked a favourable environment for invention and innovation in the metallurgical industry in Victorian England. Later investors hoped that they too might do just as well, and continued to hope so long afterwards and despite many disappointments on the way.

The swing towards an innovation-oriented society is yet another manifest example of a positive feedback loop, and for as long as the loop gain exceeds unity it will produce a rapid 'runaway' switch towards a high technology industrial environment. The result is the early stages of the characteristic 'S' curve of growth, with an ever increasing rate of investment and technical development. Thus what is happening is described best as a series of 'nested' positive feedback loops: an overall process (in favourable cases) increases the probability that innovation will be adequately resourced and rewarded, and this in turn progressively increases the probability that the positive feedback controlling the evolution of each individual invention will be able to reach the threshold of the critical greater than unity loop gain which will enable it to grow exponentially.

> Ian Ross, sometime President of the famous Bell Laboratories, once said, 'There are two types of technology: exponentially developing technology and unimportant technology.'

Often several independent positive feedback loops simultaneously control the growth of an invention, for example due to reinforcement at the operational level and the social level coexisting. In this case the mathematical analysis is more complicated, but the switching action can occur even when none of the loops considered independently has a loop gain greater than unity. In general the more independent positive feedback loops there are operating the more likely the switching action is to occur, as would perhaps be expected.

However, in the end all such processes reach saturation, fall away in time from any approximation to exponential growth, and develop progressively more slowly, corresponding to the top of the 'S' curve. They do so when, due to whatever circumstances, the conducive environment goes away. This could be quite general, for example due to loss of confidence resulting from a severe downturn in economic activity, a slump or recession, which makes it seem increasingly improbable that any new invention will make a profit. This is not as significant as it may appear in the time-scale of the industrial revolution as a whole, for downturns always turn up again in time and the effect is only temporary. More fundamentally the slowing of growth in a particular industrial sector or area of innovation comes from its eclipse as a result of technical change or from having reached the limits of its potential.

In the case of steel, there exists an upper bound to the world's propensity to consume, and as that limit is approached the cost of marketing steel gets higher and higher. Similarly basic physics and chemistry set a lower limit to the cost of manufacture, and as that limit is approached the investment needed for each further cost reduction grows out of hand. From seeming like a licence to print money in the third quarter of the nineteenth century the steel industry was transformed into a worldwide loser a hundred years later.

> Due to substitution by other cheaper (because less energy-hungry) materials, such as plastics, the total propensity to consume steel is actually declining, an example of industrial substitution, but to take that into account would complicate the argument too much.

For the business sector concerned this destroys the atmosphere of well-rewarded innovation, and the pace of change slows, producing the flattened top of the 'S' growth curve, although by this time the industry has grown large, so modest expenditure on innovation remains possible. Research laboratories and institutes, a hangover from happier days, exist and will cling to life, and these too may, for a time, sustain at least a trickle of invention. Neither of these 'inertia' phenomena is in the least likely to be sufficient to maintain a loop gain greater than unity, however, and that is all that really matters.

Such is the ultimate fate that awaits all thrusting new industries based on innovation, as steel once was. As with human mortality, no exceptions are possible. Silicon chips, computers, telecommunications, biotechnology, indeed all the industries which today seem set upon a rocket-like ascent into the commercial stratosphere are impelled forward by the action of positive feedback with loop gain greater than unity, but just as inevitably as with steel, and for similar reasons, one day the loop gain will begin to fall and then the 'S' curve for them too will make its final flourish, the great days will be done. The social reinforcement will be in the process of fading away.

> It is said that George Santayana (1863–1952), the writer and critic, on learning that he was terminally ill, cabled his

> publisher, 'I have long known that all men were mortal but have always assumed that an exception would be made in my case. What now?' The reply is not recorded, but doubtless the publisher's main concern would centre on the fact that copyright is extinguished fifty years after the death of an author.

However, even right to the end some development of the product is likely to continue, often making only small improvements but more especially aimed at manufacturing cost reductions. These late-phase development programmes are best located in the operating divisions, by which they are also funded, and carried through by people with detailed knowledge of the product whose experience extends over many years. Possibly they are managed directly by the manufacturing function, but in any event they see manufacturing and marketing as the source of their instructions.

Thus the 'S' curve of growth, found in so many and varied circumstances, is the signature of a positive feedback loop, beginning the process of switching between its two stable states as its loop gain is raised above unity and coming to the final state as the loop gain declines due to inevitable saturation processes. The great sea-changes of technology are no more than this. The Technical Director of the mechanical calculator company, put out of his employment by the unthinkably rapid development of the competition, was the unknowing victim of a positive feedback loop established by both operational and social reinforcement of the electronics technology. Needless to say, it is impossible to prove rigorously that wherever an exponential or 'S' growth curve is seen there is necessarily positive feedback at work. It would be feasible for some person of Olympian detachment to achieve a similar profile by open-loop control, so it is safe to say no more than that an 'S' curve, or the exponential growth which is its precursor, normally indicates a positive feedback process. The detail of the feedback loop may be hard to disentangle, but proven exceptions to this empirical rule are difficult to find.

It is because major technology changes take place driven by the action of a positive feedback loop that—like having a row, participating in an arms race or falling in love—they seem to have an 'unstoppable' quality. In all these cases a sense of being driven along by forces greater than one's own power is typical. It is in fact precisely their own actions that each participant senses, but processed by having passed through the feedback loop, and amplified in their effect by that. For those involved no open-loop control can produce a 'feel' of ever quickening acceleration in any way comparable. To participate in such a positive feedback switching action is to feel almost powerless to do more than try to steer its headlong trajectory. That is why the scientist opening up a new branch of knowledge, the engineer pioneering a new technology, or the businessman developing a new market all believe themselves driven, not wholly autonomous. It is sure to be exciting, even if it never feels quite safe.

Finally, so much has been said about invention in this chapter that it would be unsatisfactory to conclude without a brief summary of the natural history of the inventive process. Aside from the stage in its life cycle that an invention is at, there are also different kinds of inventions and for each a best way of seeking it can be identified; thus three distinguishable patterns of innovation exist.

The first may be called 'more of the same'. Existing technology trends can usually be extended a little further into the future. For example, in electronics it is a fair bet that the microcircuit chips will continue to grow more complex and will operate faster. Similarly, structural materials used in aircraft get progressively lighter for a given strength, diesel engines get more powerful for a specific weight and consumption of fuel, and so on. This kind of innovation is predictable and reasonably certain. Because the risk is low it is the way industrial R&D organizations prefer to work for most of the time, and small companies, with limited capital resources, generally restrict themselves to innovation of this kind. The returns are modest, however, and any advantage it gives over competitors is short-lived, because they can quickly do it too.

The second style of innovation is more complex, and may be identified as 'the passing over of quantity into quality' (the phrase may seem familiar; it comes from Friedrich Engels, though in another context). When 'more of the same' innovation has gone a long way it can turn a familiar product into something quite different. For example, when microcircuit chips had grown sufficiently in complexity they gave birth to microprocessors—the computer on a chip—which were something wholly new, and began a cycle of development in their own right. This was one example of the passing over of quantity into quality—another is the development of radar as a result of the evolution of radio receivers and transmitters. Things of this kind are much less common than 'more of the same', but they can still be foreseen and planned for, and are often tackled by major strategic development programmes. When successful they give advances capable of sufficient protection by means of patents to yield a real and enduring competitive advantage, and the fortunes of some companies have been built on such things. However, getting there can demand considerable resources.

Finally, the third category of innovation has been called 'the knight's move'. It does not result from steady progress in a straight line, but is the result of an out-of-line jump to something wholly new. Just somebody's bright idea, it is impossible to predict or plan for. In the nature of things, 'knight's move' inventions mostly give rise to technology push developments, and will share all the problems of this mode of innovation. Rarely will they correspond to market pull, although of course when they do they are worth their weight in gold. Although 'knight's move' inventions may originate almost anywhere, including the research laboratories of universities, they usually require considerable resources to enable the resulting product to generate sufficient market pull to achieve a successful launch. For this reason the effective exploitation of 'knight's move' inventions is mostly the domain of large organizations. University or small company inventors who innovate in this way are best advised to protect their intellectual property through patents and copyrights, but then to seek a large industrial partner who can carry the fight to achieve success.

To summarize, the processes of invention are varied, and they will succeed only if the work is done by the right kind of people in the appropriate working environment, and what 'right' means in this context depends on the kinds of inventions being sought. However, the successful development and launch of a new product does not depend on the ingenuity of the research laboratories alone, but critically on the establishment of a positive feedback loop, in which market pull is the critical component, the effect of which is to propel the innovation into a permanent significance. In short, with positive feedback the new thing becomes an established part of the fabric of our lives; without it, nothing more impressive than a 'nine day wonder' can result.

11

The big switch

According to Derek de Solla Price, the industrial-scientific revolution began in the middle of the seventeenth century and thereafter gave a close imitation of exponential growth for the next two hundred years.[1] During this period many things have shown the constant 'doubling time' characteristic of exponential growth over long periods, and some still do. Doubtless there are doctorates to be earned by discovering how the positive feedback loops work in each case and proving that the loop gain is greater than unity.

Among examples of exponential growth (giving the doubling time) are:

World population ... 40 years
Number of universities ... 40 years
Number of important discoveries ... 20 years
World population of university graduates ... 10 years
Number of science journals ... 10 years
Number of telephones ... 10 years
Available phone circuits across the Atlantic ... 5 years
Complexity of a silicon chip ... 15 months

Others who have studied this great transition in human affairs[2] have come up with approximately similar conclusions as to its beginning and subsequent course, although not all make as explicit a connection

1 Derek J. de Solla Price, *Science Since Babylon* (1961).

2 T. S. Ashton, *The Industrial Revolution* (1948).

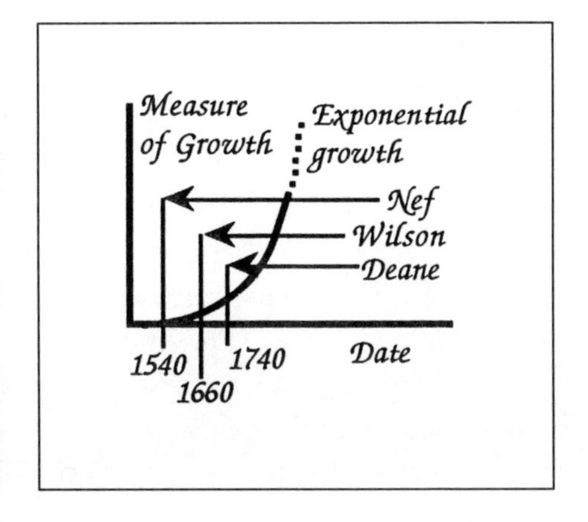

Fig. 13 When did the industrial-scientific revolution begin?

between the scientific and industrial changes. The principal argument between historians seems to be about when the industrial-scientific revolution actually began. In England it was obviously very well under way by the dawn of the nineteenth century, but the precise start date is disputed, and the view that it began around 1760, which appears in many earlier books, is now challenged.

Thus Phyllis Deane appears to argue for 1740,[1] Charles Wilson for 1660[2] and J. U. Nef for a date as early as 1540.[3] But the process of growth approximated in those early days to the exponential law; between 1780 and 1850 growth of national product per head in England grew exponentially at a rate doubling every fifty years.[4] For a process of this kind there is no well-defined start—the graph just rises smoothly and continuously, accelerating upwards. Followed back to its beginnings, at a certain point it becomes obscured by the normal year-to-year economic fluctuations caused by such things as the weather, determining good and bad harvests. To be able to find a 'start' for the industrial-scientific revolution it would be necessary to agree some arbitrary definition for what 'start' meant—maybe when the national product was 'clearly' (two or three times, perhaps?) greater than the average of the preceding fifty years. Such a 'start date' would be pretty

1 Phyllis Deane, *The First Industrial Revolution* (1965).

2 Charles Wilson, *England's Apprenticeship, 1603–1763* (1965).

3 J. U. Nef, 'The Industrial Revolution Reconsidered', *Journal of Economic History* **III** (1943).

4 R. M. Hartwell, *The Causes of the Industrial Revolution* (1967).

meaningless, all in all. Instead, de Solla Price adopts 1665, the year when the first regular scientific journal made its appearance, but this too is just his preference. Truth to tell, the industrial-scientific revolution has no particularly plausible start date, but it began nevertheless; it eased itself into existence.

> A few in the scholarly world have held that what does not have a well-defined start date ipso facto did not begin and therefore cannot have existed. Evidently they have yet to come to terms with phenomena, of which there are many, that emerge gradually from confusion. The end of the industrial-scientific revolution will be similarly imperceptible; can it be that some will argue it has never finished?

One historian of technology, Jean Gimpel, has argued persuasively that 'the Industrial Revolution' that we speak of was in fact the second of its kind, the first having begun during the so-called 'dark ages' in Europe and having come to full flowering in the twelfth century.[1] His work has not been as influential as it deserves, perhaps because of his unrelieved and unmitigated pessimism about the late twentieth-century prospects for Europe, which seems ill-supported by his historical researches. It has long been recognized that the 'dark ages' were in fact a period of previously unparalleled technological advance and Gimpel's thesis therefore has considerable plausibility. However, that there may have been an earlier, if much smaller, 'industrial revolution' does not change the arguments presented here.

Carlo Cipolla argues from quite a different standpoint that ours is the second major revolutionary period of human history, the first being the agricultural revolution, which ran from about 8000 to 2000 BC.[2] That earlier great change converted the human race from hunter-gatherers living in small tribal groupings into agriculturists living in proto-feudal nations with the institutions of kingship, law, priesthood and aristocracy, the remains of which we still see about us. A curious parallel can be drawn between the two times of change, even although the first proceeded so much more slowly. Before the agricultural revolution the sustainable human population of Earth is thought to have been 20 millions, but afterwards it rose to a fairly stable but much

1 Jean Gimpel, *The Medieval Machine* (1978).

2 Carlo Cipolla, *The Economic History of World Population* (1962).

higher number, perhaps some 500 millions, a twenty-five-fold increase on the initial figure. With the industrial-scientific revolution the world population began to rise again, soon growing exponentially. In 1990 world population was estimated at 5,300 million, but it is certain that growth is no longer exponential, and the ultimate saturation level is now being approached. If the present revolution were to produce the same 25:1 ratio of population change as the last (and there is, of course, no known reason why it should) world population would stabilize around 12,500 million. As it happens, this is in the middle of the estimated range in a United Nations report of 1990, which suggested 11–14,000 million by the end of the twenty-first century.

Be that as it may, so far as the industrial revolution is concerned all that can possibly be agreed is that it began as an exponential growth process, gradually making itself visible above the random year-to-year fluctuations, and was clearly in evidence in England by the eighteenth century. However, since no exponential process can continue indefinitely, but ultimately must slow, it is of interest to speculate at what date industrialization (and also the penetration of science into the fabric of society) will reach its saturation. To argue that it will do so, in other words that the industrial-scientific revolution will one day draw to a close, is no longer controversial, but there is no general agreement as to when this will happen.

Yet why should it end? There are many reasons. The most important of all is human. In all the present developed societies the number of professionally qualified scientists and engineers has increased sharply in recent history, doubling roughly every ten years. This growth has been not only in absolute terms but also as a proportion of the total population, which at its fastest rate doubled only every forty years.

> The growth in numbers of qualified scientists and engineers (QSEs) is itself due to a positive feedback process, because of the following effects (among others): (i) the more QSEs there are, the more are available to teach new entrants to these professions, hence the more QSEs there are; and (ii) the larger the size of the science and technology sector of the economy the better the visibility of the sector and of work opportunities for new entrants, hence the larger the entry evoked, hence the larger the size of the science and technology sector. In each case the loop closes on itself and the feedback is positive.

What this means is that throughout the industrial-scientific revolution the proportion of qualified scientists and engineers in the population has increased steadily. Obviously this would have to come to a final grinding halt when the graphs of growth crossed and the proportion reached one hundred per cent. For the United States, in theory this could have occurred around AD 2100 if the exponential growth patterns of the first half of the twentieth century had persisted unchanged, but they already show signs of saturation, which pushes the date further into the future. In reality, of course, it will never happen. The growth in the population of qualified scientists and engineers will tail away much sooner, because not everybody in the population has the aptitude or inclination for these professions.

So, one symptom of the approaching end of the industrial revolution will be a developing shortage of technically trained people. Attempts will be made to increase the supply by making more places available at universities and training institutes, historic barriers of male chauvinism will be broken down (so that the potential among women can be exploited to the full) and all kinds of assistance (ranging from better availability of less qualified helpers to better equipped laboratories and computer work stations) will be introduced to 'stretch' the scientific and engineering talent available. In capitalist societies the pay for technical people will drift upwards relative to other categories. All of these trends are visible in the developed world now, varying somewhat from country to country due to the varying degrees of understanding and political competence with which they are managed.

Another, no less important, causative factor of the end of the industrial-scientific revolution is the saturation of demand, both qualitative and quantitative. Take the number argument first; when an innovation comes to market—a new product or service, or an advance in manufacturing which provides established products at much lower cost—the sales volume will increase rapidly, to peak at the point of maximum growth rate. There comes a time, though, when all those who want the new product have bought, the number in use hardly increases, and after that the only sales that will be made are to replace products which wear out, fail, or are used up. This can be at a low level, depending on the life of the product, although it can be helped, to a degree, by promotion of fashions in products or by other kinds of designed-in obsolescence.

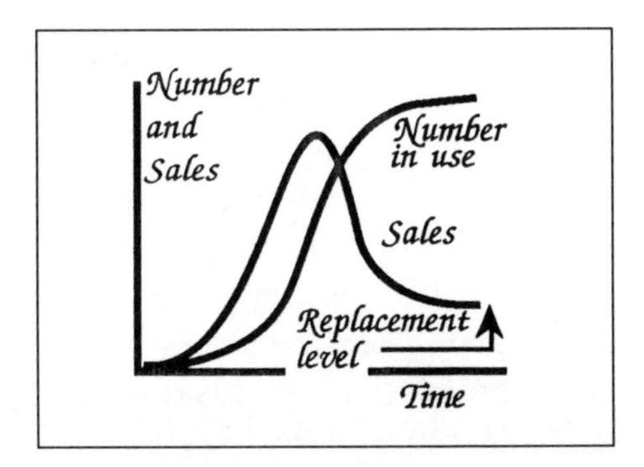

Fig. 14 Growth and saturation of an innovation market

Some businesses get used to a growing market and size themselves to meet it. Domestic electronics, for example, has lived by a succession of waves of innovation. Since the 1950s there have been black-and-white television, transistor radios, colour television, audio hi-fi, audio tape recorders, video tape recorders, CD audio, satellite television and consumer video cameras. Each had its own 'S' curve of growth, with a sales peak on the sharply rising part of the curve. Successive peaks, added together, resulted in a reasonably constant work load for the industry.

There is, as might be expected, continual pressure to come up with the next 'winner' but not all innovative products succeed; among the failures are quadraphonic sound, video disc recordings and DAT (digital audio tape, a hi-fi audio tape recording system). Candidates tipped for future success include a couple of audio recording systems (this despite DAT), new video disc records (such as CDi), video phones (telephones where you see the respondent as well as hearing them) and high-definition television (HDTV). These may fail or gain acceptance; time alone will tell. However, failed programmes for new products do not deter entrepreneurs from making a second or even third attempt, after a few years, with something essentially similar. This happens because the proposed product must have had considerable technology push to get it off the ground in the first place, and the fact that it did not attract market pull on its first outing does not detract from an awareness of its technological glamour. Earlier failure to generate market pull is typically attributed to poor marketing or sales, or to details of the product characteristics which were unacceptable to potential buyers.

Sooner or later (and it could be a century hence or a couple of decades) the industry will run out of new markets and have no option but to stabilize itself at a smaller size, dictated by the then replacement rate of products. The same will happen to all present day innovation-based industries in time, from computers to motor cars; it is not a question of whether, only when. And what causes these transitions? The question has already been answered for individual inventions and it is no different in principle across a whole society in transformation. The bright lights will simply go out one by one, and for reasons which vary little from one to another.

Sometimes it is assumed that there is no limit to human ability to consume goods and services, but this is manifestly absurd. Individuals vary widely, but there is an upper bound (however large) to the amount of food we can eat and the variety of clothes or number of wrist-watches we wish to possess. The number of cars we drive, how many television sets our houses can accommodate, all these things have their limit, sadly from the point of view of those who make them.

The assumption of unlimited demand, and therefore of unlimited growth, is a product of an epoch of poverty and dies when plenty is the rule. Appetites are large but finite; in principle they can be satisfied and this alone would cause markets to saturate, but in reality the limit comes much sooner, when the cost of another acquisition outweighs the desire to own it. As the depletion of cheaply available natural resources and rising price of labour increase the marginal cost of innovative products and services this 'turn-off' mechanism becomes all the more effective, a phenomenon which new technology may offset for a time but not forever.

Equally important is a qualitative saturation. To illustrate what this means, once again the history of computing in our time yields a clear example. Computers first began to be widely available in the 1960s; at that time it was universally the received wisdom that the installed computer would always prove to have too little power for the work it would be asked to do. 'Calculate how much power you think you will need and then double it' was accepted as a good rule, and even then one quickly ran short. In years gone by, so commonplace was this phenomenon that manufacturers would sometimes risk installing twice the computing capacity that certain customers thought they needed, locking half of it out of operation. Soon after, when the customer realized his mistake, the whole computer power could be brought quickly into use with minimum inconvenience.

The range of tasks that computers could be set to do, and the software to enable them to do it, were both developing fast at the time. However, as the decades passed this progressively ceased to be true. The computers available began to be fully up to the simpler tasks, such as word processing and elementary accounting, and the evolution of the software packages towards ever growing functional complexity slowed. In a reasonably stable environment it became possible to specify the computer one needed quite closely, and not to be disappointed with the result. So in these areas of activity the qualitative need had saturated, and indeed those activities which still seem to have an insatiable demand for computing power grow fewer with each year, and are now restricted to the likes of motion graphics, virtual reality, meteorology, cryptography and some kinds of computationally intensive scientific calculation. The tide has passed through and the major part of the qualitative demand growth is over.

Similar things apply in quite different activities. For example in transportation, *Concorde* which flies at Mach 2 makes it possible to cross the Atlantic in three and a half hours, so that taking into account time for check-in, immigration formalities and travel from city centre to airport at both ends, the fortunate passenger can go from central London to down-town New York in about seven hours. If a new aircraft flew at twice the speed (necessarily at the cost of greatly increased fuel consumption) the transit time would come down, but by less than a quarter, which to many might seem a hardly worthwhile reduction. It is doubtful that an economic service could be run if the ticket cost was more than marginally higher, so it would be hard to meet the cost of the extra fuel. Transatlantic flight is consequently reaching its qualitative saturation. An improvement in transportation from city centre to airport would have more impact on journey times.

One could go on and on. Thus, early in the twentieth century many private cars had top speeds of only around sixty kilometres per hour. Now most production cars will exceed one hundred and fifty, yet it is unlikely that speeds will increase much more for legal and environmental reasons. That parameter of private transport is reaching qualitative saturation and will stabilize near present values unless some wholly new technology emerges. Surprisingly, even in the military domain similar things hold true; there is a limit to the size of nuclear warhead that it is worth deploying, a limit to the level of threat against a warship which it is worth defending, and so on. In time it is the fate of all technical and industrial developments to reach the social and economic limits to their growth in sophistication. However far they may go and however long it may take, nothing is for ever; merely to state the proposition is to see its evident truth.

Taken both together it is the quantitative and qualitative saturation effects which will play a major part, along with the human and social factors, in bringing the present revolutionary changes in society and the economy to an end. What looks like exponential growth in the early phases of the industrial revolution is only the start of yet another 'S' curve, therefore, although one which nobody alive in the twentieth century will see in its final stages. Like the agricultural revolution before it, the industrial-scientific revolution has slid gently into historical prominence, will endure for a while, and then will fade as gently away, virtually completed perhaps by the end of the twenty-first century. Of course something which fades away with the gradualness of the 'S' curve has no more a well-defined end than a clear beginning. After a time people will realize that it is over and done, but historians of the future will have just as much scope for futile argument about the exact date when it finished as they have had about when it began. It is important, however, to emphasize that this future date when the industrial-scientific revolution comes to an end will not correspond to a collapse or decline in science, technology or industrialization, certainly not their abandonment, but only to a slackening off towards zero in the rate of growth of all three.

In the distant future, historians will teach that from the mid seventeenth century for a period of some four or five hundred years humankind went through a great process of economic, social and intellectual transition. This great and revolutionary accomplishment carried our kind, they will say, from living in absolute monarchies which were sustained by a world picture based upon an established religion, and where the overwhelming majority of people were engaged, one way or another, in agriculture, to an ordering of society wholly different, to...what?

At present we might be tempted to respond that the end-point of the transition will be liberal capitalist republics (or constitutional monarchies), established without any explicit ideology or religious foundations of more than symbolic importance, where most people will be engaged in the manufacturing or service industries. This is what that important, but now sadly underregarded, futurologist Herman Kahn seems to have believed. Yet to say that would be no more than to describe the point at which we have presently arrived, and the great change remains as yet only two-thirds completed, or so it appears.

Herman Kahn (1922–83) was a student of the future who attempted to use scientific techniques in his attempt to foretell what lay ahead of us. With a few others, notably Henry H. Arnold (1886–1950) who set up the RAND Corporation, Kahn established the modern concept of 'futurology'. Doubtless this twentieth-century Nostradamus made his mistakes, but some of his predictions were uncannily close to the mark, notably the collapse of communism and the rise of the Asian economies (although he did not get the date right in either case).[1] One is almost persuaded that some people really do have the gift of prophesy. Examples that come easily to mind are Edmund Burke's detailed and accurate written prognostication of the course of the American and French Revolutions, and the vision of the late twentieth century formed near its beginning by H. G. Wells (1866–1946).[2]

Currently Wells has fallen into disrepute because he often enthused about what, with the benefit of hindsight, were the worst aspects of his vision of the future[3]—particularly its intolerance of alternative world views—but that does not invalidate his precognitions or make them less remarkable. He is also accused of racial bias, but this is on the basis of his writings in the early part of the century, when prevailing social attitudes were very different. Wells was a man of his time, and if in retrospect his views on race are repugnant they must be seen in their historical context. To be fair, he changed his mind later, and on the credit side Wells was an early public supporter of the principles of feminism, despite very mixed

1 Herman Kahn, *The World Economy from 1979* (1978).

2 H. G. Wells, *The Shape of Things to Come* (1933).

3 Michael Coren, *The Invisible Man* (1993).

experiences with the many women in his own life.

In social, political, economic and religious terms we have no certain idea at all what things will be like at the end of the industrial-scientific revolution, a time in our future which may well be just as remote from the present day as the victories of the Duke of Marlborough or the United States Declaration of Independence are in our past. Is it conceivable that agnostic liberal democracy is merely the filling in the historical sandwich, between one age of authority which preceded it and another which will follow? Is it perhaps no more than a form of society which suits particularly well an age of transition and incessant change? Or, by contrast, have we moved from the age of kings into the era of democracy only to travel still further in the same direction, perhaps to a super-libertarian society of which we cannot yet conceive? It is not easy to offer a persuasive answer. Sadly, one would perhaps be driven to admit that the authoritarian outcome is by no means impossible. In a period of rapid change open-loop control by a central authority is too slow to adapt, and therefore at a disadvantage compared with societies where closed-loop control effects rapid transformations. This is well illustrated by the death of communism in the Soviet Union. However, if at some future time technical and economic change is far slower and the needs of society more predictable, the adaptive advantage of capitalism and bourgeois democracy may be much reduced.

Be that as it may, what is clear is that we are currently living in a great era of transition, the industrial-scientific revolution, and that we are probably somewhat more than halfway through it. This is a wholly untypical period in the life of humankind, with just one plausible historic parallel, the agricultural revolution, and that some seven thousand years ago. The initial exponential pattern of growth suggests that it came about because developments in science and industry, at first in England and soon afterwards in the rest of Europe and the United States, gave rise to multiple positive feedback processes that produced a continuing and relentless acceleration of the subsequent impetus to change. At some date, possibly for England in the early part of the seventeenth century, the loop gain for the positive feedback grew to the point where it exceeded unity, after which the process of change took on an apparently invincible character.

What cannot be denied is that the seventeenth century was an exceptional time in English history, characterized by profound conflict and disorder. Kings had been overthrown many times before, but the essential political structures of the country had evolved smoothly until then without any too marked and general discontinuity, at least since the Norman conquest. The period of change that the sixteenth century brought seems different in kind. Already by the 1560s there had been a succession of revolutions and counter-revolutions in religion, which had shaken the traditional spiritual, intellectual and moral sources of social authority. In the hundred years that followed there was a failed attempt at a royal monopoly of power, three civil wars, and a brief military dictatorship. The king was then restored to the throne, thanks to General Monck's decision to take the Army out of politics rather than make himself dictator, but that by no means restored the social order of fifty years before; indeed it proved no more than an interlude of relatively subdued social tensions, and not of long duration.

> George Monck (1608–70) fought as a Royalist at the outset of the First Civil War, but was captured in 1644 and imprisoned. Released two years later, he joined the Parliamentary army. Changing sides like this was not unusual at the time; for many people it was not a very ideological war. In 1660, after Cromwell's death (1658) and the failure of his son Richard, General Monck led his troops from Scotland to London, restored the Long Parliament and opened negotiations to bring back the king. A grateful Charles II created him Duke of Albemarle.

When the politically inept James II succeeded his subtler brother difficulties became acute once more. Stuart kings of England were of two kinds: moral but inept schemers (Charles I, James II) or amoral, subtle politicians (James I, Charles II). Subtlety without too much morality proved the more successful strategy. James II's difficulties grew, culminating in the Monmouth rebellion and the so-called 'Glorious and Bloodless Revolution' of 1688, a spontaneous uprising of the English people in the Protestant cause, or a successful (though well-disguised) Dutch invasion, according to which historian one reads. Maybe it was both. The previously established order of English society had been overthrown between 1560 and 1660, and although in the next century the Hanoverian settlement proved enduring and a new established order came into being, it was by no means the same as the old. Nor should the historical fact of a century of social upheaval be taken lightly, for it was during this time that the industrial-scientific revolution achieved unity loop gain and began its exponential take-off.

Looking beyond the Atlantic rim, where the industrial order of society first saw the light of day, the need for a failure or absence of effective central power to enable an industrial revolution to begin is clearly illustrated by the different destinies of China and Japan. In the nineteenth century efforts were made, under Imperial sponsorship, to industrialize the Chinese Empire in order to remedy its technological, and hence military, backwardness compared with the European powers. Since Shi Huangdi, the first Sovereign Emperor (221 BC), and despite changes of dynasty and occasional setbacks, the Chinese Empire had been a classic bureaucracy, exercising a monopoly of power. It remained so in the nineteenth century, and in this social context no self-sustained industrial revolution proved able to take off. Whatever positive feedback may have existed to enhance industrial and scientific innovation, it was insufficient to provide the critical loop gain, greater than unity, needed to trigger the process of change and the switch to a new kind of society.

By contrast, after the Meiji restoration (1867–8), Japan experienced a rapid (although by no means painless) period of industrial and scientific development, with many characteristic parameters showing exponential growth, indicating strong positive feedback. Although to uninformed Western eyes Japanese traditional society, headed by its emperor, might seem quite like a smaller version of China, and although indeed there were periods in Japanese history when it was fashionable to emulate everything Chinese, in fact the two societies were radically different.[1]

It is beyond doubt that Japanese history, society and institutions are very difficult to understand for an outsider, and in particular the significance and role of the emperor or *tenno* is very hard to comprehend.[2] Of course, excellent histories and cultural studies of Japan exist in English, but they must be read with an awareness that apparent parallels between Japanese and European institutions may not be quite what they seem. For example, the Emperor of Japan who died in 1989, and is widely known in the West as Hirohito, did indeed have this

1 George A. Sansom, *A History of Japan* (1958–63).

2 Thomas Crump, *The Death of an Emperor* (1989).

name before his accession. However, the person Hirohito ceased to exist at the Emperor's consecration; once he became *tenno*, for the Japanese he had no need of a name because he was unique. On his death, there being many dead emperors, a name became essential again, and a time-honoured procedure exists by which one is chosen. He has therefore been officially designated as the Showa emperor, and in future will always be known as such by Japanese. Similarly the Meiji emperor was not known by this name until after his death. This is but a minor example of the strangeness (to the Westerner) of Japanese institutions.

There is archaeological evidence for the occupation of Japan from as early as 8000 BC. Traditional histories describe the foundation of the state in 660 BC by the Emperor Jimmu, who is, needless to say, entirely mythical. Reliable records of Japanese history start around the fifth century AD, by which time a Yamato emperor was in place, although ruling through a loose coalition of tribal heads rather than as monarch of a unitary state. In 604 the Prince Regent, Shotoku Taishi, tried to impose centralized government on the Chinese pattern, culminating in the Taika 'reforms' of 646 and the Taiho laws of 702. A period of increasing imperial authority followed, culminating in the move of the capital from Nara to Kyoto (then called Heian) in 794. The first decades of the Heian period were the high point of centralized power, although the imperial family was dominated by, and intermarried with, the Fujiwara clan, who were often the real movers and shakers.

However, soon the imperial authority began to ebb away, private ownership of land was re-established bit by bit, private armies began to reappear and tribal authority gradually reasserted itself. The class of samurai—independent rural warriors—came into being, and by the eleventh century the imperial power was already a fiction, giving way to a feudal system headed by a shogun. The shogun's office was essentially military and he has been described as a dictator. Some who held the title doubtless were, but in many cases this would exaggerate their power, which was more like that of a paramount chief among tribal leaders, and a few were no more than figureheads. In parallel with the office of shogun the imperial line continued, however, and in 1334 the emperor revolted against the shogunate, reasserting imperial power in the so-called Kemmu restoration. Two years later, having demonstrated unparalleled political insensitivity, the emperor was driven from Kyoto by the shogun, who established a puppet emperor in his place, with the result that for fifty-six years Japan had two nominal emperors. From that day to this, the survival of the imperial institution in Japan has probably depended upon the fact that no subsequent emperor ever again tried to grasp at political power. Even so, and particularly as the head of the Shinto religion, the emperor has retained vast influence and prestige, his position closer to that of a medieval pope than an emperor in the Chinese or Western sense.

> The dominant religions of Japan are Shinto, which originated in very early times, and Buddhism, introduced from Korea in AD 538. It is common among Japanese to adhere to both, and they are not seen as conflicting. Shinto, which recognizes spiritual powers in every aspect of life, is the religion of the 'here and now'.[1] It offers good fortune in the things of this world: health, prosperity and happiness. For this reason marriage is usually a Shinto ceremony, as are the blessing rites when crops are sown or any new business enterprise undertaken. Its temples hold no representations of gods; this is a pantheistic religion. Simply go there, the Japanese say, clap your hands to attract the attention of the supernatural powers, say your prayer, leave an offering, and you will be fortunate. By contrast Buddhism (which like Christianity exists in a number of sects ranging from the traditional to the charismatic) is about what is beyond this life and eternal.[2] Its impressive temples contain great images not of a god but of the Enlightened One (Buddha) in a meditative posture. There are Buddhist saints, monastic orders and an extensive literature of sacred writings, some of it very scholarly. Obviously, a wise Japanese chooses to have a Buddhist funeral.

Thus, from the fourteenth century to the nineteenth, Japanese society was feudal, with a shogun as its political head but considerable power in the hands of the *shugo*, or local rulers, and later the *daimyo* (great names), and also with a samurai class who enjoyed some personal freedom. It lived by interaction, bloody dispute and negotiation between quasi-independent parties (the closed loop) rather than by fiat

1 Genchi Kato, *A Study of Shinto* (1971).

2 Christmas Humphreys, *Buddhism* (1962).

of the centre executed by a pervasive bureaucracy (the open loop). Because no monopoly of power was firmly established in Japanese society after the fourteenth century there was only weak open-loop political control from the centre, and local feedback, both positive and negative, was increasingly free to operate. During the first half of the nineteenth century the power of the Tokugawa shogunate declined further, and a degree of internal political chaos began to develop. Peasant uprisings became commonplace and were repressed with vigour. The samurai and even the *daimyo* were increasingly in debt to the merchant class. All of this undermined traditional restraints on behaviour. The situation was right for establishing positive feedback mechanisms which could radically change society.

The final, and crucial, factor in the disordering of nineteenth-century Japan was the abandonment, forced on the country by the United States, of the long-standing policy of national seclusion. In 1852 the United States Navy sent Commodore Matthew Perry, one of its most experienced officers, on a mission to Japan, a country which had been totally secluded from the outside world since 1639. After firing of his ships' guns over Tokyo as a display of naval force and having presented his letter from President Fillmore to the *tenno* (who at the time had no political authority), in March 1854 Perry signed a treaty with the Japanese in which they agreed to protect shipwrecked sailors, supply coal to United States ships and open two ports to international trade.

The display of superior technology by the Americans at that time included armoured steam-powered ships, impressive weapons of all kinds and even a small steam railway. It all made a profound impression, and those among the Japanese with enough flexibility of mind to accept the idea quickly realized that their traditional life style was doomed. A coalition of samurai (from Satsuma, Choshu, Tosa and Hizen) began a civil war under the pretext of restoring the emperor, and after a brief but sanguinary fight they drove the discredited shogun from office. Thus Japan turned again towards the outside world. In typically Japanese style, under the pretext of restoring a very old form of government something very new was brought into being. After a brief interlude of oligarchy, in 1889 a new constitution established a constitutional monarchy with (at first limited) representational government. This presented few problems, since for the better part of a thousand years their emperor had exercised no political power. Naturally, the religious significance of the *tenno* was untouched; he remained an awesome spiritual power in his own person—not merely the wielder of such a power, but the power itself. To most Japanese he still does.

As in England, so in Japan, the industrial revolution had begun its exponential development at a time of social disorder when central power was weakened. Now the reformers were assuredly in the saddle, and the new age in Japan was in process of birth. With little help from outside other than what they themselves sought, the new generation in Japan created their own social revolution, building their country into a major industrial and military power within half a century. By the 1980s Japanese economic strength had become the envy of the world, although to achieve it once-fair parts of their country had been overbuilt, overindustrialized and polluted. To be fair, large tracts of Eastern Europe have been similarly devastated, but in that case to no discernible economic advantage.

In China, by contrast, things happened very differently. Emperors might be deposed, dynasties come and go, but the bureaucracy continued to function and the imperial system remained in place, as it had since the Qin. Despite well-meaning efforts at the top, no industrial revolution happened throughout the eighteenth or nineteenth centuries. Only after the revolution led by Sun Yat-sen which overthrew the Qing (Manchu) dynasty (1911) did the open-loop command structure of the empire slowly relax its grip sufficiently for things to begin to change. From 1917 to 1921 a transformation in Chinese thought and culture known as the 'May Fourth' movement took place. Its consequences were varied: an intensified nationalism, increasing awareness of Western liberal ideas leading to an attack on the Confucian model of social order, enthusiasm for science and technology and a new vernacular style in literature.

Sun Yat-sen (1866–1925) was born to a peasant family. He studied medicine in Canton and Hong Kong, graduating in 1892. In 1895 he fled abroad after a conspiracy against the imperial regime was betrayed. While in Japan, Sun founded the Alliance Society (1905) and issued a manifesto containing an early version of his 'Three Principles': of nationalism, democracy and land tenure reform. After the revolution of 1911 Sun became president of the new republic but was forced to resign a year later and never regained office.

Central power was re-established in China with the coming of communism in 1949, which in due course led to the usual economic stultification. There were many struggles, culminating in the so-called 'Cultural Revolution' which led to widespread social disruption and overthrow of authority. From the mid-1980s, however, under the influence of Deng Xiaoping, capitalist economic policies were progressively reintroduced, whilst still maintaining an authoritarian political structure and an obligatory State-sponsored belief system. The result has been impressive economic growth, but as yet the final outcome cannot be seen.

It appears, then, that an industrial revolution does not begin in a society where the centre has strong effective control of the actions of individuals, still less in a well-ordered and tranquil one. The examples of England, Japan and China are not alone in teaching this. The French time of civil troubles came about a century after the English and the industrial revolution was similarly delayed there. The example of Germany is little different, the period of political chaos engendered by the Revolutionary and Napoleonic wars leading to the process of change which manifested itself in an impressive German industrial revolution, particularly apparent after unification in 1871. It is noticeable that the delay before take-off is shorter for follow-on nations than pioneers. French and German entrepreneurs had the English example to aid their confidence and thus raise the loop gain accelerating industrial growth.

As for the United States, a country constitutionally constructed on the rights of the individual and the division and restraint of central powers, the case need only be stated to be made. The United States industrial revolution was born between the American Revolution (1775–83) and the Civil War (1861–65). From 1810 the United States economy grew as never before. The westward extension of the frontier was matched in the North by unprecedented industrial advance. The discovery of large deposits of gold and silver provided risk capital to accelerate the pace of business. A national thirst for education, aided by the appearance of affordable newspapers, led to a rapid fall in illiteracy, raising work-force quality. Productivity improved by leaps and bounds in the factory system, by then well established.

In essence, it seems that the industrial revolution does not start where there is a monopoly of power. However, it would be wrong, on the basis of the American experience, to associate the birth of an industrial revolution too closely with the existence of democratic institutions, since neither England, Germany, Japan nor even France had these in developed form throughout their own critical period. It seems that an independently minded aristocracy or oligarchy will do quite as well as bourgeois democracy; enough individuals must have freedom of action, and access to capital and other resources, for the positive feedback to be effective, but universal liberty and political autarky appear not to be essential. There must be competition between reasonably free and independent entrepreneurs, able to command resources adequate to the task, yet at the same time the number of players can be quite small, at least at first. Nevertheless, although bourgeois democracy is not essential for an industrial-scientific take-off it is one of the most effective means of ensuring that change is not blocked by monopolistic central power.

Yet why should it be essential that there be a degree of social flexibility so great that in a traditional society only the turmoil of war can create it? Any answer must be speculative, but the crucial factor is that the take-off can only occur when positive feedback is present with greater than unity loop gain. There may be one such feedback loop or many, although the latter is more likely, in which case they must achieve unity gain working together, even if they are too weak to do so independently. The two common categories of positive feedback—operational and social—have already been described, and in a favourable case both will be present. To recapitulate: at the operational level, some inventions fit together so that one supplies the needs of the other, thus the silicon chip improved computers making possible better silicon chips. Social feedback arises if invention itself is generally valued and the bringing of new inventions to market is well resourced and rewarded. Prior successful examples help to establish this environment. However, it seems plausible that the primary interest of well-integrated central power is to keep processes of change in society to a minimal, or at least manageable, pace. To stabilize existing social parameters the organs of the State, particularly the bureaucracy and the legal system, will normally apply negative feedback. Only that change is welcome which does not appear to threaten the established order, and whatever may be thought even to risk passing beyond this boundary is discouraged, penalized or repressed. These negative feedback processes will tend to cancel any locally generated positive feedback associated with a particular innovative process, reducing the loop gain below the critical unity threshold. A pervasive and well-integrated central bureaucracy may be able to do this so generally that all technological innovation, beyond a slow evolution which is tolerable to them, is entirely repressed.

Historical examples of this dampening down of the innovative process below the threshold required for a positive feedback 'trigger' effect are without number. In medieval Europe the building of water and wind mills, the basis of the current phase of technical innovation, was subject to strict licensing. Gimpel, for example, attributes the slowing down of technical innovation in the late Middle Ages in part to the formation of craft guilds who vigorously opposed changes in traditional ways of working.[1] This can be seen as an example of collusion between an established industry and government, on the pretext of maintaining standards of craftsmanship. Neither party wanted radical change. Something rather more extreme happened in Japan, where the Tokugawa shoguns vigorously repressed forms of innovation, particularly in military technology, which seemed to threaten the established Japanese social order. In the twentieth century, in Eastern Europe detailed regulation by the communist State made innovation almost impossible. It became widely accepted amongst industrial managers there that new technology would have to be imported from the West, and this despite a flourishing scientific establishment.

In the West itself some argue that, whatever the original intention might have been, the patent laws are used as much to protect existing technology as to promote new. Much past business activity has certainly been aimed at inhibiting innovative competition, and only relatively recently has the State begun to take the innovators' side. Government regulation and licensing, aimed in theory at the public good by way of protection of the environment, prevention of chaotic and disorderly economic behaviour and sustaining employment in existing activities, has the practical effect of damping down innovation by the introduction of stabilizing negative feedback.

A case history from England will illustrate the pattern. Francis Ronalds was born in 1788, the son of a City merchant. In 1816 he

1 Jean Gimpel, *The Medieval Machine* (1978).

built the world's first practical electric telegraph, capable of nearly instantaneous communication over theoretically unlimited distances. Like most new inventions the telegraph had some problems at first, but it soon worked well enough. It was demonstrated successfully to large numbers of people transmitting at the slow but usable rate of two words per minute, and was certainly capable of further development to serve its purpose better still. A patriotic man, Ronalds offered his invention to the Admiralty, thinking that they would be enthusiastic about using it to communicate between Admiralty House and His Majesty's ships at anchorage in the Royal Dockyard, Chatham. At the time the Admiralty did so, if at all, by means of a crude visual signalling system, known as the 'Murray telegraph', involving hand-rotated black and white wooden boards, viewed from a distance by telescope.

Ronalds wrote to Lord Melville, the First Lord of the Admiralty, on 11 June 1816. On 5 August, after sending them a reminder, he received his reply from Mr Barrow, the Secretary, thus: 'Mr Barrow presents his compliments to Mr Ronalds and acquaints him with reference to his note of the 3rd inst. that telegraphs of any kind are wholly unnecessary and that no other than the one in use will be adopted.' Ronalds took it with philosophical detachment and published a description of his telegraph in 1823. For a quarter of a century he received no recognition of any kind, but was knighted near the end of his life, after the opening of the Atlantic telegraph.

Later, of course, the electric telegraph (but not Ronalds' version) became the basis of nineteenth-century communications and an indispensable adjunct to the railways. From its success grew modern newspapers and the telecommunications and electronics industries as we now have them. Few inventions could be classed as more significant, yet the Admiralty's rejection of the idea was not irrational from their standpoint. Having, over many years, developed a command system which worked perfectly well without the use of telegraphs (because they had to), for the Admiralty to have adopted the new technology would have had incalculable effects on the way the Royal Navy conducted its business, not all of them positive or easy to manage or foresee. Better to keep things as they were, and concentrate on detailed improvement, which they knew how to do, at least in principle.

The electromagnetic telegraphs of Morse and Vail (in the United States) and Cooke and Wheatstone (in England) both date to 1837, after Ronalds' work had fallen into obscurity. Amusingly enough, something quite similar to Ronalds' experience with the Admiralty also happened to Cooke and Wheatstone. The directors of the London and Birmingham Railway were offered the new electromagnetic telegraph to control traffic out of Euston station working over the inclined plane up to Camden Town, in those days hauled by a stationary winding engine (which had to be told when to wind). They rejected it in favour of an extremely loud power-operated whistle! What the inhabitants of the Euston area thought of this device is not recorded. The setback proved only temporary however; the electromagnetic telegraph went into service in 1839 on the Great Western Railway, perhaps because its engineer, Isambard Kingdom Brunel, liked novelties. The line ran from Paddington to West Drayton, later extended to Slough, and for the first year of its operation made more money by charging a shilling a head to view the 'telegraph cottage' (where the equipment was housed) than by charges for telegrams.

An established and functioning bureaucracy will always prefer incremental improvement to radical change, it seems. By contrast, in more chaotic social conditions, where control from the centre, either by government or other powerful interests, is weak or ineffective, the stabilizing effects of negative feedback are less in evidence. This may make life difficult for the population as a whole, but innovators are able to effect change with less inhibition, crossing the unity gain threshold in the positive feedback loops which set the pace of change. What happens then is a discontinuity in history, and the material from which legends are built.

12

On Bifrost Bridge

If life is about the attempt to control, to manage the world about us constructively and not simply be a passive victim, if politics and economics are no more than attempts at that control on a grander scale, then we had better learn something about the way it should be done. Yet of all the valuable lessons the theory of control offers, the most important are few and simple:

i. There are two basic strategies of control, open-loop and closed-loop. The open-loop form simply involves taking direct control action, its nature decided before the event and its application unheeding of the outcome as it unfolds.

By contrast, closed-loop control is the strategy in which the consequences of each action are continuously monitored from the moment it is taken and future control activities are modified accordingly.

Feedback control is further subdivided into negative feedback, in which the sense of the control action is such as to steer the system ever closer to the achievement of a specified goal or aim, and positive feedback, in which action taken is in the opposite sense, promoting divergence and change.

ii. For reasons which must be sought in psychodynamics, we are all of us inclined to see open-loop control as moral, efficient and admirable and those who practise it as skilful, charismatic, heroic even, and endowed with what are still too often thought of as 'the manly virtues'.

We reward them highly, although as often with power, status, esteem and reputation as with money. Later the best of the open-loop practitioners may be eligible to be counted among the mighty dead, and to exert their influence on our thoughts even from beyond the grave.

In the Arts and Science this predilection for the open loop may not matter too much. It will cause us to value the second-rate but creative above the first-rate exponent, so much is true, but it will do little other harm. By contrast in the management of the economy it has proved a snare since at least the time of the pharaohs, leading to perpetual hankering after a command economy and to a deep-rooted unwillingness to trust the operation of markets. In consequence entirely possible levels of wealth generation and prosperity are all too often missed, and life is materially harder than it need be.

Worse still, though, is the impact of this honeymoon with the open loop on politics. In social affairs open-loop control is our obsession and our vice, a triumph over the prospect for mutuality of the malign belief that there are those who know best what is good for us. Scepticism time and again proves an inadequate defence. The great charismatic leader of the *Volk* (or the proletariat) who promises the millennium but in the event causes the death of millions, the 'scientific' rule by the Vanguard Party which brings only disillusion and hardship, the morally flawed President whose reputation is saved by timely assassination—we are needlessly vulnerable to them all because they thrive on our wish to believe that out there, somewhere, is the heaven-sanctioned leader, the all-wise father who will set the world to rights by his own mere motion, the open-loop practitioner who will resolve all our problems with a careless certainty. And we go on believing in them long after reason says they should bewitch us no longer. So we have our myths of great lost leaders, magical super-heroes from King Arthur to Owain Glyndwr, from Wolfe Tone to Charles Stewart Parnell, Jeanne D'Arc to Napoleon Bonaparte and Leon Trotsky to John F. Kennedy. From their deaths legend builds around their names, until we come to believe that if only they had been given the chance, had lived and been able fully to exercise their powers, they would have put all wrongs to right, chained the Fenris Wolf, and made this world into an earthly paradise. But the truth is that they would not and could not, partly because history is not like that, but mostly because they were only human after all. Which is why far and away the best of the great leaders are the ones long dead, those who sleep under the hill, ready (so it is said) to come once again to our aid at the time of our greatest need. Let them sleep on, do not disturb their endless dream; they threaten us less as they are.

iii. Closed-loop control with negative feedback is quite another matter. It is the control strategy of stability, always adjusting to achieve a predetermined aim, parameter or target. A myriad of negative feedback loops within us keep us viable by setting the physiological variables on which our lives depend. Similarly, electronic and mechanical negative feedback systems keep the parameters of our homes, our cars, the aircraft in which we fly and the industrial and agricultural processes that generate our wealth, all to their appropriate values. Attempts by governments and central banks to stabilize and regulate the economy depend on negative feedback actions.

Socially, our first infant experience of this pervasive power is in the enfolding care of our mothers, which keeps us loved, fed, clean and secure. Because the associations of negative feedback are therefore maternal and female, like that early loving care it is too easily taken for granted. The ground of our being, it does not seem specially remarkable or to merit unusual reward. Sometimes it can feel stifling, because we recall that at the end of infancy we had to break with it in order to do our own, our open-loop, thing. It is vital to our autonomy to forget that mother may have played a positive role even in preparing for that break too.

Making everyday life run smoothly, achieving modest but important goals, keeping the world from want—these are each accomplished by negative feedback loops, working through the routines of business, services and social administration. They are wholly admirable but, for the most part, modestly rewarded and their practitioners will never be eligible to take a place among the mighty dead.

iv. Although negative feedback can at its best work wonders of precise and flexible control, it is subject to problems, and the worst of these come when there is significant time delay in the feedback loop. If it takes time for the feedback to act it will overshoot its aim; if that time is still longer the system may be wholly unstable, hunting wildly about the proper value and never settling at all. When this happens Nyquist's insights teach that simply being more energetic or trying harder with the same strategy of control—increasing the loop gain, in short—will do no good at all. In fact reducing it might make things better.

Problems of this kind are often encountered in every area of attempted closed-loop control; the visible sign of excessive loop gain ranges from the tremor of Parkinson's disease, which disables the movement of the limbs, to the trade cycles of boom and bust in the economy which disappoint legitimate expectations, impoverish nations and ruin lives. Assuming that the loop gain is set no higher than necessary to achieve the desired control, the only radical solution to the problem is to reduce the time lag in the control process. The market is usually a good regulator of the economy just because of the immediacy with which it acts, quickly matching wants to what is offered and thus minimizing the prospect that this particular control will hunt, but it fails sometimes when some factor of production imposes an undue delay.

v. Positive feedback is control for change and little that is at all dramatic takes place without it. Provided that the loop gain exceeds the magic threshold of unity it makes sudden transitions happen. Whether it be falling in love, going to war or transforming society by an industrial revolution, if the feedback is sufficient all can seem virtually inevitable. In the business world, exciting growth of a company is impossible without a positive feedback loop.

Such a system has only two stable states, that in which it begins and the one to which it finally settles when the process of transition ends. The smallest disturbance of the initial state can begin the process of change, the state switch. Between its stable conditions there is no resting point to be found, and during the interval in which it is in the process of changing, this bi-stable system gives every appearance of being driven forward by some inexorable outside force.

It may seem to people caught up in this process of switching, the positive feedback state flip, that their lives are out of control, driven, the plaything of greater powers. In truth, though, the power that we feel is our own, reflected back to us from the feedback loop; however it may seem, the Devil is not really out there, cranking the handle of our lives. If we wish no longer to feel the victims of forces we do not understand, the entirely possible art must be learned of engendering positive feedback where we want it and not elsewhere. The loops that drive us toward disaster must be weakened or broken, and those enhanced which build what our hearts desire.

Were these simple insights to become a routine part of what every educated person takes for granted we would all of us be better able to understand many things. We would know why it is that in politics we so often fail to achieve the good we hope for, however altruistic our motivations. In our private lives we would be more aware of what was happening to us when we fell in love or had a row, and perhaps we would be less likely to lose our money on ill-advised schemes for pig breeding or making silicon chips. If just this much of the formal science of control could be taken over into common knowledge it would deepen most people's understanding of the world in which they live and help them to achieve more often their personal and collective goals.

All of that would, however, be no more than a start. The theory of control has grown so extensive that the little presented here is a very small part of it indeed, no more than scratching the surface of a massive corpus of knowledge, if even that. It was my purpose merely to present ideas which are ripe and ready now to be absorbed into common knowledge, just the things it is high time we all made part of our ordinary understanding of the world. To do so is not the end of the story, for there is more, so much more, and perhaps much of that too we shall all have to come to terms with one day. But that must be for another writer, and another book.

Of all the limitations that I have imposed on myself perhaps the most significant is that hidden, but underlying everything I have written, is a very simple category of linear or near-linear mathematics. No apology is needed; much of science and technology is grounded in similar assumptions or the most tentative and modest departure from them. Things are said to be linear if effects are proportional to causes, that is if doubling a stimulus produces double the result, for example. For a few phenomena this is precisely true, for quite a lot more it is a good enough approximation, but most things that science studies do not really fit it well at all. Until recent times, when dealing with situations like that the mathematician began to move warily, although not yet at the end of his resources.

Conventional mathematics can be extended usefully by using not the direct linear relationships but variation according to the higher powers—squares, cubes and so on—of the stimulus. A yet further step is to use the sum of the different powers, each multiplied by a suitable constant. Thus, the exponential growth curve is the sum of one plus the first power of time (the linear term) plus half the square of the time, plus one sixth of the cube, plus one twenty-fourth of the fourth power, and so on to an infinite number of terms. It might be thought that an expression with an infinite number of terms would be of little practical use, but provided that each term is smaller than the last (so that they eventually tail off to nothing) the series of numbers has a sum total which is finite, and therefore tractable. In mathematical jargon such a series is said to be convergent. Provided that it is, many useful things can be done with it. With power series of this kind ordinary mathematics still works, and we can use the calculus invented by Newton and Leibniz, so they are extremely useful and can be used to model quite a lot of nonlinear things tolerably well.

Until recently virtually all of science and technology relied on this kind of mathematics, and most still does. However, it retains certain limitations: all the things it represents are mathematically 'well behaved'. They change smoothly and do not hop about in a discontinuous fashion, for example; also everything remains finite all the time, and if we plot graphs of what is going on they are smooth curves, just like the exponential and 'S' curves of growth earlier in this book. Yet in the real world the phenomena are in a small minority which satisfy well-behaved descriptions of this kind, so it follows that almost all we know in science is at best only an approximation to what we see. In the typical 'normal science' style of denying what is awkward up to the point where it can be denied no longer, until recently many who work in science would simply, and quite genuinely, have been unable to see the truth of this statement, let alone accept it. Now it would be questioned only in the scientific backwaters.

We have long played the game of science using approximations to the truth we see because the mathematics employed was tractable only that way. We pressed into use as best we could the limited methods we had when forming our theories, forcing them into situations where the fit between what we could observe and what we had the power to analyse could hardly be good. The truth is that from the beginnings of science until a few years ago, only in the circumstance of well-behaved mathematics have the sums given answers that we could use. By contrast, stray far outside that magic domain and classical paper-and-pencil mathematics hardly works at all. Looked at this way it is a miracle that our science has succeeded as it has, but that is because of the amazing degree of human ingenuity which has been brought to bear on the problems of using a quasi-linear analysis to describe a nonlinear world. We are like Nasrudin, the sage of Middle Eastern legend, who one night was found in the road outside his house looking for his lost latch-key under a street lamp, not because that was where he thought he had dropped the key but because the light there was so much better for the search.

> Uncounted stories are told of Nasrudin, some witty and all instructive. Perhaps a real person as the Turks claim, more likely mythical, Nasrudin is a folk hero who teaches that wisdom and folly lie very close to each other. He demonstrates the spirit of the Sufi (and also distantly echoes the insights of Zen, with its *koan* or joke as a path to enlightenment).
>
> 'Mullah Nasrudin, Chief of the Dervishes and master of a hidden treasure, a perfected man. Many say: I wanted to learn, but here I have found only madness. Yet, should they seek deep wisdom elsewhere, they may not find it.'—so wrote the master Ablahi Mutlaq, called 'The Utter Idiot', in his *Teachings of Nasrudin* (1617).[1]

Combine all this oversimplification with the scientific base of Newton's laws of motion and the result is a beguiling but false picture of the universe, which was, even so, universally believed by scientific people in the eighteenth and nineteenth centuries. According to this view the universe is simply particles of matter in motion and interacting, and those interactions, fully worked out, explain everything that ever was or will ever be. Logically, if the position and motion of all the particles in the universe, every atom, were completely known, then the state of the universe could be calculated for any time in the future, everything to come would be totally determined, prediction in principle a mere computation. Even more remarkable, and absurd, in this universe time must be reversible.[2] The logic is impeccable: if the position

1 Idries Shah, *The Exploits of the Incomparable Mullah Nasrudin* (1966).

2 Peter Coveney and Roger Highfield, *The Arrow of Time* (1990).

of every particle in the universe were unchanged but its motion were to be exactly reversed, then everything would be as before, governed by precisely the same mathematical equations, but now with time running the opposite way. By this simple means the universe would thus reverse in time, faithfully retracing all its past states in due order.

In such a universe grotesque and impossible things would happen. Dead people would be dug up from holes in the ground (with much ceremony by other people walking backwards), would then come to life, grow progressively younger as the years passed, gradually forgetting much that they knew, and finally would attend establishments called schools (or maybe sloochs) where almost all learning would be extracted from them. At last, growing smaller and smaller, they would lose the power of speech and the ability to walk, and finally pass into their mother's wombs. Such an idea is grotesque and ludicrous, yet it was once scientific orthodoxy, though an uncomfortable one, that such a universe was fully possible.

Newton's time seemed reversible,[1] but real time as we live it is not, as every sensible person always knew full well and as thermodynamics made scientifically obvious and respectable from the middle of the nineteenth century. The universe cannot run reversed, if only because the second law of thermodynamics dictates heat must flow from the higher temperature to the lower and that disorder will increase and that these are things which are in no way reversible, so that therefore time itself is not reversible. That mad reversible Newtonian universe was a natural consequence of preoccupation, to the exclusion of all else, with reductionist science and a mathematics of continuity. It was a typical constraint of the quest of normal science to the place where the light seemed good, and for a while it served us well, despite the paradox at its heart. The Newtonian model fuelled the enlightenment, it made rational men believe that first deism and later atheism was the only scientifically credible view, and some think so still. Yet it was not only wrong, but in some respects absurd.

The dictatorship of reductionism is long gone now, but the limi-

1 Only because the scientists of the Newtonian epoch did not understand the significance of errors of observation and experimental uncertainties. See Leon Brillouin, *Science and Information Theory* (1962), particularly Chapter 21. Some mathematics is required to read this book.

tations of our mathematics lingered on for a while, into the twentieth century. What finally transformed it all was the coming of the computer. At first these new machines were primarily used for 'more of the same' type innovations, taking the calculations we had long been doing by hand and automating them so that they could be performed faster and with much less effort. Before long, though, particularly as the power of computers increased and our understanding of the software needed to vivify them improved, they began to show clear signs of the 'passing over of quantity into quality', as their users began tackling calculations that never could have been done by humans unaided because they were simply too laborious and too extended. Needless to say, many of these were concerned with the nonlinear and discontinuous problems classical mathematical techniques could not touch but which the computers were able to crack by a tedious process of detailed point-by-point calculation.

A sense of excitement began to permeate the world of computation. Suddenly it had become possible, for example, to calculate the complexities of the turbulent flow of air around parts of an aircraft in a way that had been quite inconceivable by classical analytical methods. Traditionally calculation had always been abandoned at a certain point in the design of aircraft, in favour of lengthy experimentation with carefully scaled models in a wind tunnel; now at last there was the prospect of calculating out the whole design, and using the wind tunnel only as a back-up to the computed results. The civil engineers were the next to benefit, not only able to design more complicated structures with greater accuracy, but even able to build mathematical models which remained valid as the structure collapsed, so that the response of a building to earthquake or fire could be predicted in advance and the danger to life minimized. All of this, however, was only a start; as the power of the computers and the virtuosity of those who used them grew still further, new areas of science began to surrender to the power of their attack, deeper insights were gained and new scientific paradigms began to form as a consequence of a computational 'knight's move'.

The most widely publicized of these new initiatives is chaos theory.[1] In contemporary scientific language chaotic events are not at all the

1 Ian Stewart, *Does God Play Dice?* (1989).

same thing as random happenings. Chaos (in the scientific sense) is strictly ruled by cause and effect, but in a way that gives rise to extremely complicated behaviour, so very sensitive to the conditions in which it starts that despite being entirely deterministic it cannot in practice be predicted. The famous example always quoted is the weather, which is often (but not always) governed by the laws of chaos. Under these conditions it is said that a butterfly flapping its wings over the Amazon could, through a complex process of chaotic dynamics, cause a hurricane over the United States. The point, of course, is that although perfectly deterministic, such processes are so ticklishly sensitive that the next time a butterfly exercised itself in the same place (and perhaps the next million times) precisely nothing at all would follow by way of consequences.

This statement has implications for science more profound than many people yet realize. Confidence in scientific theories has always depended on their ability to predict what would happen in certain circumstances. Thus our theories about the solar system are thought 'proved' because they enable us to predict events like eclipses of the sun and moon. But of course in a situation of chaos the power to predict is, by definition, gone. How do we establish confidence in a new scientific hypothesis then? If our predictions do not work out, is this because the theory is wrong or is it a natural consequence of chaos? Problems of this kind mean that a new hard look has to be taken at the underlying assumptions on which science is built. Nobody has altogether come to terms with it yet, but it is hard to believe that we are not being propelled into another revolutionary phase in science, and perhaps one of the most profound and far-reaching in its consequences that has yet been seen.

Yet these chaotic processes are by no means rare; they are all around us. If we return for positively the last time to the bath taps with which this book has been so unreasonably obsessed, the dripping tap is a perfect example. When a tap is very nearly turned off, drips will issue steadily and at annoyingly regular intervals, as anybody who has had to share a room with one will recall. Turn it on a little more and a small but steady stream of water will issue. Both the regular dripping and the steady stream can be described by well-behaved mathematics, but in between these two states a tap can mostly be induced to demonstrate chaotic behaviour. As it is very slowly turned off the thin stream of water gets less and less until it suddenly begins to break up, for a moment flowing steadily then breaking into drops, only to flow again a moment later. It behaves in a way that seems to defy all prediction no matter how long it is studied. This is chaotic behaviour, deterministic but disordered, or, more accurately, ordered in so complex a way that it is beyond our immediate comprehension. Yet at the heart of chaos is a paradox, and it is this. Although chaos itself is so complex that it defies description, chaotic models of events can be generated by mathematics of remarkable simplicity. A seemingly unfathomable sequence of events which totally defeats the mathematics of our fathers' day may be generated by a few simple statements easily handled by a desk-top computer. Until now we had all thought that complicated things necessarily had complex explanations, but today we know that there is no such direct relationship.

Many of the things that we might wish to control and predict, the economy perhaps and the weather certainly, are at least partly chaotic. Their management will consequently present problems far beyond those reviewed in this book, and indeed the theory of control of chaotic systems has scarcely begun to evolve as yet. One approach to weather forecasting, currently being tried, is to identify whether at a particular time and location the weather is following a well-behaved or a chaotic pattern. If the former, predictions can be made with confidence, but if for a time chaos rules it is known that the prospect for prediction is little better than mere chance. At least identifying the state of chaos tells us when not even to try to predict.

It seems that we have crossed some kind of invisible threshold in understanding as a result of the new kinds of mathematics which the computer is making available to us, and much that is strange and unexpected is being revealed. The process has probably no more than begun, and chaos theory is merely its first fruit. We are all unsure as yet, but it seems as if there may be more, much more of mystery in process of revealing itself, many things about which it is impossible at present to speak with any authority. Even so, many begin to feel that the universe is likely to prove an even stranger place than we already knew it to be.

The state of chaos is characterized by an exceptional sensitivity of events to their initial conditions, and contrasts with the well-behaved process, which has a comfortable predictability. Many things in nature appear to have both a chaotic domain in certain parts and a well-behaved domain in others—the weather is one example and chemical reactions are another. Thus a domain of chaos and one of well-behaved reactions may be side by side, and if so something quite strange often results. Evidence seems to be accumulating that at the edge of chaos, on the border between the ordered and the chaotic states, something very unexpected indeed occurs. Perhaps because of that very sensitivity to small things at the onset of chaos, systems which occupy this debatable ground seem actually to be capable of self-organization, that is of building more complex structures out of simpler.[1]

This is complexity theory, and to go further down that path would be beyond the scope of a book about elementary notions in control theory. Its emergence is very recent and hard, as yet, to evaluate. Complexity theory may herald the emergence of a major new scientific paradigm which alters much of our present thinking, but then again it is also entirely possible that it may not. A self-organizing process at work in the universe, promoting order out of disorder—can such a thing really be? How does it square with the gloomy pessimism of the second law of thermodynamics, with its prediction of the inexorable spread of disorder? For the present we must echo the words of the Buddha (in response to being asked by a disciple whether God exists): 'As to that, I preserve an honourable silence.' We seem to be at a turning point in science just now, an uncomfortable moment where the future shape that it will take is more than usually unpredictable; the only thing we can say with assurance is that it will surprise us.

> A fine mess Science has got us into! Now we are asked to believe that the universe began with the Big Bang, an event in which all space and time, matter and energy came into being together. About the future there is dispute, but many cosmologists hold that the universe will end in a Big Crunch, far ahead in time, when it all collapses down to a point again. This would be the end of all things, the Last Day, when even time itself is extinguished. But now it gets still worse: we are beginning to be persuaded that an organizing power is loose in the universe, a creative principle putting patterns together

1 Roger Lewin, *Complexity—Life at the Edge of Chaos* (1993).

> against all probability, a power which could perhaps be the very origin of life itself. I just hope nobody jumps to any unwarranted conclusions, that's all. It's so unfair—ideas like this are not what we were led to expect of Science. Is nothing reliable?

But all of this is a look far ahead, and for the moment the more pressing task is to come to terms with what we currently know and can state with confidence. If the world were dominated by the randomness of chance neither civilization nor life itself could long endure, but happily that is not how things are. The power to control is our fragile but enduring barrier, ever renewed, between that total disorder and the continued wellbeing of humankind. The infant in the cot discovers its own separateness and defines its identity by efforts to control what seems painful in its early world. On the larger scale, even in unlikely areas such as the evolution of scientific research, it turns out that important issues of control determine the course things must take. Above all, politics and economics are about the attempt to apply human powers of control to the states and societies in which we live.

Stability in our lives, wherever we encounter it, is the product of negative feedback. Rapid change, by contrast, is most likely and most enduring when it is positive feedback that spurs it forward. The greatest such change influencing all our lives is a revolution in science and industry that has had our world in its grip these three hundred years.

In medieval times the inhabitants of Christendom lived in a universe they believed strictly bounded in space and time. The world of the people whose lives were passed in that era was limited every way in extent, its dimensions impenetrably bounded by the crystal spheres that carried the stars overhead. The story all began on the First Day of the Book of Genesis, when God said 'Let there be light!' and then created everything that was—the waters, the land, the creatures on the land and the first Adam, made in His own image, to command them all. Nor could any but the most ignorant or profane doubt that the world would surely end on Doom's Day, when the great God in all His majesty would call everyone who had ever lived to rise from the sleep of death and come to their account and judgement.

But that was long ago, the cosmology of another age, and after the scientific revolution a new world vision began to seem inescapable to people of that later time. It was Newton now who cried 'Let there be light!' and in consequence all the world's picture of creation soon changed completely. Now the universe was infinite, unbounded and fundamentally unchanging, having come from an unfathomable past and moving on into a possible infinity of future, the Earth a small planet orbiting an insignificant star. If it were true that, long ago, God had indeed created all, then surely his role had been no more than that of the Celestial Clockmaker, who puts the mechanism together so perfectly that it could run on forever along lines that He must necessarily perfectly foresee. After that He could go away, not needing to intervene in what He had done because it was inescapably obliged to follow, in the minutest detail, the exact path that He, in His infinite wisdom, had established by choosing its very first disposition and motion. There was no further need of God.

Now the centuries have passed and another change of view is coming upon us, no less total. We begin to approach the last phase of the scientific and industrial revolution and the cosmic picture is in process of transformation yet again. This time it is not the god-like Newton who leads us but the unassuming Einstein who has wheedled the secrets out. Not everything is yet understood and many problems remain, it is true, but this period of uncertainty will not last. A hundred years from now there will surely be a general scientific consensus again, to which universal allegiance will be due, imperfect perhaps, but its shortcomings—if such there be—not apparent. What will it be? Let us speculate.

It seems likely to teach that there was indeed a beginning to the universe, and that there will be an end. The ocean of existence between them, the likely duration of space and time itself, will be vastly greater than the medieval mind could have appreciated, but even so it will not be without calculable limit. Thus time will have a stop, and as for space, the universe may be infinite in dimension yet, in a relativistic paradox, it is bounded also, because of its hyperdimensional curvature. So it seems that we are in the process of rediscovering the crystal sphere that encloses us, though inconceivably enlarged compared with those our predecessors thought they saw.

Nor is this all, for other subtle limitations are becoming more apparent year on year. We understand now that there is an absolute maximum speed with which anything can move—the velocity of light—which necessarily limits what we can know of distant things because of the time it takes anything at all from them to get to us. Of the stars and galaxies in the outer reaches of the universe we can say with certainty only how they were long ago; we know nothing of their present condition, not even if they still exist. At the other extreme, in the quantum mechanical realm of things that are very small, there is an inescapable uncertainty which sets a limit to what we can be sure we know. Experiment will not come to our aid much longer, for the great particle accelerators which have told us so much about the ultimate structure of matter are reaching their last generation and soon will reveal mysteries no more. Even the absolute zero of temperature, which in truth is no more than perfect stillness, seems like a barrier to us because we can approach close but never reach it. And now there is seen to be a fundamental and inescapable limit on our ability to predict the future course of events, set by the intrusion of chaos. Nor are the constraints on us purely material and temporal; the workings of the human mind no longer seem unbounded either, for the mind is surely an activity of the brain, and the brain is finite, its cells numerable. It is not only the universe, therefore, which is increasingly coming to seem inescapably finite but even human knowledge itself, the barriers growing more apparent on every side.

If I am right, and daily it seems more plausible, if indeed this is a foretaste of how things will appear to our descendants—children of that future time when the great transition creeps to its close, the positive feedback of revolution reaching its new stable state at last—then the world views of the medieval past and of that postrevolutionary future will bear a curious, mocking resemblance to each other. For though in detail they will differ as much as ever two like things could, in both of them that universe which is the habitation of humankind is perceived as strictly and forever limited, not only in its space and time dimensions but also in our capacity to comprehend it. There could be no infinities in either the medieval or that future universe, no possibility of journeys without end, neither through space and time nor yet in knowledge and human understanding. That postrevolutionary age to come will be quite another world—alien to all we know and are, it is not our world, not for us.

According to the ancient sagas of the Icelandic people, Middle Earth is the habitation of kings, nobles and farmers, whilst in the bright Halls of Asgard dwell beings so superior in knowledge and powers that they are accounted gods.[1] Over the bottomless gulf between these two realms stands the Bifrost Bridge, composed all of fire and colour and guarded by Heimdall, whose ears are so sharp that he can hear the grass grow. It is hazardous for mortals to pass over the bridge, and once begun the crossing can never be retraced.

For good or ill, the fate of everybody alive today was to be born in an era of transition, a strange unruly epoch quite without parallel in the history of our planet. Driven out by the sword of knowledge from the God-lit simplicities of Middle Earth, and not yet come to the brilliance of the Halls of Asgard which will be our long home, we are obliged to survive as best we can midway, on the Bifrost Bridge, in a confusion of light and shadow. Behind us are the verities we have abandoned, ahead the new certainties of the postrevolutionary age which is to come. Between them we journey on in doubt and wonder, controlling our wild ride as best we may.

1 The Icelandic prose *Edda* of Snorri Sturluson (written around 1220) is the source often quoted, but he had it from verbal tradition which goes a long way further back. Sturluson, Speaker of the Icelandic parliament, was murdered in a dispute about one of his procedural rulings.

Index